sister species

sister species

EDITED BY
lisa kemmerer

FOREWORD BY
carol j. adams

women,
animals,
AND social
justice

university of illinois press
urbana, chicago, and springfield

Library of Congress Cataloging-in-Publication Data

Sister species : women, animals and social justice /

edited by Lisa A. Kemmerer; foreword by Carol J. Adams.

p.   cm.

Includes bibliographical references and index.

ISBN 978-0-252-03617-0 (cloth : alk paper)

ISBN 978-0-252-07811-8 (pbk. : alk paper)

1. Animal welfare. 2. Animal rights. 3. Ethics.

I. Kemmerer, Lisa.

HV4708.S57   2011

179'.3—dc22   2010050885

dedicated to those who work across intersections of violence—who put their lived (though perhaps untheorized) knowledge of interlocking oppressions into practice to bring deep-seated change: vegans staffing rape crisis lines, feminists engaged in open rescue, those tending little home sanctuaries while working day jobs to heal battered children, those who speak out against racism while tending shelters for the homeless, and any number of other determined activists who are helping to end oppressions on more than one front.

contents

foreword
carol j. adams

How do women, especially feminists, discover the call to be involved in stopping animal suffering and why does it become so profoundly important in the shaping of their activism? How have women influenced the animal advocacy movement even though this influence is not as acknowledged as it might be?

This book provides stories from women involved in animal advocacy that answers these questions. Through their stories, the women establish that the suffering of animals is an important concern for human beings; that women's involvement in animal advocacy is consistent with other traditions of women's social advocacy; and that there are connections among forms of oppression and these connections require that we include animals in our advocacy.

The question is sometimes posed: why do women work for animals instead of women and other disenfranchised humans? The question simplifies a complex dynamic. These compelling stories, in evoking the particular nature of each of the authors' work and life, reveal the complexity. By gathering these diverse essays together, Lisa Kemmerer shows us that the either/or approach to social change (work for disenfranchised humans or work for animals) is false. One answer to the question "why animals?" is that feminism led us here. The "here" where we find ourselves, at least most of us, does not simplify through opposition (us or them, women or animals). These essayists demonstrate what countless feminist-vegan writers and activists have known for many years now. Activism for justice isn't easily divisible into "human" and "nonhuman."

At this point, with more than thirty-five years of feminist writing and activism that explicitly includes animals,[1]—with women constituting more than 60 percent (at the minimum) of animal activists—and women doing the majority of activism, personal stories that tell the how and why of women's involvement are important.

But these personal essays don't just offer insights into why and how women work on behalf of animals. Through their stories, these writers give us the opportunity to learn more about what is happening to animals.

In *The Sexual Politics of Meat*, I propose that in Western cultures built on the oppression of animals, animals are absent referents.[2] They disappear as individuals or subjects to become someone's object—to be bred, exhibited, hunted, devoured. Information about the transformation of a subject into an object is upsetting, discouraging, and depressing; this information can inspire feelings of rage, hostility, anger. This knowledge and these feelings can also be transformed into activism. Read and see how.

One important aspect of these essays is that they show how awareness leads to activism. Awareness does not exist on its own, without its companion, activism.

In terms of my feminist-vegan theory, awareness of the structure of the absent referent and the lives it destroys motivates activists to challenge it, to restore what (actually who) has been made absent. Awareness and engagement exist together. I like the way these personal essays illustrate this point. Many of them reveal a relational ethics that situates the "I" who speaks as well as the subject this "I" encounters. They show the refusal of the political structuring of human supremacy; we learn about the process by which an "object" is restored to subject status.

We all know by this point how the political structures personal lives; what these essays reveal is how we can illumine the political by personal stories. These personal essays anchor the difficult information of animals' lives under humans and they offer us a way into thinking about and relating to animals.

There is anger and passion here. How could it be otherwise?

This anger and passion is confusing to people who remain firmly anthropocentric. They ask, "Why are you angry about what is happening to animals and not what is happening to humans?" (They presume we aren't.) Or they ask, why we are doing this rather than feeding the homeless or helping battered women? And we loop back to where we began, with an either/or perspective that thinks we must always be choosing one over the other. This teleological presumption that humans are the fulfillment of evolution (superior to all the other animals), this human exceptionalism, requires that animal activists defend their choices. Of course, I have found that it is only human exceptionalists who believe you can't be doing both. I don't think animal activists need to defend why they have decided to focus in the way they have on animal issues, but illuminating how they came to what they are doing may help those who are put on edge or made slightly defensive when they realize that our activism implicates them. When they realize there are choices to be made, and some of those choices are ones they need to make, will animals remain objects in their lives or not?

As I say in *Living Among Meat Eaters,* people who benefit from the object status of animals "think change is hard. Not changing is even harder. They just haven't discovered this yet."[3]

Another thing human exceptionalists often do is to stereotype animal activists by race and class. In this book you'll see why this truly is a fundamental error; an error that reveals itself to be a project of anthropocentrism. Stereotyping animal activists arises from biases and misperceptions; it is not representative of animal activism at all. Not only is ethnic and racial diversity represented in this book, but also tactical diversity—from campaigns originating with the Humane Society of the United States to direct action, from founding a sanctuary to pioneering for animals in higher education, from activism that sexualizes women to activism that critiques activists who sexualize women.

As a result of this diversity, let me advise you not to take anything that any one of these women says as an absolute representation of animal activism. Their differences from one another in situation, tactics, and philosophy not only illustrate the diversity of the movement, they also show that there isn't one way or one voice.

If you assembled us all in a room, there would be energetic discussions and disagreements: about language choice, about the theoretical framing of animal oppression, about tactical decisions, about the use of women in animal activism and the symbolism of women's bodies. It probably wouldn't be cacophonous, but it would be lively (like this anthology). It would reflect the diversity that is central to the purpose of this anthology: To decenter any notion that we can identify just who an animal activist "type" is.

We would have much to debate and we could debate these issues because on many other things we are in agreement. We agree that human exceptionalism is a—or for some—*the* major problem of the twenty-first century.

These essays are so fascinating and important because they tell personal stories of awareness and engagement. None of them is my story; none of them is your story. For the writers they express the actuality of what she is doing and what grounds her; for the reader they represent so many possibilities, possibilities arising from awareness and finding expression through engagement.

I believe I am not alone in suggesting that when you put down this book, ask yourself, "In relationship to the other animals, what is my own story of awareness and engagement?" "What does this awareness ask of me?" And remember, in attempting to answer this question—as this anthology shows you so wonderfully—you aren't alone.

NOTES

1. For an overview of the different feminist approaches to animal ethics, see the introduction in Josephine Donovan and Carol J. Adams, *The Feminist Care Tradition in Animal Ethics: A Reader* (New York: Columbia University Press, 2008).

2. Carol J. Adams. *The Sexual Politics of Meat: A Feminist-Vegetarian Critical Theory Twentieth Anniversary Edition.* New York: Continuum, 2010. 66–67.

3. Adams. *Living among Meat Eaters: The Vegetarian's Survival Handbook.* Herndon, Va., 2008. 57.

acknowledgments

I am grateful to the women in this anthology for their honesty, for sharing their experiences and expertise, and for their energetic work on behalf of nonhuman animals and on behalf of justice more generally.

Special thanks to pattrice jones and A. Breeze Harper for recommending possible authors, to reviewers Carol Adams and Kathy Rudy, and to Carol Adams, pattrice jones, and A. Breeze Harper for helpful suggestions on short notice for the introduction.

Organizations represented in this book need support and assistance if they are to bring much-needed change. Most social justice organizations have openings for unpaid and paid help, and they always need financial support. Be informed. Be involved. Please help bring change.

sister species

introduction

lisa kemmerer

 t his anthology began when I sent out a call for papers, asking women to write about their work in animal advocacy. I had long been aware that women were the heart and soul of the animal advocacy movement, and I was determined to create an anthology that honored at least a few of these courageous women.

I asked contributors to write about animal advocacy. I sought authors working in different types of activism, for different species, in a variety of capacities, in a handful of nations. I chose women from different ages, religions, socioeconomic groups, and continents. Each of these women sent an essay about animal activism and also discussed some other form of oppression that they were addressing alongside speciesism, whether sexism, racism, homophobia, or class stratification. Unexpectedly, I discovered that I had gathered a collection of essays demonstrating the many ways in which animal liberation is inextricably linked with other social justice causes.

With essays in hand, I found myself outside my field of expertise, which focuses on animal ethics. My doctoral dissertation centers on major thinkers in several key areas of animal ethics. During the years in which I worked on this dissertation, no faculty member suggested that I explore the feminist ethic of care, or ecofeminism—though these constitute key areas of animal ethics. No one suggested that I explore how Martin Luther King or Gandhi might have informed the animal rights movement. Maybe this is because all of my teachers were white men, and they all worked within the narrow confines of patriarchal, Western philosophy. Nonetheless, as I worked, I caught glimpses of ecofeminism and the feminist ethic of care through the eyes of male authors; their comments turned me away from exploring these alternative perspectives.

Ultimately, my dissertation was published in a fat book on animal ethics that considered only white male thinkers, only white male perspectives, only white male ideas. My work was expansive, and yet it was painfully narrow. And no one working with me seemed to notice.

Only later, through activism, did I meet feminists working in the area of animal liberation, at which time I slowly began to explore this deep vein of comparatively new ideas. During this exploratory time period I picked up Karen Warren's book on ecofeminism, which caused me to drop the subject with disgust. Warren went out of her way to be inclusive of humanity, while being equally conscientious about excluding nonhuman animals. I turned to the writings of Carol Adams, thinking that her combination of feminism and animal liberation might be more palatable. My journey into interlocking oppressions began in earnest with her 2003 book, *The Pornography of Meat*, which stands at the juncture of feminism and animal advocacy, but which also explores racism and homophobia.

So there I was, manuscript in hand. How was I to write an introduction for a book on interlocking issues of social justice? I headed for the library, and this anthology has become part of my ongoing growth outward from that initial white, hetero, patriarchal perspective—a journey that has led me into richer understandings of animal advocacy specifically, and social justice more broadly.

Here is one of the key ideas that I am assimilating into my social justice advocacy: It is necessary for each of us to try to understand how privilege affects the ways we think about and engage in social justice. The way that we view the world is influenced by our lived experience—by sexual orientation, socioeconomic class, race, sex, and species, for instance (Mills and Salamon in Harper, "Phenomenology"). And this affects how we engage in advocacy. If I explore just one of these dimensions, race, I discover that "social contracts, economic systems, and citizenship, a person's consciousness and how one creates philosophies" are all "significantly shaped by one's lived experience of race" within a particular society (Mills, Yancy, and Sullivan in Harper, "Phenomenology"). For example, Barbara Flagg points to "the ability of Whites to control the cultural discourse of racial equality," including the rhetoric of colorblindness, and "Whites often employ strategies that reinstate Whiteness at the center. Here the metaprivilege of Whiteness resides in the 'absence of awareness of White privilege' . . . Whiteness does not acknowledge either its own privilege or the material and sociocultural mechanisms by which that privilege is protected. White privilege itself becomes invisible" (Flagg 5–6). In an upcoming essay on this topic, A. Breeze Harper writes that to be white is to "know and move throughout" one's racist homeland as if it were not a racist nation (Harper, "Phenomenology"). She notes that Dwyer and Jones III describe whiteness as carrying a "socio-spatial epistemology" that assumes the position of authority, through which Caucasians come to believe that their epistemologies are not specific, but are general—applicable to all people (Harper, "Phenomenology"). All of this is equally true in a sexist society and a speciesist society. Those who are of comparatively powerless races, when put in a position of power-over, tend to be no less blind to *their* privilege.

Despite my belated efforts, I have no doubt that my white privilege continues to be largely opaque from my own point of view, just as most white men are oblivious to sexism and most racialized minorities are oblivious to speciesism. I would prefer that my privileged status as a white, middle-class, abled-but-aging female not slip under the radar. This requires education—mostly not from those in our privileged category—followed up with a will to change, complete with commitment and diligence.

I am one of those many white, middle-class, female vegans whose voices dominate Western animal activism. My whiteness—my blindness and ignorance—limits my effectiveness as an activist. Race matters. (Sex matters. Sexual orientation matters. Species matters.) Ignorance of what others face, where they are coming from and where they have been, limits my ability to dialogue with others in any meaningful way. Tara Sophia Bahna-James—who self-identifies as standing among the many racialized minorities in the United States—notes that, as she adopted the vegan lifestyle, her "female, Black-identified friends" provided "the most vocal skepticism" (162):

> One friend made the connection that often veganism meant having the luxury of enough time and money to go out of one's way and engage in specific, harder-to-find consumer choices; a prerequisite that makes assumptions about class and privilege that are largely at odds with the more mainstream Black American experience. Another, more financially successful Black friend had been put off by hearing vegans make ethical arguments that analogized animal agriculture to slavery. Still another friend, whom I watched go from childhood in the projects to a law school degree by the sweat of her own brow, couldn't help but interpret what I said as though someone was asking her to sacrifice after all she'd been through. And though I'm committed to veganism, I don't necessarily disagree with their arguments. I still feel I can see where these friends are coming from, simply because I know where they've been. (Bahna-James 162)

I don't know where they've been, or even what life is like for racialized minorities in our racist communities. What are *my* chances of touching these individuals with my hopes for change when I have little understanding of *their* particular frustrations and hopes for change?

I must engage with the normative parts of my life because they are a major impediment to social justice activism. Privilege creates a consciousness that is reflected in social justice advocacy, about which we are generally unaware—as is evident if one explores the history of the feminist, environmental, and animal liberation movements. Those who hold power and set norms simply because they are male, or white, or heterosexual must be aware of their unjust power and accept different ways of being and thinking—introduced by others. People must find commonality with those of different religions, affectional orientations, races, and classes if hoped-for social changes are to be considered by those who do not share our religion, affectional orientation, race, or class.

Fortunately, there is a growing awareness that oppressions are linked. In *Sistah Vegan*, Michelle Loyd-Paige writes:

> All social inequalities are linked. Comprehensive systemic change will happen only if we are aware of these connections and work to bring an end to all inequalities—not just our favorites or the ones that most directly affect our part of the universe. No one is on the sidelines; by our actions or inactions, by our caring or our indifference, we are either part of the problem or part of the solution. (Loyd-Paige 2)

Many social activists are now discovering that certain oppressions have been imprudently ignored and that many concerned and dedicated social activists are fighting just one form of oppression while unwittingly fueling the fires of other injustices. In a single-minded quest to reduce poverty, racism, or sexism, for example, many activists lose connection with the bigger picture—the links between poverty, racism, and sexism. This harms our ability to work with a diversity of other activists, and also harms the effectiveness of outreach. For example, in A. Breeze Harper's new anthology, *Sistah Vegan: Black Female Vegans Speak on Food, Identity, Health and Society*, Harper writes of her experience as a black college student, encountering social justice activists who tried to "reach out" to Harper, but their seeming indifference to race and class (likely stemming from ignorance of race and class issues) blocked effective communication:

> When I met those "crazy, tree-hugging" environmentalists and vegetarians (and the occasional vegan) for the first time, while attending Dartmouth College from 1994 to 1998, I couldn't believe they thought they had the right to tell me I shouldn't be eating Kentucky Fried chicken or taking thirty-minute showers or buying GAP clothing. *Who the hell were they to tell me this?* I naively thought

with prejudice, *They're just bored overprivileged rich white kids who do not have real problems.* I realized nearly a decade later that they simply weren't trained or well read enough in antiracist and antipoverty praxis to deliver their message to me in a way that connected to my social justice work as a Black working-class female trying to deal with sexism, classism, and racism at Dartmouth. Though I would have appreciated a much more culturally sensitive delivery in their message—and cultural sensitivity is something I think the largely white, middle-class, eco-sustainable, and alternative-health movements in the U.S. need to work on—these kids' concerns were not only real, but substantial; it was their white, middle- and upper-class, privileged perception of health and eco-sustainability that made most of them unable to connect to working-class people and to Black and brown people like myself.

My experience with this is not singular. . . . [P]redominantly white, liberal, social-justice initiatives—from community food organizing and antiglobalization protests, to veganism, to dismantling the prison-industrial complex—are often entrenched in covert whiteness and white privilege that are collectively unacknowledged. . . . This has blunted the effectiveness of these movements' outreach and intent to people of color like myself, who perceive the tone and delivery of their message as elitist and colonizing. I believe this is one of the key reasons why so many people of color in the U.S. feel that ethical consumption is a "white thing" only and don't delve into how it will help our antiracism and antipoverty praxis.

Until I made the connections on my own, I too felt this way. (Harper, "Social" 35)

Sometimes (though perhaps rarely), when people are caught in this single-minded approach, they come to see links of oppression with only a slight nudge from others. More frequently, these links are difficult to decipher—even when others eagerly point the way. In fact, sometimes people have trouble shifting gears to see linked oppressions *because* others must point the way. When individuals are working hard to bring change, and someone tries to explain that they have fallen short of justice and equality, people often feel defensive, irritated, exhausted—broadsided by yet another weighty concern. Worse yet, one that *they* are contributing to.

The activist's path is not easy, but it is the only reasonable path for those who desire change. In the words of Melissa Santosa:

Sometimes I think, "Fuck this, if I could choose another life, I would." If it were in my logical power to deny the call to action from wherever it summons me, I would. For me, there is both choice and obligation. . . . Like professor after professor at the historically Black university I attended [said], "To whom much is given, much is expected." (Santosa 76)

While all things are relative, if you are able to access and read this book, you are almost surely among those to whom much has been given.

This anthology is about expanding understandings of social justice, about connecting dots—recognizing links of oppression. "Ultimately, we must deeply consider, do our addictions and other forms of consumption contradict our antiracist and antipoverty social justice beliefs?" (Harper "Social"). Does our diet contradict our antiracist, feminist agenda? This collection of essays stems from an understanding that social justice activism in the twenty-first century must address intersectional oppressions, and that these interlocking oppressions include—to name just a few—speciesism, sexism, racism, and homophobia. More specifically, this book

- Exposes critical connections between social justice movements, focusing on sexism, racism, homophobia, classism, and speciesism, remaining mindful that there are other forms of oppression that fit within this framework;
- Establishes speciesism as an important concern for all social justice activists, with a special focus on connecting speciesism with racism and sexism;
- Elucidates why all social justice advocates ought to adopt a vegan lifestyle;
- Encourages animal advocates to network with other social justice advocates to expose and dismantle all forms of oppression, and (at a minimum) avoid contributing to other forms of oppression because of ignorance, exhaustion, or indifference.

Toward this end, I have included four separate sections in this introduction. In the first section I provide a brief overview of the evolution of intersectional analysis in the field of social justice, beginning with feminism and pluralism in the sixties and seventies, moving through an explanation of patriarchy and linked oppressions in industrialized Western nations, exploring ecofeminism, and concluding with speciesism. In this section I endeavor to explain how aspects of feminism have been challenged and stretched across time in the hands of a diversity of human thinkers and writers, and how this process has prepared the way for understanding and incorporating interlocking oppressions through an increasingly diverse feminist movement. If you are familiar with the history of feminism, basic elements of patriarchy, and ecofeminism, you may prefer to skim the beginning of this section, focusing on the latter portion, which introduces speciesism.

Section II focuses on a handful of key ideas that run through this collection of essays: empathy, silence, trauma, and voice. After exploring these (and closely related) concepts, I employ two of these ideas, empathy and voice, in Section III (Making Change). In this section, true to the purpose of this anthology, I encourage readers to be informed, and to make choices that are consistent with a heightened understanding of linked oppressions. Social justice advocacy is not simply a career—it is a lifestyle. Martin Luther King noted that "injustice must be rooted out by strong, persistent, and determined action" (M. King 407). Living up to our own beliefs is essential. This type of advocacy requires a great deal of vigilance, introspection, and a willingness to change. Reading *Sister Species* is of little use if the information therein is not applied in day-to-day life. To demonstrate the sort of integration of daily choices and ethics, the type of conflicts that can arise in this quagmire of interlocking oppressions, and the sort of introspection and flex that is required, we close Section III with an ongoing debate over food choices at feminist and ecofeminist conferences.

Section IV introduces authors and essays. The introduction closes with a short comment on word choice and the ongoing process of expanding understandings of interlocking oppressions.

i. feminism, patriarchy, ecofeminism, and speciesism

EXPANDING FEMINISM

For thousands of years the patriarchy has waged a war against women; a war in which it controls and violates our bodies with rape, battering, forced motherhood, and conditioned self-hatred. As well as assigning women the exclusive sexual functions of reproduction and providing men pleasure, the patriarchy reduces women to instruments of labour. (Heller 351)

In the early sixties, Betty Friedan became a household name when she published *The Feminine Mystique*, in which she writes: "We can no longer ignore that voice within women that says: 'I want something more than my husband and my children and my house'" (hooks, "Black" 25). While Friedan called women to take up careers, rather than languish at home, other authors noted that the problems about which Friedan wrote were not the problems of all women, or even most women. She did not speak for "women without men, without children, without homes. She ignored the existence of all nonwhite women and poor white women. She did not tell readers whether it was more fulfilling to be a maid, a babysitter, a factory worker, a clerk, or a prostitute, than to be a leisure class housewife" (hooks, "Black" 25).

Friedan made the error of writing as if "a select group of college-educated, middle- and upper-class, married white women—housewives bored with leisure, with the home, with children, with buying products, who wanted more out of life" represented women generally (hooks, "Black" 25). She seemed to assume that all women shared her luxurious boredom when, in truth, most women would likely revel in the life that Friedan rejected. Consequently, Af-

rican American bell hooks—along with many others who did not share heterosexual, abled, white privilege—recognized the value of Friedan's contribu-
tion, but also felt that her book was "a case study of narcissism, insensitivity,
sentimentality, and self-indulgence" (hooks, "Black" 26).

The starting point of feminist theory is envisioned as universal: Women
are systematically oppressed in relation to men in patriarchal societies, societies in which "men have more power than women, and have more access to
whatever society esteems" (Flax 10). Additionally, at least since the writings of
Aphra Behn (1640–1689—one of the first professional English female writers), some white women "have thought about race and class as well as gender"
(Kirk, "Introduction" 7). Nonetheless, there has been a well-publicized form of
feminism, championed largely by comparatively privileged women (epitomized
by Friedan), who have offered a somewhat "one-dimensional perspective"
(hooks, "Black" 26):

> [M]any prominent U.S. feminist activists and writers were White, middle-class,
> heterosexual women who generalized from their own experiences. They focused
> on their subordination as women without paying attention to their privilege on
> other dimensions, notably race, class, and sexual orientation. (Kirk 16)

Some notable feminist authors demonstrated little or no understanding of
interlocking oppressions experienced by poor, Latino, lesbian, or Muslim
women, for example, and disenfranchised women came to see this narrow-
ness of understanding as "a marked feature of the contemporary feminist
movement" (hooks, "Black" 26).

Those who felt marginalized challenged feminism's one-dimensional
perspective. In the late 1970s, for example, a group of black feminists known
as the Combahee River Collective (CRC) pointed out that, in their experience,
it was "difficult to separate race from class from sex oppression," because they
most often experienced oppressions simultaneously (Combahee 39). The CRC
built their agenda around personal experiences: We are "actively committed
to struggling against racial, sexual, heterosexual, and class oppression," and
we hope to exemplify an "integrated analysis and practice based upon the fact
that the major systems of oppression are interlocking" (Combahee 38).

Some white feminist authors willingly climbed aboard. Others gave a nod,
but failed to engage with or weave these interlocking issues into their writing
in any meaningful way (hooks, "Black" 32). Still other mainstream feminists
overtly refused to include race or class in their feminist analysis, while others
attempted to shut down those who brought interlocking oppressions to the
table (hooks, "Black" 31), perhaps fearful of diverting attention from their pri-

mary focus. Embarrassingly, history has shown time and again how humans complain about the pinch in their own shoes, while failing to see that their tight-fitting shoes are trampling on someone else.

Over time, more and more feminists accepted the reality of linked oppressions. Generally speaking, it is no longer acceptable "to talk simply and naively about 'women' as women" (Birke 33). With an increased awareness that "women" represents a host of individuals distributed across lines of considerable difference, contemporary authors and thinkers often put their work in context, outlining the limitations of their viewpoint (Collins 187). One such author notes: "My own experience is not only as a woman, but is also situated in my experiences of being white, of being middle-class, of growing up in postwar London, of being a lesbian" (Birke 33). Contemporary texts for gender studies now tend to be created with an eye to diversity, including essays from women and men of varied cultural backgrounds from around the world; more often than not, these texts carry subtitles with the word "multicultural" or "global." This shift toward diversity—this reaction to a new understanding of the complexity of "women"—is not completely integrated into feminism, nor has this shift been completely satisfying. Sometimes attempts at diversity create an uneasy balance "between the imperatives of outreach and inclusion on the one hand, and the risk of tokenism and further marginalization on the other" (Lee 46).

Strong scholars continue to push for greater reform, noting that "diversity" too often holds whiteness as the norm, and that diversity is generally envisioned as assimilation into the larger, dominant culture. Transnational feminist Dr. M. Jacqui Alexander notes that "diversity" is inadequate, particularly for addressing racism and colonialism. "Diversity" too often diverts attention from the root problem: Normative whiteness. Alexander notes that neither "diversity" nor multiculturalism will achieve equality if whiteness continues to occupy the center. She notes that U.S. academic institutions increasingly have faces of color on their faculty and in their student body, but all are expected to assimilate into Eurocentric whiteness as the cultural norm. As long as the politics of diversity and multiculturalism are prevalent among the white middle class, "diversity" will continue to mimic or reflect this demographic and maintain privileges affiliated with whiteness (Alexander 118–19). While on the faculty of The New School for Social Research in New York City, Alexander fought the school's white supremacist sense of "diversity," through which they merely added faces that did not look "white," with the expectation that these racialized minorities would teach in a way that would support and perpetuate white privilege.

Overall, the School's definitions of "diversity" do not emanate from a historical reading of racialization—the historical collective aspects of debt to which black people and people of color are entitled. . . . Rather, they attenuate history into notions of individual rehabilitation and individual remuneration. The institution would want to attempt such a revision of history in the absence of any discourse about the mythologies of race and the creation of racism, hence the substitution of "diversity," racially preferring race-neutrality, meaning presumably that white people can never acknowledge the privilege they derive from the hierarchies of race; people of color and black people can never talk about racism; and progressive coalitions of white people and people of color could never undertake fruitful discussions about the ways in which privilege and disinheritance mutually imbricate each other. These discourses establish, in effect, a system of segregation that absents white men in power, even while they rule. (Alexander 140)

This is equally true of heterosexism, sexism, and speciesism.

Despite these deep, institutional tendencies, feminists and those in women's studies are now more apt to recognize that it is ineffective to seek justice for women without addressing racism, homelessness, and heterosexism: One of feminism's strengths is that it is not generally just about women (Birke 33). I think it is fair to say—certainly among scholars—that most contemporary feminists link equality between the sexes with "welfare and social-work groups, peace groups, pro-abortion groups, [and] black women's groups"; they critique "militarism, racism, and capitalism" alongside sexism (Adams, *Pornography* 163). Those working for sexual equality have generally come to understand that social justice advocates "must liberate women from the multiple oppressions that constitute their gendered identities—oppressions based on race/ethnicity, class, affectional orientation, age, ability, geographic location, anti-Semitism, and colonialism" (Warren 62).

Despite an impressive array of oppressions that activists must work against, hooks notes that black women tend to live at the bottom of the demographic barrel, with a social status that is "lower than that of any other group" (hooks, "Black" 32). Consequently, she argues that black women are not "socialized to assume the role of exploiter/oppressor in that [black women] are allowed no institutionalized 'other' [to] exploit or oppress" (hooks, "Black" 32). Here, hooks' words reveal her own privilege and a consequent blindness and lack of understanding.

PATRIARCHY, DUALISM, AND HIERARCHY

Oppression—Prejudice and discrimination directed toward whole socially recognized groups of people and promoted by the ideologies and practices of all social institutions. The critical elements differentiating oppression from simple prejudice and discrimination are that it is a group phenomenon and that institutional power and authority are used to support prejudices and enforce discriminatory behaviors in systematic ways. Everyone is socialized to participate in oppressive practices, either as direct and indirect perpetrators or passive beneficiaries, or—as with some oppressed peoples—by directing discriminatory behaviors at members of one's own group or another group deemed inferior. ("Glossary" G-4)

By definition, oppression is propagated by ideologies and institutions, and individuals are socialized to oppress certain "others." An "ideology" consists of ideas, values, and attitudes "that represent the interests of a group of people" ("Glossary" G-3). Oppressions, then, are by definition linked—linked by common ideologies, by institutional forces, and by socialization that makes oppressions normative and invisible.

Contemporary societies tend to be distinctly patriarchal, and contemporary oppressions therefore tend to be rooted in patriarchal ideologies and patriarchal institutions. Patriarchy is "the systematic organization of male supremacy" (Stacey 53) so that "men hold power and are dominant figures" ("Glossary" G-4). Patriarchy provides a "male-dominated, male-identified, male-centered, and control-obsessed" social structure (Johnson 34). Certain attributes are common in patriarchal societies, such as false dualisms, which provide a framework for domination and subordination, oppressor and oppressed, and support a social structure in which certain groups have power while others are comparatively powerless.

Patriarchal dualism feeds into contrived hierarchies of power, which provide those on top with "access to whatever society esteems" (Flax 10). Dualism also undermines human relations (Lahar 96): Through dualism, those living in patriarchies tend to categorize in terms of opposites, beginning with male and female, and extending to a plethora of other contrived divisions, such as white/other races, human/animal, culture/nature, and reason/emotion. Most people in Western patriarchal cultures are conditioned to "see human differences in simplistic opposition to each other: dominant/subordinate, good/bad, up/down, superior/inferior" (Lorde, "Age" 526). But why would Africans and Caucasians be viewed as separate and distinct when all human beings have emerged from common ancestors in Africa? It would make more sense to view all Americans as African Americans, since evidence suggests that humans originated in Africa. Similarly, patriarchy's ideology of false dualisms encourages us to view Barack Obama as "black," though with one white parent and one black parent he is just as genetically white as he is black.

Despite the obvious shortcomings of dualistic thinking, cultures around the world tend to dichotomize sex into male and female (Lorber 27). At the root of this false dualism lies the erroneous assumption that there are only two sexes. While XX and XY genes predominate in the animal world, this karyo-type does not even begin to express the variety of karyotypes possible, even if we focus only on the human animal. In humans, we find 45 X, 47 XXX, 48 XXXX, 49 XXXXX, 47 XYY, 47 XXY, 48 XXXY, 49 XXXXY, and 49 XXXYY (Callahan 62). Roughly 60,000 boys are born annually with one or more extra X chromosome (Callahan 63). About half as many babies are born with a 45 X karyotype (Callahan 64), while still other babies are born with a variety of karyotypes among different cells within their bodies (Callahan 65). All of these people tend to suffer because of dualistic thinking—because others have cre-ated a false dichotomy of male and female biology into which they cannot fit.

Western patriarchy adds to this biological dualism the idea that there are certain characteristics that go with each of these exclusive and exhaustive sex options. If you are assessed to be biologically female, then you will be expected to be feminine. Conversely, if those born before you decide that you are male, you will be expected to be masculine. Society pressures children, from birth, to conform with one or the other—masculine or feminine. But human ways of being are rarely bifurcated cleanly along sex lines: Most of us are a mix of masculine and feminine ways and inclinations. Most of us suffer from being pushed, one way or another, through social molds into which we do not easily fit.

Dualistic separations of human/animal and nature/culture are as unten-able as racial and sexual dualisms. Humans are animals—mammals, pri-mates—and humans are part of nature. Furthermore, each "species ramifies into many differences, including human beings," who are born into a variety of breeds/races and cultures (Radford Ruether 469). Simplistic dualisms, because they are untenable, impede our ability to relate to the world around us—including one another—and it is therefore critical that people "address and redress" dualistic thinking (Lahar 96).

Dualism is central to interlocking oppressions: Patriarchal societies don't merely divide, they conquer. In a "dualistic worldview, men and women are not simply defined as polarities, but all that is associated with women is devalued and subordinated" (Kheel, *Nature* 38). This means that "emotion, animals, na-ture, and the body" are all devalued in relation to "those things associated with men," including "reason, humans, culture, and the mind" (Gaard, "Living" 5).

In *The Pornography of Meat*, Carol Adams uses the terms "A" and "Not A" to describe this common feature of patriarchy. On the "A" side, patriarchal cultures hold men, whites, culture, human beings, minds, civilization, production, and capital as the norm. Audre Lorde adds young, thin, heterosexual, Christian, and financially secure to the "A" category (Lorde, "Age" 527). Those who do not qualify as an "A" fall into the subordinate "Not A" category: Women, nonwhite racialized minorities (a term which I borrow from A. Breeze Harper), nature, nonhuman animals, bodies, primitive peoples, reproduction, and labor (Adams, *Pornography* 50), as well as plump, older, nonheterosexual, and non-Christian individuals. Patriarchal societies thereby empower certain individuals at the expense of others: Devalued individuals are viewed as a means to the ends of the dominant group. In order to maintain this power structure, and further selfish interests, those in power strive to "maintain a strong distinction and maximize distance" between dominant and subordinate individuals (Plumwood 23).

Oppression is propagated by ideologies and institutions, whereby individuals are socialized to oppress and be oppressed. This creates a system of linked oppressions. Martin Luther King Jr. demonstrated an understanding of linked oppressions forty years ago when he said,

> I am cognizant of the interrelatedness of all communities and states. I cannot sit idly by in Atlanta and not be concerned about what happens in Birmingham. Injustice anywhere is a threat to justice everywhere. We are caught in an inescapable network of mutuality, tied in a single garment of destiny. Whatever affects one directly, affects all indirectly. (M. King 399)

Neither can activists afford to struggle against one group of "Not A" individuals while remaining ignorant of other oppressed groups. While no one can speak for all who are oppressed, neither can social justice advocates work from isolated corners, divided and fragmented, yet hoping to bring deep and lasting change: The "liberation of all oppressed groups must be addressed simultaneously" (Gaard, "Living" 5).

Increasingly, groups of feminists are coming to see that the "struggle for women's liberation is inextricably linked to abolition of all oppression" (Gruen 82). Indeed, many people have come to understand that feminism cannot move forward without addressing other isms—especially isms that are manifest within the ranks of feminist circles: "Racism, the belief in the inherent superiority of one race over all others and thereby the right to dominance. Sexism, the belief in the inherent superiority of one sex over the other and thereby the right to dominance. Ageism. Heterosexism. Elitism. Classism" (Lorde, "Age" 527). Many social justice activists—many feminists—continue to work against one form of oppression while feeding the flames of another, without noticing that the blowtorch behind the flames must be turned off before we can have any hope of putting out the resultant fires.

ECOFEMINISM

Ecofeminists see the oppression of women, people of color, children, lesbians and gays and the destruction of nature as linked and mutually reinforcing in a system of domination which is legitimized and perpetuated by various institutions such as the state, the military, religion, the patriarchal family, and industrial capitalism. We fight for the freedom and self-determination of all oppressed peoples as well as for a harmonious relationship with nature: We realize that until we are all free from social and ecological exploitation, no one is free. (Heller 351)

In 1972, in a book with a title that translates as "Feminism or Death," French author Françoise d'Eaubonne called women to "lead an ecological revolution to save the planet," coining the term "ecofeminism" (Merchant, *Earthcare* 5). She looked to a change in relationships between women and men to bring about a change in relations between humans and the natural world, which she believed would reverse ecological destruction and preserve life on the planet (Merchant, *Earthcare* 5).

Ecofeminists focus on interconnections between the domination/oppression of women and the domination/oppression of nature, noting that the "hatred of women and the hatred of nature are intimately connected and mutually reinforcing" (Y. King 458). Ecofeminists are aware that "the perpetrators of violence throughout the world are, by and large, men, and the victims of this violence are primarily women and the natural world" (Kheel, "License" 110). Ecofeminist analysis is generally much more expansive than environmentalism and feminism: "Conceptual interconnections are at the heart of ecofeminist philosophy" (Warren 24). While the science of ecology "aims to harmonize nature, human and nonhuman," ecofeminism draws on ecological, socialist, and feminist thought, incorporating a handful of social justice movements, such as feminism, peace activism, labor, women's health care, antinuclear, environmental, and animal liberation (Y. King 458; Gaard, "Living" 1).

For example, many ecofeminists now argue that environmentalists could more effectively protect the natural world from large corporations dumping externalities—carbon monoxide, chemicals, and animal waste—on poorer, nonwhite neighborhoods, if they were willing to stand up against racism. Their insights into the workings of patriarchy have been supported by recent findings. For example, in 1987 the United Church of Christ's Commission for Racial Justice (CRJ) discovered that two-thirds of U.S. Blacks and Latinos "reside in areas with one or more unregulated toxic-waste sites" (Riley 472).

> The nation's largest hazardous-waste dump, which has received toxic material from 45 states, is located in predominantly black Sumter County, Alabama (de la Pena and Davis 1990, 34). The mostly African American residents in the 85-mile area between Baton Rouge and New Orleans, better known as Cancer Alley, live in a region which contains 136 chemical companies and refineries. (Riley 472)

In the United States, "poor people of color are disproportionately likely to be the victims of pollution," including toxic waste (Riley 472); race is "the most significant variable" in distinguishing communities with toxic waste from those without (Riley 475, 472). The CRJ coined the term "environmental racism" to describe waste management policies that favor moneyed Caucasians at the expense of "others."

Race is a key factor in determining the level of environmental pollution that individuals are likely to experience in their neighborhood; another is economic status:

> The evidence is strong. If you are a person of color, you are much more likely to live in an area where toxic dumps, landfills, incinerators, and polluting industries are or will be located. It is also less likely that the pollution will be cleaned up, and polluters probably will face lighter punishments than if they were located in white neighborhoods.
>
> Similar results are found at the international level. Poor countries are more likely to suffer environmental degradation—deforestation, desertification and air and water pollution—than wealthy countries, and the poorest residents of those countries, the poorest of the poor, are likely to suffer the most. (Des Jardins 240–41)

Sex is also an important factor because the natural environment is "inextricably connected to rural and household economies," which tend to be governed by women (Warren 3). Development and destruction of the natural environment therefore create "particular burdens for women," especially in underdeveloped countries (Des Jardins 245). Women constitute 80 percent of Africa's farmers, and are therefore directly affected by deforestation and soil erosion (Riley 478). Women are also primarily responsible for gathering fuel and water, and women in Africa, Asia, and South America are increasingly faced with water and wood scarcities, forcing them to "spend up to forty-three hours per week collecting and carrying water," and traveling many miles to find fuel (Warren 7). Additionally, toxic substances that are dumped into water and backyards "impair women's reproductive systems, poisoning their breast-milk, their food and their children" (Heller 351). In short, women suffer disproportionately in relation to men because of "both social domination and the domination of nature" (Y. King 462).

In Western patriarchal culture, both women and nonhuman nature have been devalued alongside their assumed opposites—men and civilization/culture. Nature tends to be objectified, "controlled and dissected"; nature is an object to be exploited for "natural resources" (Merchant, "Dominion" 47). Women and nature are placed together in the "Not A" category, and are often seen as objects for exploitation, "things" to be used for the benefit of the "A" category—white, property-owning males. Ecofeminists—at least in theory—oppose all forms of domination, and reject "the notion that any part of the world, human or nonhuman, exists solely for the use and pleasure of any other part"—they reject power-over (Vance 133–34). Dichotomies and hierarchies, contemporary ecofeminists note, are alien to the natural world—nature is interconnections (Y. King 461). No individual or species is privileged in the world of nature: All eat and are eaten; all become sick and die in their turn. Humans are part of an interconnected continuum of life (Merchant, *Earthcare* 204).

In light of environmental racism and sexism, many ecofeminists call attention to the fact that environmentalists, feminists, and those fighting racism and poverty are plucking at different straws in the same broom: "The global environmental crisis is related to the sociopolitical systems of fear and hatred of all that is natural, nonwhite, and female" (Riley 473).

SPECIESISM

As often as Herman had witnessed the slaughter of animals and fish, he always had the same thought: in their behavior toward creatures, all men were Nazis. The smugness with which man could do with other species as he pleased exemplified the most extreme racist theories, the principle that might is right. (Singer 257)

Failing to notice a lack of Latino and African American representation in Congress is a result of systemic oppression—racism. Indifference to the fact that white men dominate large corporations is both racist and sexist. A lack of concern about the plight of a "breeding" sow on a factory farm is also a result of normative systematic oppression—speciesism.

Historically, women, animals, and children have legally been defined as the property of males. Patriarchy (where men control women) and pastoralism (where men control nonhuman animals) "are justified and perpetuated by the same ideologies and practices" ("Sexism"). For example, both women and animals have historically been considered less intelligent, less rational, and therefore more primitive and closer to nature than men. Reducing women and nonhumans to something less than civilized men of intellect has allowed men to exploit women, nonhuman animals, and nature. Objectification, ridicule, and control of reproduction are all linked to patriarchal denigration and exploitation of females—including human females—and nature. Nonhuman animals are systematically marginalized, objectified, and exploited by human beings of both sexes, of every color, age, and ability, and from every socioeconomic background.

In Western patriarchal cultures, nonhuman individuals tend to be associated with human females and nonwhite racialized minorities, but they are even lower on the contrived human hierarchy of being (Adams, *Pornography* 45–46). "The oppression that black people suffer in South Africa—and people of color, and children face all over the world—is the same oppression that animals endure every day to a greater degree" (Alice Walker quoted by Adams, "Feminist" 207). Humans are all in the "A" group in relation to nonhuman animals.

Speciesism is systematic, institutionalized oppression. Exploitation and slaughter of nonhuman animals in Western nations is a "group phenomenon," forced onto the vast majority of cows, turkeys, pigs, and chickens simply because of their species. Cattle and pigs are collectively viewed as expendable—eatable. Rabbits and rats are treated like Petri dishes rather than living beings. Fox, chinchilla, mink, and beaver are called "furbearers"—resources, clothing. Tigers, elephants, dolphins, and chimpanzees are bought and sold for zoos, circuses, television programs and advertisements, and marine parks as entertainment, as props, as means to human ends. "Humankind's root cultural relationship with animals is that of aggressor to victim," and this victimization is systemic—"deeply ingrained in human institutions" (Scholtmeijer 235, 256).

In the definition of oppression offered above, at the start of the section titled "Patriarchy, Dualism, and Hierarchy," "institutional power and authority are used to support prejudices and enforce discriminatory behaviors in systematic ways" ("Glossary" G-4). In the case of speciesism, institutional power and authority are used to support and perpetuate the oppression of nonhuman individuals. For example, the U.S. government created a food pyramid, which erroneously claimed that animal products are central to a healthy diet. Similarly, both animal agriculture and science industries propagate the myth that animal exploitation is "necessary for human health and wellbeing" (Luke 311). Many people still believe both of these blatant untruths—the vast majority of students in the classes that I teach believe this expedient capitalist's untruth. The U.S. system of justice has created and maintains laws whereby nonhuman animals have no legal standing, but are defined as "property," as wives and slaves once were. Other animals (including mice, rats, and birds) are not included in the current, legal definition of "animal" in the United States, thereby denying these individuals the slight protection provided by U.S. animal welfare laws in order to allow scientists to use these sentient beings in any way they see fit, without pausing for fear of legal sanction (Luke 303). Institutional power and authority also lie behind discriminatory laws that prevent animal advocates from using free speech to protect hunted animals (Comninou 134). Institutionalized support for the systematic oppression of nonhuman animals is also evident in the recent Animal Enterprise Terrorism Act, as well as in the mainstream media, both of which mislabel animal advocates—social justice advocates—as "terrorists."

Because the oppression of nonhuman individuals is normative, it is largely invisible, and most of us are complicit in one way or another. While social justice activists now widely recognize that the poor, elderly, and nonwhite racialized minorities are harmed (along with women) by patriarchy, these same activists are too often unable to similarly recognize the harm of patriarchy on nonhuman animals—even ecofeminist theorists (Gaard, "Living" 6). Very few social justice activists understand speciesism or the harmful exploitation that stems from such marginalization and cruel domination of nonhuman animals.

This remains the case despite obvious links across forms of oppression. For example, men equate sex with women and hunting in both language and tactile experience. Bullets are called "balls," firing is referred to as "discharge," and hitting a body with a bullet is called "penetration"; firing prematurely is called "premature discharge" (Kheel, "License" 91–92). This makes yet more sense given that hunting ethics are often "predicated on the need to harness an aggressive, sexual energy and to channel it in appropriate ways," allowing for "the continuation of man's aggressive drive" (Kheel, "License" 92, 95). As a teacher, I impatiently listened to a young man boldly defend the importance of hunting because he found the experience to be orgasmic. In Western patriarchal culture: "Without the pursuit of orgasm, sex typically is thought to have no meaning or narrative structure; without the intent to kill, the hunt, we are told, has none as well" (Kheel, "License" 91).

Patriarchal metaphors "simultaneously feminize nature and naturalize women" (Adams, "Introduction" 1). Marriage grants a man "legal license to his wife's sexual and reproductive services, [while] the model of animal husbandry grants agribusiness and wildlife managers access to the bodies and reproductive services of other-than-human animals" (Kheel, *Nature* 231). Women and nonhuman animals are exploited for their reproductive abilities, and both are devalued as they age and wear out—when they are no longer able to reproduce. Susan Griffin provides a noteworthy example of how both women and nonhuman animals—largely female nonhuman animals—have been molded and exploited across centuries by men for the sake of men (Griffin 67–70). Factory-farmed animals are the objects of egregious oppression, exploitation, and violence—and the vast majority of factory-farmed animals are females. Sows and cows are repeatedly forced into pregnancy through artificial insemination. After they carry their offspring and give birth, they desperately try to protect their newborns. Nursing milk is stolen from cows, who must be reimpregnated each year (because cows lactate—like women—only after giving birth). In contrast, sows are simply reimpregnated immediately after birthing, while hens are manipulated into cycles of ovulation so that people can steal and consume their reproductive eggs.

Because of their biology, female farmed animals are more rigidly confined for a longer period of time than male farmed animals (who are simply sent to slaughter as adolescents). Given the horrors of factory farming, those slaughtered young are lucky. Farmed animals are genetically and physically manipulated from birth to premature death, and they are looked down on in Western, patriarchal cultures as dumb and unnatural. "Not only men but women and animal protectionists exhibit culturally conditioned indifference toward, and prejudice against, creatures whose lives appear too slavishly, too boringly, too stupidly female, too 'cowlike'" (Davis 197). Similarly, environmentalists generally find nothing to concern them in the sufferings and premature deaths of domestic animals "bred to docility, tractability, stupidity, and dependency" (Davis 201). Females—sows and cows and hens and women—suffer because of their sex in Western patriarchal culture, where female bodies are exploited as sex symbols, for reproduction, for breast milk, and/or for reproductive eggs. As such, farmed animals are at the very bottom of the contemporary, Western hierarchy of beings—and this is speciesism. (For more on factory farms and females, please see the Appendix.)

Factory farming is not the only Western business that cruelly exploits females *because* they are females. Wyeth-Ayerst Laboratories, Inc. produces an estrogen replacement product called Premarin (also sold under the name Prempro). Premarin is made from the urine of pregnant mares who are tethered in stalls for four or five months out of each year specifically for this purpose. Their foals—some 40,000 strong—are shipped off to be fattened and slaughtered at just four months old, a time when they would normally be close at the sides of their mothers. Premarin is marketed based on the archaic assumption that a woman's biology is problematic, that there is something inherently not quite right about female processes, and that women therefore require the care of medical professionals—traditionally males (Ehrenreich 6). Premarin is on the market because people have been led to believe that a woman's natural ways of aging are a sickness in need of cure. This attitude toward aging is indubitably linked with the exploitative view of females as childbearers, which makes aging and menopause problematic and undesirable. "Marketed as a cure for menopause, Premarin hurts both female horses and female humans in order to provide profits for a pharmaceutical corporation" ("Sexism").

Overtly associating women with nonhuman animals, as I have just done, is unsettling to many. Such association is viewed as offering a "more substantial threat to women than identification with nature" (Scholtmeijer 233), perhaps because nature is recognized as noble and magnificent, while nonhuman animals—especially farmed animals—are viewed as expendable property—dumb and despicable. "The suggestion that the otherness of nonhuman animals can inform the otherness of women, therefore, appears to be counterproductive, to pull women down into a condition of defeat along with the animals" (Scholtmeijer 234). Consequently, feminists have too often bolstered the "otherness" of nonhumans in the hopes of extricating women from this ignoble association, liberating "white women and people of color from the onerous equation with animals and otherness," while leaving nonhuman animals to remain as exploitable "other" (Scholtmeijer 257; Adams, "Feminist" 204). (I experienced this type of reaction from feminists at a conference in Stony Brook University. At the time, I did not understand their aggressive objections to identifying the links between the oppression of women and the oppression of female farmed animals.)

By distancing themselves from other exploited females, such feminists endeavor to pass exploitation on to other exploited individuals, those whom they perceive as being yet lower on the hierarchical ladder (Kappeler 335). Such indifference to the exploitation of those whom they perceive as lesser mirrors the larger culture of hierarchy and oppression. In so behaving, these feminists "mirror patriarchal oppressors" (Dunayer, "Sexist" 19). Women, including feminists or ecofeminists, who prefer to ignore that nonhuman animals who are exploited for their reproductive abilities are oppressed females "closely resemble men who prefer to ignore that women are human" (Dunayer 19). Women who prefer not to recognize a cow as an objectified female also resemble early feminists who focus exclusively on white, middle-class women. Feminists who "engage in this kind of denial, [who] support and participate in the oppression of the less powerful" in hopes of elevating themselves, are "not only hypocritical" but also engage in a "profound betrayal of [feminism's] deepest commitments" (Adams and Donovan, "Introduction" 8). To avoid such pitfalls, in light of linked oppressions, feminists and ecofeminists "must specifically address the oppression of the nonhuman animals with whom we share the planet. In failing to do so," activists and theorists adopt "the sort of exclusionary theorizing" that they ostensibly reject (Gruen 61). For those who seek freedom "from violation by the powerful—power and privilege must not be more widely shared, they must be radically dismantled" (Kappeler 335). Instead of feeding nonhuman individuals to the patriarchal monster in the hopes of saving themselves, women must turn the monster away.

Those who fail to recognize speciesism as one of many linked oppressions are likely blind to shared attributes between feminists, animal activists, and other social justice advocates. Like those fighting sexism and racism, animal liberationists call attention to a lack of any morally relevant distinction between "A" and "Not A" individuals by which humans might legitimately exclude certain nonhuman individuals from basic legal protections and privileges enjoyed by human individuals. Farmed animals have a central nervous system and show recognizable signs of physical distress and psychological trauma—similar to those of humanity—when they are physically harmed and/or tightly confined on factory farms, and when their young are snatched from their protective care. Animal species (such as kangaroos, crocodiles, cattle, and chickens) appear different on the surface—like human races and sexes—but share core similarities such as a need for "food, shelter, space, and freedom to move about" (Merchant, *Earthcare* 204). Animals (human and nonhuman) feel pain, can suffer, and ought to be treated accordingly—pain and suffering are always morally relevant. Social justice activists who are not on board with animal activists ought to belatedly "acknowledge the pain and suffering currently experienced by many other-than-human animals, including those who are raised to be eaten" as morally unacceptable (Kheel, *Nature* 233).

Protecting nonhuman animals places limits on human power, and will put an end to ill-gotten gains (a term used by animal rights philosopher Tom Regan)—just as emancipation of African slaves curtailed white power and put an end to the ill-gotten gains of Caucasian Americans. This is the reason for such strong resistance to animal liberation even among other social justice activists. Animal activists are often met with derision from those who wish to continue their accustomed diet, those who do not want to rethink their leather shoes, toiletries, or treasured forms of entertainment. Feminists and civil rights activists who ask others to change for the sake of justice—to give up ill-gotten gains—are often met with similar insults and raucous rejection.

Though other social justice activists rebel against a movement that requires all of us to make significant changes in daily choices—particularly dietary choices—it is increasingly difficult to advocate for women, the poor, or immigrants, for example, with a clear conscience while eating cattle and their offspring and consuming their nursing milk. Animal activists are exposing the links that connect the oppression of nonhuman animals with human oppression. For example, in *Slaughterhouse*, which focuses on factory-farmed animals in industrial slaughter facilities, animal activist Gail Eisnitz found it impossible to ignore human rights violations and labor injustices. Racking up "nearly thirty-six injuries or illnesses for every one hundred workers," Eisnitz notes that "meat packing is the most dangerous industry in the United States" (271). Eisnitz spoke to many slaughterhouse employees who reported acid-spattering (261), arms torn off (272), lost hands (272) and death—which was "compensated" with a mere $1,000 (272). "Knowing that they can—and will—be fired for complaints about injuries, illness, and working conditions, employees are scared silent" (274). One employee commented that slaughterhouses "exploit Hispanic workers because they can't really speak out. They hire a lot of illegals, too. Some are just children—twelve and thirteen, maybe fourteen years old" (262). She found these horrific conditions again and again in U.S. slaughterhouses, in a nation where most citizens expect the government to oversee labor, a nation where few citizens are aware of the affects of the financial ties between agribusiness and the U.S. government.

Those who buy animal products support the abuse of these laborers. Those who buy animal products ought to ask whether or not they would like to work in one of these slaughterhouses, or in a battery hen operation. If we would not like such a job, we ought to choose other food options, shifting job opportunities to places of employment whose policies and methods do not grate against our conscience.

Animal activists have also begun to link animal-based diets with environmental devastation. It is now clear that those who care about the natural world are better off committing to a vegan lifestyle than moving to an economy car (Eshel 1). Choosing to consume animal products—when one can remain healthy with an entirely plant-based diet—"has dire environmental consequences such as deforestation, soil erosion, heavy water consumption, unrecyclable animal excrement, and immense demands on energy and raw materials" (Adams, "Feminist" 214). Those who would suggest that individual animals do not matter in light of larger ecological problems do not know (perhaps do not want to know) that speciesism has caused—and continues to cause—ecological devastation.

That said, those who enjoy socioeconomic class privilege are often unaware (as I tend to be) that many, many people do not have ready access to healthy, vegan food choices. I have the option of growing a little garden outside my home. We have three health-food stores in town that provide vegan alternatives, and I have a car to use to pick up groceries from these stores. Poorer neighborhoods, where people likely live without transportation, often do not have health-food stores with vegan options—or even supermarkets with fresh vegetables—let alone organic produce:

> Access to locally grown fresh fruits and vegetables, proper nutritional information, and community gardens is currently challenging for many whose food choices are limited to Jack in the Box, White Castle, convenience stores, or grocers that do not sell fresh produce. In addition, TV food advertisements

aimed toward people of color convey unhealthier items than those aimed toward whites, which potentially makes unlearning current concepts of food and nutrition difficult. (Harper, "Social" 39)

Scholars such as Kwate and Eisenhauer note that poorer neighborhoods more often provide a liquor store and a greasy but cheap fast-food restaurant. If farmer's markets are located near working-class neighborhoods, critical food scholars like Dr. Alkon note that most socioeconomically poorer people simply cannot afford these alternatives.

While remaining aware of the white class privilege that can lie behind a healthy vegan diet, readers who have not yet noticed what bell hooks missed in the quotation above, assessing the position of African American women, may now be in a position to do so. Though women of color tend to live near the bottom of the demographic barrel, they do not have a social status "lower than that of any other group" (hooks, "Black" 32). Furthermore, nonwhite racialized minorities *are* "socialized to assume the role of exploiter/oppressor" and they *are* provided with an "institutionalized 'other'" to exploit and oppress (hooks, "Black" 32). While poor women of color are likely to have few if any human "others" to oppress, *all* human beings are systematically socialized to oppress cattle, chickens, snakes, mice, dogs, and other nonhuman individuals. After the fashion of Sojourner Truth, wouldn't cows and chickens likely ask feminists: "Ain't I a female, too?" And would not dogs and snakes ask: "Ain't I a living being, too?"

SUMMARY

The various strands of feminism have faced many challenges as they have emerged to address a host of different social justice issues. Many of these strands have evolved to accommodate an ever-growing understanding of linked oppressions. Feminism is stronger because feminists were willing to rise to meet challenges posed by people like bell hooks. As a result, feminism has become more diverse, more inclusive—more relevant to more people. Listening to the criticisms of others—and being self-critical—has been and remains central to the survival, growth, expansion, relevance, and applicability of feminism.

Some feminists have effectively challenged other social justice movements, including animal advocates, for sexist campaigns such as PETA's famous naked march. And animal advocates are now challenging feminists, as well, not only for excluding billions of females from their protective canopy, but for turning their heads away, for continuing to make choices that lead to the oppression and premature death of these many beleaguered mothers and their offspring. The challenges for feminism's many strands in the twenty-first century are not the same challenges that faced feminists in the last century. Now that scholars and activists have firmly linked speciesism with sexism, the many feminisms have arrived at yet another critical juncture: How will feminists meet the challenges posed by animal advocates?

Advocacy is better served when fellow activists are able to respond in ways that do not build walls or burn bridges. Change takes time and tends to come hard to human beings. Those who understand this human tendency are more effective activists.

Challenges between activists are most appropriately met with sincere inquiry. If we wish others to hear our message when we bring social justice issues to the table, we must listen to other activists when they do the same.

ii. empathy, silence, trauma, voice

> Those of us who stand outside the circle of this society's definition of acceptable women; those of us who have been forged in the crucibles of difference—those of us who are poor, who are lesbians, who are Black, who are older—know that survival is not an academic skill. It is learning how to stand alone, unpopular and sometimes reviled, and how to make common cause with those others identified as outside the structures in order to define and seek a world in which we can all flourish. It is learning how to take our differences and make them strengths. For the master's tools will never dismantle the master's house. They may allow us temporarily to beat him at his own game, but they will never enable us to bring about genuine change. (Lorde, "From" 587)

I have often wondered how empathetic women have the courage to repeatedly expose themselves to trauma—entering animal labs, factory farms, and slaughterhouses to witness and record insidious treatment of nonhuman animals—while maintaining a semblance of emotional and psychological equilibrium. Authors in this anthology provide an answer: Empathic people face misery head-on, not only to bring about much-needed change but as a means of coping. In a world where unconscionable violence and pervasive injustices are the norm, they have come to see activism as the lesser of two miseries. *These women have found that their only hope for peace of mind is to walk straight into that pervasive misery and work for change.*

To understand this brave response, it is important to understand violence in patriarchal cultures. Violence runs across lines of oppression. (How else can large populations be kept subservient to smaller populations who are alienated by a dualistic, hierarchical social structure?) Violence, generally enacted by males, disproportionately affects children, nonhuman animals, nonwhite racialized minorities, and women—especially women who are members of nonwhite racialized minorities. Violent men sometimes purposefully create terror in women by threatening a beloved child, cat, or parakeet (Adams, "Woman-Battering" 72). Men sometimes harm or kill nonhuman animals, using them as pawns to establish or maintain power and control over women.

In the racist, sexist United States, nonwhite racialized minorities—and women in particular—are subjected to more than their share of horrific violence, but no human being would wish to trade places with nonhuman animals in factory farms or laboratories. "Whereas women may feel like pieces of meat, and be treated like pieces of meat—emotionally butchered and physically battered—animals actually are made into pieces of meat" (Adams, *Sexual* 46). While women may be called "pet" (as if they exist only to entertain men), nonhumans legally *are* "pets." The legal status of women and nonwhite racialized minorities has improved markedly in the past fifty years; matters have grown considerably worse for nonhuman animals.

Violence against those in the "Not A" category "cannot be understood without a feminist analysis" (Adams, "Woman-Battering" 80). Violence is central to patriarchy, and Western society's various forms of systemic violence are interconnected. Recognizing similarities across forms of oppression such as racism, child abuse, speciesism, and sexism, for example, is essential to "recognizing the interrelatedness of all violence" (Adams, "Woman-Battering" 80). We can curb this tendency only if all forms of violence are exposed and challenged—rape and slaughter, rodeos and brothels. We cannot expect to put out the fire by removing only one coal.

Violence tends to force silence on those who would otherwise speak. Audre Lorde writes about fear that rules lives and requires silence (Lorde, "From" 583); Adrienne Rich writes of "lies, secrecy, and silence" that have been used to "perpetuate the exploitation of women" (Kheel, "From" 259). Indeed, women are systematically silenced to prevent them from speaking out against oppression: "Beginning in preschool, girls are told to be quiet much more often than boys," even though, as one might expect in such a system, boys tend to be "much noisier than girls" (Kilbourne 139). From a young age, girls are trained to be "quiet, small, and physically constrained," leaving girls "afraid to speak up for themselves or to use their voices to protect themselves from a variety of dangers" (Kilbourne 139).

Authors in this anthology recall a past tendency toward silence and describe their struggles to find voice. They explain the importance of honesty, of speaking up, of using voice to keep us all "uncomfortably conscious" of oppression, asking tough questions—even when we don't have all the answers. In "Talking Back," bell hooks explains her need to create a "writer-identity" to pull herself from institutionalized, systemic silence ("Talking" 81), and calls attention to the healing, empowering affect of finding voice—how voice leads women from exploited and manipulated object to liberated subject: "Moving from silence into speech is for the oppressed, the colonized, the exploited, and those who stand and struggle . . . a gesture of defiance that heals, that makes new life and new growth possible. It is that act of speech, of 'talking back,' that is . . . the expression of our movement from object to subject—the liberated voice" (hooks, "Talking" 81).

All of those in the "Not A" category tend to be objects that can be exploited by those in the "A" category. Objectification is a defining aspect of linked oppression: "Objectification permits an oppressor to view another being as an object" (Adams, *Sexual* 47). Sexist men view women as objects (for sexual gratification, household labor, or as status symbols); racists view other races as objects (slaves, cheap labor, athletes); speciesists view nonhuman individuals as objects (meat, livestock, pets). Objects "do not speak, objects do not feel, and objects have no needs. Objects exist only to serve the needs of others" (Kheel, "From" 260). In Western medicine, women have been objectified as something to be "investigated, analyzed, solved" (Ehrenreich 6). African Americans and the poor have been used as test subjects, as in the infamous Tuskegee experiments. And billions of nonhuman animals have been objectified as Petri dishes.

Amid this pervasive violence, in spite of their own painful objectification, women in this anthology convey a deep and abiding empathy. Alison Lance describes herself as a voodoo doll, taking each blow for doomed nonhuman animals. Empathy leaves these authors wide open to trauma, especially in a patriarchal world of pervasive violence. Many contributors discuss how they have dealt with destabilizing experiences of trauma. Perhaps, most notably, Karen Davis explains her prolonged struggle to maintain balance in a world of irrational violence.

These authors provide insights into the links that connect empathy and silence on the one hand, with trauma and voice on the other. Their essays indicate that social justice activists in general, and animal advocates in particular, must work to expose the injustices they have learned to see—even though this injustice brings yet more trauma—so that this tension can be noticed, and eased. To correct social problems, we must expose them to the light of day.

> Like a boil that can never be cured so long as it is covered up but must be opened with all its ugliness to the natural medicines of air and light, injustice must be exposed, with all the tension its exposure creates, to the light of human conscience and the air of national opinion, before it can be cured. (M. King 404)

Authors in this anthology who are working on behalf of social justice *immerse* themselves in the horrors of oppression—they know what is going on, help those who are suffering, and inform the larger community. For the women whose essays are included in this anthology, immersion in the ugliness of injustice, in the hope of change, seems preferable to turning away. Bahna-James expresses this choice well in her essay when she refers to "accessing vulnerability" as a "source of power."

Essays in this volume indicate that there is a reward for courage and determination in the face of helplessness and suffering: Walking into pain in the hope of bringing change moves a person from helplessness and despair to empowered activism.

iii. making change

I have found that the happiest people are those who do the most for others. (Washington 281)

Most of us know at least one beleaguered activist who endlessly faces injustice in the hope of bringing change, battling every day against the indifference of the masses, sometimes disillusioned with humanity, but never willing to give up hope. In fact, at least a few readers are likely to fit this description. Those who are such activists know that the overwhelming array of desperate problems that face social justice activists can "numb and immobilize us," can foster a bitter and disillusioned view of humanity, or cause individuals to concentrate energies "too narrowly" (Lee 48).

Activists quickly learn that it is impossible to be thoroughly educated on all relevant matters; we cannot "address everything fully at the same time" (Lee 48). By definition, we cannot simultaneously offer an all-out battle against sexism and racism, or prostitution and marital rape, or the veal industry and the egg industry. By definition, an all-out battle requires exclusive attention, and most activists tend to specialize, to launch an all-out attack on just one aspect of the many linked oppressions. Specialization enhances effectiveness, so activists tend to specialize.

But activists must not work against one another in their single-minded dedication to one specific cause. Those fighting to protect horses must not eat cattle. We do well to specialize, we do not do so well if we specialize without knowledge of interlocking oppressions—or without the application of that knowledge.

Audre Lorde notes that "the quality of Light by which we scrutinize our lives has direct bearing upon the product which we live, and upon the changes which we hope to bring about through those lives" ("From" 583). I have found this to be very true: "Deep personal and social change requires self-criticism" (Birkeland 49). Social justice advocates must "revision"—look again—"in order to correct or improve" advocacy and our lives more generally (Adams, "Introduction" 5). We must all "reach down into that deep place of knowledge" so that we can "touch that terror and loathing of any difference that lives there. See whose face it wears," and thereby expand the circle of justice (Lorde, "From" 588). All of us have more to learn about interlocking oppressions. I have just begun this somewhat startling journey, and I am unhappy to remember where I stood just a few years ago. I have been part of the problem—I still am, but I am working for change within, and I know that this inner change will enhance my ability to invite change to the larger world. Martin Luther King found that a "[s]hallow understanding from people of good will is more frustrating than absolute misunderstanding from people of ill will" (M. King 404). Those who seek greater justice in our world need to work toward a deeper understanding of oppressions. Activists need to develop the kind of understanding that will lead to a lifestyle—a way of being—that works against *all* oppressions.

It is also important that each of us "be fully aware of the limitations of our specific agendas" (Lee 48). This requires us to be open to change as a response to what other social justice activists say—especially those advocating against parallel interlocking oppressions. We cannot end just one form of oppression, so we need to be on board with other activists. If we are not, we doom social justice activists to perpetually pulling up the innumerable shoots that spring from the very deep roots of oppression. Furthermore, blindness to one's own privilege and ignorance of the struggles that others face (in a homophobic, racist, ageist, ableist, sexist society) are major impediments to social justice activism. Those who are privileged must give way so that others can take the lead, bringing new social justice concerns and methods to the activist's table.

APPLICATION: CONTROVERSY OVER DIET

If we acknowledge the connection between these systems of exploitation, we will have to make a change in the way we live—in what we eat, in what we wear. And it is simply not convenient to make such a change. . . . Yet if we can see the intertwining oppressions of women of different colors and different nations, if we can understand how racism and classism function like sexism, if we can understand in essence, that it is the claim of difference that authorizes these oppressions—what prevents us from understanding the oppression of other animal species? (Gaard, "Ecofeminism" 301)

While it seems likely that most social justice activists will agree that oppressions are linked, few such activists incorporate this understanding into their reading lists, discussions, economic choices, or daily lives. Those who fight sexism know little about homelessness, and those who fight racism know little about factory farming. Similarly, those who work on issues of poverty often fuel the flames of sexism and speciesism, and animal advocates too often express racism. In fact, most social justice advocates know almost nothing of speciesism and therefore reject animal advocacy outright (rather than nod agreement while continuing as before). An ongoing debate between feminists, ecofeminists, and animal advocates exemplifies this speciesist tendency, and reveals a lack of understanding about speciesism on the part of many feminists and some ecofeminists.

Many feminists and some ecofeminists employ inclusiveness to exclude nonhuman animals. For example, some feminists and ecofeminists defend animal-based food offerings at events by arguing that not all who attend are vegan, and that those putting on a conference should not force a particular diet on participants, alienating those who choose a different diet. To do so, they argue, would infringe "on women's rights to choose," and fail to show "deference to the cultural traditions of women of color" (Gruen 82).

Ecofeminist Karen Warren falls into this category. She focuses her argument on minority groups, such as those living in the Arctic, whom she claims are unable to choose a vegan diet. She therefore argues that requiring a vegan or vegetarian diet is, in the words of Andrew Brennan, "ethical colonialism" (Warren 129).

Warren misses the point. Although there are people who have no choice but to eat what is readily available, this is irrelevant to food offerings at feminist and ecofeminist conferences, which are seldom if ever held in the Arctic. In fact, I do not believe that these conferences are held in locations where finding food is a common problem. Nor do these conferences offer whale blubber or caribou flesh so as to be inclusive of those who live in the Arctic. Yet Warren's arguments (and those of others who oppose offering a vegan diet at feminist and ecofeminist conferences and meetings) indicate that conference organizers ought to serve foods that participants are accustomed to eating. Foods offered at feminist and ecofeminist conferences generally represent nothing beyond that which the dominant culture is accustomed to, ignoring all other "ethnic and racial traditions around food" (Adams, "Feminist" 211).

Warren sidesteps the critical question: Can those putting on ecofeminist or feminist conferences serve nonvegan foods and remain true to their mission and ideals? Perhaps even more critically, can Warren continue to eat and serve yogurt and salmon and maintain personal integrity?

Warren's argument conveniently forgets that "cultural traditions are exactly those institutions at which legitimate feminist critiques are aimed"

(Gruen 82). Why would it be necessary to challenge cultural traditions that maintain male dominance over women, but not cultural traditions of human dominance over nonhumans?

Of course the absence of vegan foods at feminist and ecofeminist conferences is just the tip of the cow's exploited teat. Feminist and ecofeminist conferences, to be consistent with much contemporary theorizing, will need to offer only fair-trade coffee and chocolate, hire well-paid labor, avoid foods that are individually wrapped (which require extra processing and result in excessive waste) and avoid Styrofoam altogether. To be consistent with much of what feminists and ecofeminists are saying at their conferences, they will not only need to provide foods that minimize suffering, but also offer only products that minimize waste and human exploitation, that require less processing and more community involvement. If Warren is going to hold her ground, she will have to decide whether feminist and ecofeminist politics are exclusive: By providing eco-friendly, vegan foods at conferences, are feminists and ecofeminists engaging in cultural insensitivity and exclusivity? And if so, does this mean that Warren and her supporters must provide, at their conferences, environmentally damaging, exploitative products unless or until eco-friendly alternatives are readily available for everyone?

From the standpoint of linked oppressions, it is of critical importance that Warren's arguments, designed to justify serving animal products at feminist conferences, ignore egregious suffering and innumerable premature deaths caused by those who choose to eat animal products in industrialized nations. Warren's speciesism is perhaps most evident in her conclusion where she sums up and reiterates her viewpoint: "For animal welfarists, moral vegetarianism is like an event everyone can and should practice always. To fail to do so is always to commit a moral wrong. This is not a view I share" (Warren 143). Is feminism "like an event"? Veganism is no more of an event than is feminism. Much like feminism, veganism is a way of being based on a certain understanding, but unlike feminism, this understanding leads people to boycott animal products when alternatives are available because choosing nonhuman animal products exponentially increases suffering.

Despite her misunderstanding of the nature of veganism, common sense would likely lead Warren to agree that anyone in the industrialized, technological world who attends a feminist conference has the ability to choose a vegan diet—at least while he or she is at the conference—and thus holds a political responsibility to make dietary choices that are consistent with his or her overall commitment to social justice. Inasmuch as animal products in Westernized nations are brought to the table only by exploiting those who are less powerful—usually in an extremely gruesome manner—those who stand against exploitation of the less powerful by the more powerful will need to select vegan food options whenever possible.

If we apply Warren's above statement to feminism, by simply replacing "animal welfarists" with "feminists," and "moral vegetarianism" with "equality between the sexes," we can see her speciesism yet more clearly: "For feminists, equality between the sexes is like an event everyone can and should practice always. To fail to do so is always to commit a moral wrong." True. Well said. Like many feminists, Warren recognizes the importance of protecting women—even at the expense of culture—but she is not similarly committed to the protection of chickens or pigs. In short, Warren is speciesist, and Warren's seeming ignorance of speciesism allows her to view flesh eating as a merely personal choice, rather than a political choice. She fails to recognize the consumption of animal products as yet another form of systematic oppression—one that she fuels every time she consumes animal products (Adams, "Feminist" 200). Carol Adams highlights this point: Serving "animal flesh at feminist conferences requires that feminists traffic in animals—that is, buy and consume animal parts," and this indicates that participants "endorse the literal traffic in animals: production, transportation, slaughter, and packaging of animals' bodies" (Adams, "Feminist" 197). I assume that feminists would not consume human flesh to appease the world's dwindling number of marginalized cannibals.

Sadly, collectively, feminists "seldom see the practical connection between the liberation of women and that of animals," and pitifully few "feminist gatherings are vegetarian, let alone vegan" (Gruen 82). Luckily, other ecofeminists (and feminists) include animals in their moral circle. Carol Adams notes that hierarchy—power over—"is clearly a part of our relationships with the other animals, otherwise we could not experiment upon them, display, hunt, kill, and eat them" (Adams, *Pornography* 18). She notes that feminist and ecofeminist pluralism ought to prevent all of us, including Warren, from siding with "human-skin privilege in order to avoid white-skin privilege" (Adams, *Pornography* 18). Consistency *requires* a vegan diet:

> The differing ethical stances regarding the flesh of human animals versus the flesh of nonhuman animals illustrates that the issue is not whether a community can forbid an action but who is to be protected from being consumed. Since a communitywide vegetarianism is seen as problematic but a community ban on cannibalism is a given, it is obvious that theorizing about species is at this point in time receiving different discursive space from theorizing about race, class, gender, and heterosexism. (Adams, "Feminist" 210)

Similarly, ecofeminist Greta Gaard writes that "the most ethical course is clearly the path of least subordination [and] a vegetarian diet is ethically preferable to a carnivorous diet because a vegetarian diet involves the least amount of subordination, domination, and oppression" ("Ecofeminism" 298). Therefore, for those who are not dependent on killing animals in order to survive, "vegetarianism is an integral part of ecofeminist praxis" (Gaard, "Ecofeminism" 301). Marti Kheel also encourages those working against oppression to commit to a vegan lifestyle as an important method of "reducing . . . suffering and for contributing to the overall well-being of the natural world" (*Nature* 233). A voice of inclusiveness also comes from Josephine Donovan, offering a common-sense reasoning: "We should not kill, eat, torture, and exploit animals because they do not want to be so treated, and we know that" (185).

Obviously, people with limited options must eat what is most readily available, but feminists and ecofeminists cannot hide behind "ethical colonialism" to justify speciesist food choices at conferences and maintain intellectual integrity. It is hard for those who hold power to relinquish power—it is hard for most humans to change basic daily habits—but as A. Breeze Harper notes in her essay in this anthology, feminists and ecofeminists cannot ask of others what we are not willing to do ourselves. In light of interlocking oppressions, feminists and ecofeminists must take a stand on behalf of all who are oppressed, rather than seek loopholes in the hope of defending their habitual diet while continuing to ask others to make fundamental changes in their understandings and lifestyle on behalf of women and other oppressed human minorities.

iv. authors and essays

Some of the authors in this volume have been social activists since they were young, and have seldom turned their hand to writing. Other contributors were called away from writing their essays to rescue a flock of hens, investigate a new tip from an informant, or travel abroad for an extended tour of education and outreach. In such cases, I felt privileged to work with rough material to create polished essays.

In the process of unexpectedly collecting this unusual assortment of essays, I have learned firsthand how one can come to see and understand intersections between animal advocacy and other social justice causes by hearing others. For example, through the essays they submitted, Harper, Park, and Iyer helped me see more clearly how racism is linked with speciesism. By reading the experiences, feelings, and understandings of others, I have learned a great deal about the many ways in which sexism, heterosexism, racism, and class privilege form interlocking oppressions. These essays are, first and foremost, about learning by listening to the understanding of others.

In a boldly personal and deeply philosophical essay, pattrice jones, a young "lesbian/feminist/anti-racist/pro-peace/anti-poverty activist," remembers how she "insisted that everything—racism, sexism, homophobia, capitalism, militarism, etc., etc.—was connected . . . but somehow managed to leave animals out of the equation." She ponders her reluctance to recognize milk products as sexist exploitation, touching on a hot button between feminists, ecofeminists, and animal liberationists—is diet personal or political? Further, jones connects trauma with action, noting the "shifty slippage" behind the "ease with which we forget" the traumas that "others" have suffered and calls us to speak in ways that keep truths about the suffering of others "uncomfortably conscious."

An early obstetrics text noted that a woman "has a head almost too small for intellect but just big enough for love" (Ehrenreich 72). Males are prototypical in patriarchal Western science; in 1980 it was still the case that "not a single chapter in the Handbook on Adolescent Psychology was devoted to girls. . . . [R]esearch was done on boys and assumed to apply to girls as well" (Kilbourne 130). So it was that Twyla François' mother was "ignored in a medical system that was not designed for women," and while her grandmother, aunt, and mother perished from cancer, their male doctors never explained that the consumption of animal products is linked with cancer. Facing cancer herself, François realized that her voice and her authentic self had been crushed by a patriarchal society that "coerces young women into being what they are expected to be—submissive and unquestioning, maintainers of the status-quo." She reclaimed her life, delving into the trenches on behalf of farmed animals and finding commonality between female humans and female farmed animals.

Ingrid Newkirk's essay shows the spunk and pluck that lies behind People for the Ethical Treatment of Animals (PETA). She rejects categorization at the outset (even male and female), and ponders a world without compartmentalization—a community of beings—but categories inevitably resurface. Newkirk observes that she works largely with females (and for females), raising the question of essentialism: Is there some innate difference that lends females to animal advocacy? She also notes that women tend to control kitchens, which she refers to as "fonts of power"—vegan power. Newkirk even urges readers to move toward the compassionate side of human nature—"the side that women are not ashamed to show." (At some point, one suspects that demolishing categories is perhaps not Newkirk's primary concern.) Newkirk's essay asks the proverbial question: What does it take to bring change?

"People of color" is a category created by false dualities—a legacy of European racialized colonialism, whereby the many nuances of humanity are divided into "color" and "white"—neither of which describes either category in any meaningful way. How does it make sense to lump every African

American and every Korean American together, while keeping every Swiss American and French American separate . . . unless that Swiss or French American has noticeable Chinese or South American ancestry? Although racism unifies those who are oppressed by racists, each individual's experiences are unique. Although women suffer from sexism and nonwhite minorities suffer from racism, there are a plethora of huge differences between the experiences of individual women and individual racialized minorities that shape an individual's life. Why does skin color (biology) trump culture, class, education, age, nationality, and all other determinants of who we are—all other categories?

Harper's American roots reach back farther than my own: On her mother's side, her blood reaches back to a lineage of black slaves owned by Thomas Jefferson. In contrast, I am a second-generation American and Miyun Park is the daughter of immigrants. While I have learned about slavery only as a matter of grade school curriculum, Amie Breeze Harper takes America's shameful history of slavery personally and identifies this ongoing legacy in what she terms "racialized neocolonialism and environmental and nutritional racism" (Harper, Personal). Park is perhaps more cognizant of America's involvement in the Korean War than she is of U.S. slavery. But it would also be possible that neither Harper nor Park—as an African American and a Korean immigrant, respectively—are concerned about either of these topics. We cannot know people's interests or inclinations based on their race. We *can* know that race and its byproducts (i.e., racialization, racial formation, racism, normative whiteness) will have shaped the lives of both Harper and Park in the United States.

Amie Breeze Harper turns attention to "animal whites"—the tendency of the animal rights movement to be powered by middle-class Caucasians who remain collectively oblivious to linked oppressions, particularly the issues of racism and poverty. Harper reflects on her childhood, and calls attention to the power of finding voice, of speaking honestly, and notes a lack of engagement on the subject of racism among most white animal advocates. She asks: "How can any of us be exempt from the same critical reflexivity and emotionally difficult self-analysis that we demand from speciesists?"

Miyun Park is a Korean American, and as such, she is stereotyped among the model immigrants who "work hard, send their children to college, [and] rise rapidly in American society" (Daseler 46). This "dubious distinction" (model minority) denies individuality, imposes expectations, and "biases relations with other minorities" (Daseler 46), but this stereotype has likely been part of Park's life—along with racism. Labeled "nothing" in kindergarten, "Gook" in public, and "yellow" on her birth certificate, Miyun Park's essay offers an insider's view of "other" in which she focuses on "it"—cruelty and indifference, prejudice and inequality—the wrongness of exploitative, damaging relations.

Indian American Sangamithra Iyer highlights the inadequacies of dualisms. She seems "white" to the locals of Cameroon, but is a "person of color" in the United States and Europe, where the slightest visible indication of any nonwhite racial mix disqualifies an individual from white privilege. Iyer's essay focuses on capitalism and poverty, speciesism and racism (especially environmental racism); she links the profits of the powerful with the suffering of the masses. Additionally, Iyer, who becomes a foster mother for three chimpanzees orphaned by the bushmeat trade, offers musings on motherhood and trauma. She notices the plight of poverty-ridden mothers in Cameroon and recalls the many unfortunate mother cows exploited by the dairy industry.

While women may or may not be more empathic than men, Iyer makes clear that empathy is not unique to the human animal. Iyer brings us back to the topic of trauma: Trauma caused by animal research and by big industry (dairy, logging, and oil), trauma caused to orphans (both chimpanzees and humans) and to mothers (both chimpanzees and humans), trauma linked with poverty—sickness and premature death—and the trauma caused to earth and wildlife by capitalistic industries. Her essay shows us how personal experience and understanding bring change and reminds readers how easy it is to overlook the affects of our actions.

Hope Ferdowsian remembers her father quietly weeping as he recognized the dreadful affects of oppression and trauma on a stray dog—the same dreadful affects he had seen in his own mother. Ferdowsian is the daughter of an Iranian who relocated to the United States in order to avoid religious persecution, carrying with him an understanding that exploitation and suffering are always undesirable. In her work, she compares the affects of trauma in human beings and chimpanzees (a new and fascinating area of noninvasive research). She recognizes the potential of these new studies to help even the most calloused people understand just how wrong it is to treat other animals as if they have no feelings.

Martin Luther King Jr. warned that if the church did not move away from smug complacency, the church might "lose its authenticity, forfeit the loyalty of millions, and be dismissed as an irrelevant social club with no meaning for the twentieth century" (M. King 409). He wrote: "I see the church as the body of Christ. But, oh! How we have blemished and scarred that body through social neglect and through fear of being nonconformists" (M. King 408). Elizabeth Jane Farians pulls Christianity into the spotlight in an essay that explicitly and implicitly demonstrates critical links between sexism and speciesism. Farians chose to work within the church to institute long-term changes and reverse some of Christianity's "spiritualization of violence" (Kheel, "License" 88). In the process, she reminds herself "to keep cool," that she is "making progress," and that she is "doing this for nonhuman animals." Like many women who work for nonhuman animals, Farians perfects the art of self-effacing in her dedication to the cause. Lurking under the cloak of the model female in order to bring change to a patriarchal institution, Farians informs us that who she is and how she is treated is irrelevant—she is "here to bring change for nonhuman animals."

Tradition is somewhat sacred in the West. In fact, tradition trumps life itself—so long as that life is not human. While respect for tradition does not prevent feminists (or other social activists) from taking a stand against female genital mutilation (FGM), child marriage, or the seclusion of women (none of which are inherently deadly), this respect for tradition too often prevents any meaningful response to hunting, trapping, fishing, rodeos, and ranching, for example (all but one of which are inherently deadly). Speaking from inside the Ojibway community, artist Linda Fisher expresses dismay at the innumerable "leather goods, feathers, and trinkets made of animal parts—bear claws, cougar teeth, turtle shells, and whale bones" that she sees at traditional ceremonies. She questions whether the Native American tendency to focus on hunting is essential to her community's heritage, and explores the recent attempt of the Makah (Western Washington) to renew their "ancient tradition" of whaling.

Latino playwright, performer, and educator Tara Sophia Bahna-James describes the important role of theater in social activism. Her paradoxical acceptance of unity through diversity parallels feminist thinking and drives Bahna-James' art-based activism: "True compassion is not something we can feel merely for a few select individuals, groups, ethnicities, or species. True compassion acknowledges a connection to All; true compassion is inherently inclusive." Bahna-James refocuses our understanding of "other" to include those who do not share our personal point of view, and also to include those "parts of ourselves that we don't wish to see." She describes how theater carries us across contrived boundaries, noting the helpless feeling that sometimes overwhelms activists, and introduces vulnerability as power.

"I believe that nonhuman animals suffer in ways that no human has ever dreamed of or experienced, and that there are elements in human nature that exult in creating strange new worlds of misery." Karen Davis, who wrote these lines, grew up in a community where animal abuse and racial prejudice were as invisible—and rampant—as child abuse and sexism. In college, Davis became fascinated with Nazi concentration camps, and her empathy—her ability to identify with the oppressed—moved her into a psychological state that pushed her out of school. She later returned to school, refocusing on the civil rights movement, noting the incongruity of her college's separate-but-equal policy and coming to an "intellectual awakening" that placed her in "opposition to much of conventional society's way of thinking." In her empathic examination of linked oppressions, Davis describes her journey from a powerless and sensitive youth, through dangerous levels of despair and collapse, into an empowered faithfulness to animal advocacy.

For lauren Ornelas, animal liberation is not about compassion, it's about justice, and she notes that "animal advocates will draw more people, and become part of a more viable movement, when we explicitly connect animal, human, and environmental injustices. We are all comrades." Consistent with her words, Ornelas launched the Food Empowerment Project (FEP), a vegan project focusing on "animals, workers, and the environment." The FEP is designed not only to chip away at corporate animal exploitation, but also to encourage community gardens, change how fieldworkers are treated, and shine a stark light on environmental racism. Through food, Ornelas notes that she has "found a movement in which almost anyone could participate."

In "Letter from Birmingham Jail," Martin Luther King, Jr. commented that "law and order exist for the purpose of establishing justice and that when they fail in this purpose they become the dangerously structured dams that block the flow of social progress" (M. King 404). Our Western speciesist legal system protects humans (mostly property-owning humans) over and against all other creatures. Billions of dollars back institutions that exploit animals, and officers of the law support corporations at the expense of activists. Christine Garcia, a lawyer working in the field of animal law, exposes injustice in the U.S. legal system, and in the process, introduces animal liberationist as "other." She recognizes nonhumans as the "most abused individuals on the planet," and the U.S. government forms most of her opposition in her efforts to protect these many sentient beings. King once wrote that laws are unjust when they "deny citizens the First-Amendment privilege of peaceful assembly and protest" (403). Garcia notes: "Police protect the university's legal right to test on animals, not the citizen's right to protest animal experimentation. Officers (the government) never arrest scientists or administrators at the request of picketers, even when picketers are harassed while protesting." She quips: "Judges need to be reminded that even animal activists are protected by the constitution."

Allison Lance tries not to let speciesist legal systems get in her way: She is determined to rescue and aid nonhuman animals using whatever methods are readily available and likely to be effective. Some of Lance's actions seem modeled on M. L. King's description of "nonviolent direct action," which he asserts "seeks to create such a crisis and foster such a tension that a community which has constantly refused to negotiate is forced to confront the issue" (M. King 401). Even peace-loving King recognized the importance of breaking unjust laws in a world where "everything Adolf Hitler did in Germany was 'legal' and everything the Hungarian freedom fighters did in Hungary was 'illegal'" (M. King 404). Activists, King declared, should "dramatize the issue [so] that it can no longer be ignored" (M. King 401). Lance does just that.

Lance's essay pushes the limits of "conscientious citizen," "dedicated activist," and flies in the face of essentialist stereotypes of female animal activists motivated by empathy and compassion. A bold scrapper with a sense of humor, a woman who considers human childbearing to be both selfish and thoughtless, Lance is willing to go beyond nonviolent action, heeding the words of Malcolm X: "We're not for violence. We're for peace. But the people that we're up against are for violence. You can't be peaceful when you're dealing with them" (Malcolm X 417). Lance confronts killers with two strong arms and raises critical questions about the place of violence and illegal action when working in a violent world, a world where animals are killed by the billions, daily. Lance's essay will resonate with women who are deeply tired of patriarchy and its insidious, pervasive male violence and control and with animal activists who are sick of the pervasive and ongoing exploitation and killing.

v. note on word choice

Linguistic practice, like other human practices, is even more deeply speciesist than sexist. Humans, after all, have a verbal monopoly. (Dunayer, "Sexist" 17)

In pulling this anthology together, I tried to remove sexist, racist, homophobic, classist, and (most notably) speciesist language. It is important not only to change how we write (in order to purge prejudices and oppression from our language), but also to explain why we have made such changes. In this section I explain a few of the changes that I have made in the course of compiling this anthology and why I have made them.

For many centuries we talked only about "breeding" when talking about procreation in *other* species. Now the term is sometimes applied to humans, but there is a marked tendency to accuse women of breeding without mention of men, who are equally breeders. In this text, any reference to breeding *includes* humans and *equally* refers to men.

There is no such creature as a "farm animal," except human beings, who have spent considerable time farming down through history. Other species, such as turkeys and pigs, are exploited on farms, by humans. As such, they are "farmed" animals. Similarly, there is no such thing as a "veal calf" or a "lab animal," though there are millions of calves and mice who are systematically exploited by ranchers, experimenters, and consumers. There is also no such thing as seafood, only sea creatures who are exploited by others for food or profit. In this anthology, I have tried to locate and correct these common misrepresentations.

People also tend to refer to nonhuman animals as "it" or sometimes "he," regardless of the individual's sex. This one-sex-fits-all approach objectifies and denies individuality. In fact, nonhuman animals who are exploited for food industries are usually females. Such unfortunate nonhumans are not only exploited for their flesh, but also for their nursing milk, reproductive eggs, and ability to produce young. When guessing the gender of a nonhuman animal forced through slaughterhouse gates, we would greatly increase odds of being correct if we referred to such unfortunate individuals as "she."

In Western culture, we most often refer to nonhumans as things, rather than as individuals. For example, we might say, "The dog that chased the ball was black." I have tried to note these conventions, and change "that" to "who": "The dog who chased the ball was black." Nonhuman animals are individual beings, they are a "who," not an "it" or a "that." I hope that I have caught and changed most of these common but demeaning habitual references to nonhuman animals. (For a more comprehensive look at speciesism through language, see Joan Dunayer's *Animal Equality: Language and Liberation*.)

Finally, the word "animal" also refers to humans: We are animals, mammals, primates. Therefore, I have tried to replace "animal" with "nonhuman animal," or "other animals," for example, when referencing animals who are not human beings. In my own works I tend to use the word "anymal" to refer to all animals excluding the species of the speaker, whether chimpanzee, whale, or *Homo sapiens*. This avoids the human tendency to exclude themselves from the animal world. (For more on this, please see "Verbal Activism: 'Anymal'" at http://www.animalsandsociety.org/assets/library/593_sa1413.pdf.)

In watching carefully how this anthology might either help or harm other species through the use of language, I hope that readers will remember that humans are also animals, lest we falsely distance ourselves from others. Such false distancing facilitates exploitation of other species: cows and hens, bears and chimpanzees, mice and rabbits. Largely to avoid cumbersome sentences, I have not made this change for "animal" when used in conjunction with a second word, such as "animal liberation," "animal welfare," "wild animal," "animal advocate," "animal testing," "animal research," "animal shelter," "animal protection," "animal law," "animal products," "companion animal," "animal cruelty," "animal control," and "animal suffering."

The language of this anthology attempts to be inclusive, understanding that language is equally a tool for oppression and a resource for liberation. The complex interweaving of oppressions that are highlighted in this anthology call us to reconsider common, unexamined uses of language. It is important to note that these linguistic habits are as true for me as for many authors and readers of this anthology. I offer this text in the spirit of doing the best we can, of evolving consciousness, of a shared journey toward a richer understanding of systematic, interlocking oppressions.

REFERENCES

Adams, Carol. "The Feminist Traffic in Animals." *Ecofeminism: Women, Animals, Nature.* Ed. Greta Gaard. Philadelphia: Temple, 1993. 195–218.

———. "Introduction." *Ecofeminism and the Sacred.* New York: Continuum, 1995. 1–9.

———. *The Pornography of Meat.* New York: Continuum, 2003.

———. *The Sexual Politics of Meat: A Feminist-Vegetarian Critical Theory.* New York: Continuum, 1994.

———. "Woman-Battering and Harm to Animals." *Animals and Women: Feminist Theoretical Explorations.* Ed. Carol Adams and Josephine Donovan. Durham: Duke University Press, 1995. 55–84.

Adams, Carol, and Josephine Donovan. "Introduction." *Women and Animals: Feminist Theoretical Explorations.* Ed. Carol Adams and Josephine Donovan. Durham: Duke University Press, 1995. 1–10.

Alexander, M. Jacqui, and ebrary Inc. *Pedagogies of Crossing Meditations on Feminism, Sexual Politics, Memory, and the Sacred, Perverse Modernities.* Durham: Duke University Press, 2005.

Alkon, Alison Hope. "Growing Resistance: Food, Culture and the Mo' Better Foods Farmers' Market." *Gastronomica* 7:3 (2007): 93–99.

Bahna-James, Tara Sophia. "Journey toward Compassionate Choices: Integrating Vegan and Sistah Experiences." *Sistah Vegan: Black Female Vegans Speak on Food, Identity, Health and Society.* Ed. A. Breeze Harper. New York: Lantern, 2010. 155–68.

Birke, Lynda. "Exploring the Boundaries: Feminism, Animals, and Science." *Animals and Women: Feminist Theoretical Explorations.* Ed. Carol Adams and Josephine Donovan. Durham: Duke University Press, 1995. 32–54.

Birkeland, Janis. "Ecofeminism: Linking Theory and Practice." *Ecofeminism: Women, Animals, Nature.* Ed. Greta Gaard. Philadelphia: Temple, 1993. 13–59.

Brett, Jim. "Rosalie Barrow Edge (1877–1962)." Commonwealth of Pennsylvania Department of Environmental Protection: Heritage. 27 July 2007. <http://www.depweb.state.pa.us/heritage/cwp/view.asp?a=3&Q=443908>

Callahan, Gerald, N. *Between XX and XY: Intersexuality and the Myth of Two Sexes.* Chicago: Chicago Review, 2009.

Collins, Patricia Hill. "Where's the Power?" *Gender Inequality: Feminist Theories and Politics, 3rd Ed.* Ed. Judith Lorber. Los Angeles: Roxbury Pub., 2005. 184–88.

Combahee River Collective. "A Black Feminist Statement (1977)." *Women's Lives: Multicultural Perspectives, 4th ed.* Ed. Gwyn Kirk and Margo Okazawa-Rey. New York: McGraw-Hill, 2007. 38–43.

Comninou, Maria. "Speech, Pornography, and Hunting." *Women and Animals: Feminist Theoretical Explorations.* Ed. Carol Adams and Josephine Donovan. Durham: Duke University Press, 1995. 126–48.

Daseler, Robert. "Asian Americans Battle 'Model Minority' Stereotype." *Gender Basics: Feminist Perspectives on Women and Men.* Ed. Anne Minas. Belmont, Calif.: Wadsworth, 2000. 45–49.

Davis, Karen. "Thinking like a Chicken." *Women and Animals: Feminist Theoretical Explorations.* Ed. Carol Adams and Josephine Donovan. Durham: Duke University Press, 1995. 192–212.

Des Jardins, Joseph. *Environmental Ethics: An Introduction to Environmental Philosophy, 3rd ed.* Belmont, Calif.: Wadsworth, 2001.

Dobson, Andrew. "Ecofeminism." *The Green Reader: Essays toward a Sustainable Society.* Ed. Andrew Dobson. San Francisco: Mercury House, 1991.

Donovan, Josephine. "Animal Rights and Feminist Theory." *Ecofeminism: Women, Animals, Nature.* Ed. Greta Gaard. Philadelphia: Temple, 1993. 167–94.

Dunayer, Joan. "Sexist Words, Speciesist Roots." *Women and Animals: Feminist Theoretical Explorations.* Ed. Carol Adams and Josephine Donovan. Durham: Duke University Press, 1995. 11–31.

———. *Animal Equality: Language and Liberation.* Derwood, Md.: Ryce, 2001.

Dwyer, Owen J., and John Paul Jones III. "White Socio-Spatial Epistemology." *Social & Cultural Geography* 1:2 (2000): 209–22.

Ehrenreich, Barbara, and Deirdre English. *For Her Own Good: Two Centuries of the Experts' Advice to Women.* New York: Anchor, 2005.

Eisenhauer, Elizabeth. "In Poor Health: Supermarket Redlining and Urban Nutrition." GeoJournal 53 (2002): 125–33.

Eisnitz, Gail. *Slaughterhouse: The Shocking Story of Greed, Neglect, and Inhumane Treatment Inside the U.S. Meat Industry.* New York: Prometheus, 1997.

Eshel, Gidon, and Pamela A. Martin. "Diet, Energy, and Global Warming." *Earth Interactions* 10:9 (2006). Online. Internet. June 25, 2010. http://pge.uchicago.edu/workshop/documents/martin1.pdf.

Flagg, Barbara J. "Whiteness as Metaprivilege." *Washington University Journal of Law and Policy* 18:1 (2005): 1–11.

Flax, Jane. "Women Do Theory." *Women and Values: Readings in Recent Feminist Philosophy.* Ed. Marilyn Pearsall. Florence, Ky.: Cengage Learning, Inc., 1993. 9–13.

Gaard, Greta. "Ecofeminism and Native American Cultures: Pushing the Limits of Cultural Imperialism?" *Ecofeminism: Women, Animals, Nature.* Ed. Greta Gaard. Philadelphia: Temple, 1993. 295–314.

———. "Living Interconnections with Animals and Nature." *Ecofeminism: Women, Animals, Nature.* Ed. Greta Gaard. Philadelphia: Temple, 1993. 1–12.

"Glossary: Glossary of Terms in Common Use." *Women's Lives: Multicultural Perspectives, 4th ed.* Ed. Gwyn Kirk and Margo Okazawa-Rey. New York: McGraw-Hill, 2007. G1-G6.

Griffin, Susan. *Woman and Nature: The Roaring inside Her.* New York: Harper Colophone, 1978.

Gruen, Lori. "Dismantling Oppression: An Analysis of the Connections between Women and Animals." *Ecofeminism: Women, Animals, Nature.* Ed. Greta Gaard. Philadelphia: Temple, 1993. 60–90.

Harper, A. Breeze. Personal letter to the author. June 30, 2010. No pagination.

———. "Phenomenology of Race and Whiteness: Knowing, Feeling, and Experiencing the Vegan 'Exotic.'" *The Food Justice Reader: Cultivating a Just Sustainability.* Ed. Alison Alkon and Julian Agyeman. Forthcoming. Cumberland, R.I.: MIT Press, 2010.

———. "Social Justice Beliefs and Addiction to Uncompassionate Consumption." *Sistah Vegan: Black Female Vegans Speak on Food, Identity, Health and Society.* Ed. A. Breeze Harper. New York: Lantern, 2010. 20–41.

Heller, Chaia. "Take Back the Earth." *Earth Ethics: Environmental Ethics, Animal Rights, and Practical Applications.* Ed. James P. Sterba. Englewood Cliffs: Prentice Hall, 1995.

hooks, bell. "Black Women: Shaping Feminist Theory." *Women and Values: Readings in Recent Feminist Philosophy.* Ed. Marilyn Pearsall. Florence, Ky.: Cengage Learning, Inc., 25–33.

———. "Talking Back." *Gender Basics: Feminist Perspectives on Women and Men.* Ed. Anne Minas. Belmont, Calif.: Wadsworth, 2000. 78–81.

Johnson, Allan G. "Patriarchy, the System (1997): An It, Not a He, a Them, or an Us." *Women's Lives: Multicultural Perspectives, 4th ed.* Ed. Gwyn Kirk and Margo Okazawa-Rey. New York: McGraw-Hill, 2007. 28–37.

Kappeler, Susanne. "Speciesism, Racism, Nationalism . . . or the Power of Scientific Subjectivity." *Women and Animals: Feminist Theoretical Explorations.* Ed. Carol Adams and Josephine Donovan. Durham: Duke University Press, 1995. 320–52.

Kemmerer, Lisa. "Verbal Activism: 'Anymal.'" *Society & Animals* 14:1 (2006): 9–14.

Kheel, Marti. "From Heroic to Holistic Ethics." *Ecofeminism: Women, Animals, Nature.* Ed. Greta Gaard. Philadelphia: Temple, 1993. 243–271.

———. "License to Kill: An Ecofeminist Critique of Hunters' Discourse." *Women and Animals: Feminist Theoretical Explorations.* Ed. Carol Adams and Josephine Donovan. Durham: Duke University Press, 1995. 85–125.

———. *Nature Ethics: An Ecofeminist Perspective.* New York: Rowman & Littlefield, 2008.

Kilbourne, Jean. *Deadly Persuasion: Why Women and Girls Must Fight the Addictive Power of Advertising.* New York: Free Press, 1999.

King, Martin Luther, Jr. "Letter from Birmingham Jail." *Walkin' the Talk: An Anthology of African American Studies.* Ed. Bill Lyne and Vernon D. Johnson. Upper Saddle River, N.J.: Prentice Hall, 2003. 399–411.

King, Ynestra. "The Ecology of Feminism and the Feminism of Ecology." *Worldviews, Religion, and the Environment: A Global Anthology.* Ed. Richard C. Foltz. Belmont, Calif.: Thompson, 2003. 457–64.

Kirk, Gwyn, and Margo Okazawa-Rey. "Chapter One." *Women's Lives: Multicultural Perspectives, 4th ed.* Ed. Gwyn Kirk and Margo Okazawa-Rey. New York: McGraw-Hill, 2007. 11–59.

———. "Introduction." *Women's Lives: Multicultural Perspectives, 4th ed.* Ed. Gwyn Kirk and Margo Okazawa-Rey. New York: McGraw-Hill, 2007. 2–9.

Kwate, Naa Oyo A. "Fried Chicken and Fresh Apples: Racial Segregation as a Fundamental Cause of Fast Food Density in Black Neighborhoods." *Health & Place* 14:1 (2008): 32–44.

Lahar, Stephanie. "Roots: Rejoining Natural and Social History." *Ecofeminism: Women, Animals, Nature.* Ed. Greta Gaard. Philadelphia: Temple, 1993. 91–117.

Lee, JeeYeun. "Beyond Bean Counting (1995)." *Women's Lives: Multicultural Perspectives, 4th ed.* Ed. Gwyn Kirk and Margo Okazawa-Rey. New York: McGraw-Hill, 2007. 46–49.

Li Huey-li. "A Cross-Cultural Critique of Ecofeminism." *Ecofeminism: Women, Animals, Nature.* Ed. Greta Gaard. Philadelphia: Temple, 1993. 272–94.

Lorber, Judith. "The Social Construction of Gender (1191)." *Women's Lives: Multicultural Perspectives, 4th ed.* Ed. Gwyn Kirk and Margo Okazawa-Rey. New York: McGraw-Hill, 2007. 24–27.

Lorde, Audre. "Age, Race, Class, and Sex: Women Redefining Difference." *Gender Basics: Feminist Perspectives on Women and Men.* Ed. Anne Minas. Belmont, Calif.: Wadsworth, 2000. 526–28.

———. "From Sister Outsider, Poetry Is Not a Luxury." *Walkin' the Talk: An Anthology of African American Studies.* Ed. Bill Lyne and Vernon D. Johnson. Upper Saddle River, N.J.: Prentice Hall, 2003. 583–88.

Loyd-Paige, Michelle R. "Thinking and Eating at the Same Time: Reflections of a Sistah Vegan." *Sistah Vegan: Black Female Vegans Speak on Food, Identity, Health and Society.* Ed. A. Breeze Harper. New York: Lantern, 2010. 1–7.

Luke, Brian. "Taming Ourselves or Going Feral? Toward a Nonpatriarchal Metaethic of Animal Liberation." *Women and Animals: Feminist Theoretical Explorations.* Ed. Carol Adams and Josephine Donovan. Durham: Duke University Press, 1995. 290–319.

Malcolm X. "Not Just an American Problem, but a World Problem." *Walkin' the Talk: An Anthology of African American Studies.* Ed. Bill Lyne and Vernon D. Johnson. Upper Saddle River, N.J.: Prentice Hall, 2003. 412–30.

Merchant, Carolyn. "Dominion over Nature." *Worldviews, Religion, and the Environment: A Global Anthology.* Ed. Richard C. Foltz. Belmont, Calif.: Thompson, 2003. 39–49.

———. *Earthcare: Women and the Environment.* New York: Routledge, 1995.

Mills, Charles W. *The Racial Contract.* Ithaca: Cornell University Press, 1997.

O'Loughlin, Ellen. "Questioning Sour Grapes: Ecofeminism and the United Farm Workers Grape Boycott." *Ecofeminism: Women, Animals, Nature.* Ed. Greta Gaard. Philadelphia: Temple, 1993. 146–66.

Ortega, Mariana. "Being Lovingly, Knowingly Ignorant: White Feminism and Women of Color." *Hypatia* 21:3 (2006): 56–74.

Plumwood, Val. "Nature, Self, and Gender: Feminism, Environmental Philosophy, and the Critique of Rationalism." *Hypatia,* VI:1 (Spring, 1991): 3–27.

Radford Ruether, Rosemary. "Ecofeminism: The Challenge to Theology." *Worldviews, Religion, and the Environment: A Global Anthology.* Ed. Richard C. Foltz. Belmont, Calif.: Thompson, 2003. 464–72.

Riley, Shamara Shantu. "Ecology Is a Sistah's Issue Too: The Politics of Emergent Afrocentric Ecowomanism." *Worldviews, Religion, and the Environment: A Global Anthology.* Ed. Richard C. Foltz. Belmont, Calif.: Thompson, 2003. 472–81.

Salamon, Gayle. "The Place Where Life Hides Away: Merleau-Ponty, Fanon, and the Location of Bodily Being." *Differences* 17:2 (2006): 96–112.

Santosa, Melissa. "Identity, Freedom, Veganism." *Sistah Vegan: Black Female Vegans Speak on Food, Identity, Health and Society.* Ed. A. Breeze Harper. New York: Lantern, 2010. 73–77.

Scholtmeijer, Marian. "The Power of Otherness: Animals in Women's Fiction." *Women and Animals: Feminist Theoretical Explorations.* Ed. Carol Adams and Josephine Donovan. Durham: Duke University Press, 1995. 231–62.

"Sexism." *Eastern Shore Sanctuary and Education Center.* Online. Internet. Oct. 26, 2010. http://sanctuary.bravebirds.org/wp-content/uploads/2009/05/speciesex.pdf.

Singer, Isaac Bashevis. *Enemies: A Love Story.* New York: Farrar, Straus, and Giroux, 1972.

Stacey, Jackie. "Untangling Feminist Theory." *Thinking Feminist: Key Concepts in Women's Studies.* Ed. D. Richardson and V. Robinson. New York: Guilford, 1993. 49–73.

Sullivan, Shannon, and Nancy Tuana. *Race and Epistemologies of Ignorance,* Suny Series, Philosophy and Race. Albany: State University of New York Press, 2007.

Vance, Linda. "Ecofeminism and the Politics of Reality." *Ecofeminism: Women, Animals, Nature.* Ed. Greta Gaard. Philadelphia: Temple, 1993. 118–45.

Warren, Karen. *Ecofeminist Philosophy: A Western Perspective on What It Is and Why It Matters.* Lanham, Md.: Rowman and Littlefield Publishers, Inc., 2000.

Washington, Booker T. "From Up From Slavery, Chapter XIV: The Atlanta Exposition Address." *Walkin' the Talk: An Anthology of African American Studies.* Ed. Bill Lyne and Vernon D. Johnson. Upper Saddle River, N.J.: Prentice Hall, 2003. 281–89.

Yancy, George. *What White Looks Like: African-American Philosophers on the Whiteness Question.* New York: Routledge, 2004.

1

fighting cocks

ECOFEMINISM VERSUS SEXUALIZED VIOLENCE

pattrice jones

I'm sitting in a low lawn chair, wearing boxer shorts and a T-shirt that says "Feminists for Animal Rights." My legs are streaked with mud and there's a bright yellow patch on one ankle that can only be dried egg yolk. My forearms are dotted with abrasions encircled by bruises. It's sunny and hot.

From under the brim of a floppy hat, I've got one eye on a Penguin paperback and the other on a multicolored rooster who might or might not start a fight. My hat sports the colors of the Brazilian flag, but ought to be UN blue, because I'm a peacekeeper today. At any moment, I might be forced to place myself between combatants. In the interim, I wait. And wait.

Welcome to the exciting yet enervating world of rooster rehabilitation. At the Eastern Shore Sanctuary, we help roosters who have formerly been used in cockfighting to live peacefully with other birds. Although illegal in many countries, and in most of the United States, cockfighting persists in parts of Asia, on some Pacific Islands, in parts of South and Central America, and in the southern United States. In this cruel "sport," roosters are socialized to view other roosters as predators, provoked by injections of testosterone and methamphetamines, armed with steel blades attached to the stumps of their sawed-off spurs, and then matched in bloody battles from which the only escape is death. Between events, they are typically isolated in small cages or tethered to stakes adjacent to A-frame shelters.

Because cockfights are inevitably the site of illegal gambling, authorities are quicker to intervene in cockfighting than in other forms of animal cruelty. Unfortunately, their interventions usually do not aid the true victims of the crime—roosters. Most often, birds confiscated from cockfighting operations are euthanized. We are able to rescue and rehabilitate only a handful of the hundreds of former fighting cocks who are confiscated every year. For each rooster we are able to save, our sanctuary means everything. Because chickens are very close genetically to the wild jungle fowl (the living ancestors of modern chickens), many former fighters choose a feral lifestyle, sleeping in trees and wandering the woods all day. Others move into the coops, joining former egg factory inmates and big "broiler" chickens, in a more sedate lifestyle. It's their choice, as it should be.

How did a lesbian-feminist from Baltimore end up rehabbing roosters in a rural chicken yard? Just like the old joke, it all started with a chicken crossing a road. Shortly after unknowingly moving to an epicenter of industrial poultry production, my former partner Miriam Jones and I rescued a chicken from the roadside. I'd always admired birds from afar, but I was surprised to find myself growing emotionally close to this ungainly creature, who sometimes looked so much like a reptile that I knew scientists were right about birds being dinosaurs. I also noticed that she had my grandmother's eyes (as well as her stubborn charm) and that her feet were amazingly similar to human hands. I'd always felt so earthbound, but here was the evidence: People are related to birds! I was excited by this discovery, and very touched by this particular bird's growing attachment to me.

One day, Mosselle (as we called her, after my grandmother) made a new sound that seemed some kind of announcement. "Maybe she laid an egg!" I thought. I ran around looking for where she might have hidden her prize. A few days later, early in the morning, she gargled like she was choking, and I worried that she might be sick. Luckily, somebody with some sense commented, "That bird's a rooster." I had misunderstood an adolescent rooster's first attempts at crowing!

I struggled with the realization that my beloved friend was a rooster, rather than a hen. Even though he hadn't changed, it was hard not to see him differently. I struggled not to let all of the things I had heard about arrogant, posturing, aggressive roosters change the way I saw this dear young bird, who had come to count on me. This was my first inkling of the ways that gendered preconceptions alter our perceptions of chickens and other nonhuman animals.

That insight was a long time coming. "What was I thinking?!?" That's what I wonder every time I remember the years I spent as a vegetarian-but-not-vegan lesbian/feminist/antiracist/pro-peace/antipoverty activist who insisted that everything—racism, sexism, homophobia, capitalism, militarism, etc., etc.—was connected . . . but somehow managed to leave nonhuman animals out of the equation. For me, the question is not "what led me to include other animals in my activism?" but, rather, "what took me so long to include other animals in my activism?" It is a question worth answering. After we make a radical change in thought or behavior, we have a tendency to distance our new selves from our previous selves. That's understandable, but not useful. If we can't remember—much less have empathy with—our former ways of thinking and feeling, how can we make meaningful contact with those who still think and feel as we used to do? And, if we can't make contact, how can we prompt others to rethink what feel to them like intensely personal choices?

So, as much as it makes me feel queasy to do so, I'm going to try to actually answer the question of why an altruistic, animal-loving, vegetarian feminist activist, who insisted that all forms of oppression were linked, took so damn long to go vegan.

I quit eating meat in 1976, the same year I turned fifteen, came out, and went to my first gay rights rally (not in that order). When I say that I "came out," I mean that I resolved to never lie about my love for women, never deliberately pass for straight, and never deny a lover by calling her "him." To do so, I felt, would be to betray not only the women I desired, but my deepest self.

My decision to quit meat was equally simple. Somehow, through the confluence of midseventies influences, I knew that vegetarianism was a particularly healthy way to eat. One day, quite suddenly, I realized: If I didn't need to eat meat to stay alive, then eating meat was killing for pleasure. I couldn't live with myself, wouldn't be the nonviolent person I believed myself to be, if I killed other beings—beings who had their own desires—merely to satisfy my desire for the taste of their flesh.

Looking back, I see that both decisions, coming out and quitting meat, are about the interplay of desire and integrity. Sometimes integrity means being true to your desires, and sometimes integrity requires you to refuse your desires. I also notice that both decisions were about bodies and consent. A primary tenet of gay liberation is that what consenting people do with each other's bodies is nobody else's business. And, of course, eating meat is something you do to somebody else's body without their consent.

Since both of these ethical decisions were about bodies, I don't want to leave out their visceral dimensions. These were full-bodied decisions. I didn't just think, "I'm going to quit meat," and "I'm not going to lie about my sexuality." Once I had thought through the questions, my body recoiled at the notion of eating a cow or pretending to be straight. I remember very clearly the feeling of revulsion that arose whenever I summoned up the mental image of a cow and imagined eating her, which is particularly interesting in light of what I'm going to tell you a little later.

When I look back on that earnest teenager making those two seemingly unrelated decisions, it seems to me now that in both instances she was decisively rejecting patriarchal control of her body. I know now that homophobia is what Suzanne Pharr calls "a weapon of sexism," one of many means of coercing people into patriarchal families. And I know now that patriarchy (male rule) and pastoralism (herding farmed animals) coevolved, the ideas and practices of each commingling with and compounding the other.

But I didn't know any of this back in 1976. Or 1986. Or even 1996, although then I was on the brink of an emotional and intellectual breakthrough that would lead me to go vegan and become an animal advocate.

Meanwhile, I was vegetarian, not vegan. Not even reliably vegetarian. I held out well enough while I was living rough, as a teenager, supporting myself at an urban fast-food restaurant. All of us relied on free food from the restaurant to augment salaries that didn't cover rent and groceries. Sometimes, when I was really hungry and couldn't bring myself to stomach one more meal of salad and french fries, I'd break down and resentfully eat a burger or piece of chicken. I have a very clear memory of me, at about seventeen, sitting in a cheap molded plastic chair, looking out the grimy window at a grey day, choking down chicken flesh, thinking, "this is so wrong!"

Those were raw years for me, with the wounds of a troubled childhood still oozing anger and pain that anybody could see. Maybe that's why it was so easy for me to hold on to the bodily empathy in which my vegetarianism was most deeply rooted. But then I entered a period of years wherein I walled off feelings in order to focus on pulling myself out of the dangerous lifestyle into which I had drifted. I got a good job. I started night school. And I forgot about nonhuman animals.

In the early- and mideighties, I lived with lovers who ate meat and I also occasionally ate, or even prepared, meat. But when those relationships ended, I went back to being steadily vegetarian at home, and happily so. But if I had a really strong urge for a hamburger or a pepperoni pizza, I sometimes gave in, rationalizing that compromise would maintain a vegetarian diet in the long run better than rigidity.

Somehow, the ethical clarity of my original decision to be vegetarian had become muddied and muddled. I knew very well that I tended to want to eat meat when I felt angry. I knew very well that eating that hamburger would be displacing my aggression onto an innocent nonhuman. And yet I did eat that hamburger every once in a while. More often than I want to admit.

Those murderous "lapses" were mentally and morally tolerable to me, leaving me feeling only slightly more guilty than I already felt, because nonhuman animals had gone missing from my emotional landscape. Those occasional hamburgers were just "meat" to me rather than the remains of dead nonhumans with whom I actively empathized.

All of that stopped, thanks to Alice Walker. In her essay, "Am I Blue?" Walker describes going out for a celebratory steak dinner only to have the thought, "I am eating misery" interrupt her pleasure. That phrase must have stealthily planted itself in my brain, because the next time I tried to give into a craving for meat, I had no sooner taken a bite than the words "I am eating misery" echoed in my head. My stomach reeled. I spit out the half-chewed flesh and have never been tempted again.

So, for me at least, the ethical mandate had to be full-bodied—a matter of heart and gut as well as mind—in order to be truly sustainable. I suspect that's true for many people. Abstract rules are easily broken. People often do things they know they ought not to do, if they can get away with it, especially if they can tell themselves that it doesn't hurt anybody.

Which brings us to the next lesson we can learn from my past misdeeds: We must keep the real repercussions of our actions (or inaction) on actual nonhuman animals always in mind. That's true, I think, not only for would-be vegans but also for those who purport to be advocates for nonhuman animals.

The question remains: Why did I think of the decision whether or not to eat meat as an apolitical personal choice rather than a political decision (like every other decision)? The ardent activism of my teens returned with a vengeance in my late twenties, once the chore of working my way through college was behind me, and I was safely ensconced in graduate school. I involved myself in local struggles for fair housing and against police brutality and in national struggles against AIDS and for peace. I marched and chanted, led workshops, organized sit-ins and kiss-ins, distributed condoms and clean needles, and sat through endless hours of tedious meetings. Whenever I had a little extra money (which wasn't often), I gave it to PETA (the only animal organization I knew about). And yet, when one of the students in the social change class that I was teaching asked me why our lineup of social change movements didn't include the animal rights movement, I incoherently responded that I supported animal rights, but that this issue was tangential to the linked oppressions (racism, sexism, etc.) that were the focus of our scrutiny.

What was I thinking?!? As a feminist, I was well-versed in the theory behind the slogan, "the personal is political," which simply means that everything we choose to do (or not do) matters. What in the world led me to believe that every decision in life—including decisions about how to conduct one's most intimate relations—was a political decision except the decision whether or not to eat meat? I can't even say "except what we eat," since I was boycotting grapes (farm workers) and Coca-Cola (apartheid) at the time. I also believed in, although couldn't always afford to support, organic agriculture. I recognized that many food decisions were political decisions.

This very strange notion that the decision whether or not to eat nonhuman animals is a purely personal decision, uniquely exempt from the ethical and political considerations that ought to inform every other decision, is quite common and worthy of our attention. When I interrogate this notion, I find that, for me, declaring vegetarianism a political decision would have been tantamount to mandating vegetarianism for everybody, and that there were two reasons I hesitated to do this: excessive deference to religion and a misplaced application of the right to bodily self-determination.

Like many people raised to respect "freedom of religion," I used to shy away from analyzing the implications of the political ideologies that call themselves religions. Even though I was an atheist, I never challenged anybody about their religious beliefs. And though I had not yet had the pleasure of hearing Christians shout "God made chickens for us to eat!" I knew that most Christians view the eating of meat as a literally God-given right. Since I saw religion as a sacrosanct personal decision, I felt that I had no right to challenge this religious understanding. Only when I quit thinking of religious ideologies as uniquely exempt from ethical scrutiny was I free to directly challenge the human hubris implicit in most of the belief systems that men have constructed to explain the world and claim dominion over nonhuman animals.

I say "men" rather than "people" because it was men and also because those same stories have been and continue to be used to assert male dominion over women and girls. So, it's not surprising that an association between animal advocacy and feminism dates back to those hunger-striking vegetarian suffragists who were force-fed meat in a vain effort to get them to swallow male domination. Of course, control of female bodies is precisely the point of patriarchy. Maybe that's why—in spite of the fact that women have made up the majority of animal advocates from the earliest days of antivivisection agitation to the current era of open rescues—many women feel oppressed when somebody tells them they ought not to eat farmed animals. The mandate to "go vegan" can feel to some women like one more instance of others telling you what you must or cannot do with your own body. That's because, as was the case for me during my lapses from vegetarianism, the nonhuman animals are absent from the mental equation. Only if other animals enter the picture is it possible to see that eating meat is doing something to somebody else's body.

Women make most food purchases and preparation decisions. If women are going to both go vegan and withstand the demands of male family members for meat, women must be emboldened to resist their own subordination and at the same time reject the oppression of nonhuman individuals. In other words, animal advocates must balance the demand that women give up their power over nonhuman animals by encouraging them to seize their power among human animals. This sounds tricky but comes easy once you see that sexism and speciesism, having grown up together across the centuries, are codependent siblings of dysfunctional patriarchal families.

Before I illustrate this assertion, I have one more question for my former self: Why did it take me so long to extend my personal ban on meat to include dairy and eggs?

Here are some of my predictable and common answers to "What was I thinking?": I didn't know about battery cages and forced pregnancies. I didn't think about what happened to cows and hens after their bodies stopped producing economically profitable quantities of milk and eggs. I had been seduced by Elsie the Cloverland cow and other fictions designed to deceive us into believing that happy hens and placid cows live on spacious farms and are not at all inconvenienced by the friendly farmers who collect their eggs and relieve them of excess milk.

My former partner, Miriam Jones, burst my bubble a couple of years before we moved to the country and found that first chicken. We jiggled our checkbook and I was able to donate a lot more money than I had ever been able to donate before. Soon the newsletters of the animal rights organizations, farmed animal sanctuaries, and antivivisection societies began flooding our mailbox, and we learned more than we ever wanted to know. Thanks to an early childhood trauma involving a flood of blood, I have a hard time with gory images, so Miriam screened the brochures, telling me the relevant facts and showing me the photos she felt I really needed to see. One picture I really needed to see was of hens in battery cages. I quit eggs.

Dairy was more difficult. I had a really hard time believing what Miriam was reading to me. Something about the whole issue was deeply destabilizing, so much so that I half-believed that animal advocates were trying to trick me, even though I knew that was an absurd idea. What was I thinking?!? Perhaps the more apt question would be: What wasn't I thinking and why wasn't I thinking it?

To answer this question, we need to explore an incident years earlier. I really don't want to tell you about this; I had forgotten all about it until I started writing this essay. Indeed, my wish not to speak of this incident was so strong that I was even more belated in meeting this essay's writing deadline than I usually am. I repeatedly stopped right at this point in the essay, set my work aside, and forgot about it for days or even weeks. What I kept wanting to forget, what I don't want you to know, is that I did know that something was very wrong with dairy. I did see, felt uncomfortable, and then promptly forgot that cows were hurt in the process of producing milk and cheese.

Here's what happened: I went to visit my sister in Vermont, where she was living while finishing her undergraduate degree. I was in my midtwenties, just starting graduate school, and the demands of working my way through college and getting myself into graduate school had precluded any substantial attention to activism for several years. Soon I would again be the fierce fire-breathing activist I had been in my late teens, but at that moment I was disoriented, coming up for air after years of scholarly submersion to find myself living in a university milieu so substantially different than the streets of my teens that it might have been a different planet.

My younger sister was my only family connection, though she was living far from our hometown of Baltimore. Maybe that's why I was so hesitant to challenge her when she assured me that those mean-looking milk machines didn't hurt the cows. Maybe it was my overall sense of dislocation that led me to feel so dizzy as I looked down the row of milking stalls.

Or maybe there's some other reason that I can't even remember whether there were cows in those stalls as I stood there feeling silly and silenced and angry and ashamed all at the same time. Maybe it's significant that I can't even tell you whether I saw a cow at all. All I know for sure is that my sister took me to a local, probably small, maybe organic, dairy farm; I felt uneasy and we argued briefly, and then the incident disappeared from my memory along with the cows, leaving me free to continue to consume dairy products without even a twinge of bad conscience.

It would be years before cows reappeared in my consciousness, before Farm Sanctuary newsletters would combine with my own scholarly musings about daughters and dairy cows as property of husbands to finally lead me to the cows themselves, what they wanted, how they felt, how terribly unfair it was for them to be ensnared not only by our ideas about nonhuman animals but also by our ideas about femaleness. And even then it took me more than a year to get what I now call "the demon dairy" all the way out of my life, actively wrestling with what now seem to be inane rationalizations all the way.

Understand: I do not forgive myself for this; I am just reporting what happened. Nor do I seek to expiate my wrongs by confessing. No. What I want to know—what I think we need to know—is *why*. Why was that dairy farm visit so profoundly upsetting that I immediately repressed it, and my recollection of it now, years later, has all the hallmarks of a traumatic memory? Why, once I brought the issue back into consciousness, did I so strongly resist remembering what I knew, and doing what I needed to do?

I can't explain from the inside. From the outside the response is easy: "she didn't want to give up that sharp Vermont cheddar, so she put it out of her mind." But since the forgetting was not a conscious choice, I doubt that's how it happened. Perhaps, more than the loss of favored dairy products, I dreaded the sickening feeling of complicity that emerged when I finally confronted, and rejected, dairy.

I'll never know for sure why the queasy uneasiness I felt at the dairy farm slithered out of sight so easily. What I do know for sure is that this kind of shifty slippage probably helps to explain why the altruistic, animal-loving, feminist friend who sat next to me sobbing as we watched the documentary "Peaceable Kingdom" is still eating meat. Animal advocates need to understand this response more clearly so that we can understand why efforts to force people to confront their complicity in cruelty rarely lead to behavior changes.

The ease with which we forget facilitates animal abuse and all other atrocities that tend to make us sputter and reach for the word "unspeakable": child abuse, nukes, poverty in the midst of plenty. We need to learn how to speak of such things in a way that keeps them uncomfortably conscious. This requires us to see and think about the sexual and perversely sexualized exploitation of female farmed animals that is the norm in animal agriculture.

When I look closely at dairy, I see the hurtful exploitation of specifically female bodies so that some people can enjoy sensual pleasures of consumption while others enjoy the psychological pleasure of collecting profits from the exertions of somebody else's body. Cows are forcibly impregnated, dispossessed of their children, and then painfully robbed of the milk produced by their bodies for those children. No wonder I didn't want to see my complicity! Most women don't consciously perceive the everyday violence against girls and women that permeates and structures of our society. How much harder it is, then, to see the gendered violence against nonhuman animals behind the everyday items on the grocery store shelf. When we, as women, partake of that violence, we participate in sexism even as we enjoy the illusory benefits of speciesism. No wonder a glimpse of the sexist violence behind my breakfast cereal left me dizzy.

If we're going to make any headway on dairy and eggs, we've got to confront this directly. We've got to start talking to women about the sexist exploitation of female reproductive capacities to produce consumer goods that hurt women and children. We must talk about this explicitly, knowing that one in three women has been raped or battered, and may thus have strong or seemingly strange reactions to the facts. We need to confront the sickening collision of sex and violence by which nonhuman animals are electroejaculated and forcibly impregnated for human pleasures. We have to be able to look at all of the complicated and uncomfortable dynamics that drive and derive from this sexualized exploitation. Similar conflagrations of gender, violence, and pleasure smolder at the source of cultural products and activities as seemingly disparate as pornography, interrogatory torture, and cockfighting.

Which brings us back to chickens. Roosters are both the victims and the unwitting agents of human sexism. One of the most damaging aspects of sexism is the confusion between sex (maleness or femaleness) and gender (masculinity or femininity). Some people are more assertive while others are more yielding. Some are brave; some are nurturing. Sexism assigns such characteristics to gender and then asserts that gender is a natural expression of sex. Thus, girls who are assertive and boys who are nurturing are led to believe that there is something unnatural about them.

While sex is a physical fact, gender is what social scientists call a "social construct." Social constructs feel real but are, in truth, just ideas made up and maintained by members of a social group. People use other animals to make gender seem as real as sex, pointing to nonhuman animals as "proof" that certain kinds of behavior are typically male or typically female. Not surprisingly, given the wide range of animal behavior in nature, they always find what they're seeking. For many years, male field researchers studying primates explained away, refused to record, or simply failed to perceive behaviors that were inconsistent with their preconceived dominance hierarchies. (Similar biases and blind spots led scientists to miss or dismiss observations of homosexuality in hundreds of species.) People also force or trick nonhuman animals into acting out sexist stereotypes and then point to those same beings as evidence that the stereotypes reflect a "natural order." This is nowhere more clear than with fighting cocks, who are subjected to an array of abuses designed to trick them into murderous aggression.

Roosters have long been seen as embodiments of masculinity. That's how the word "cock" came to be used as slang for a human penis. International studies of cockfighters show that men and boys see fighting roosters as expressions of their own masculinity, and they feel shame if one of "their" roosters behaves normally, fleeing from an aggressor or declining to attack a retreating bird. In contrast, unnaturally aggressive birds are accorded an almost totemic respect. Cockfighters have very strong ideas about what they believe to be natural behavior for roosters, and they fail to recognize how their interventions create unnatural fights where roosters kill one another.

In nature, roosters are the sentinels and protectors of the flock. They constantly scan the skies and the horizon for predators, while joining the hens to look for food. In contrast to the myth of male stoicism, roosters tend to be more emotional than hens, probably because they need to be more sensitive to potential threats. Of course there is much overlap between the characteristics of roosters and the characteristics of hens, as well as much variation among roosters and among hens. A rooster will risk his life protecting the flock from a predator. A hen will often take the same risk protecting her chicks. Some roosters are very nurturing toward chicks; others simply ignore their offspring. Some roosters spend all of their time with hens. Others prefer the company of other roosters, or stay to themselves.

Neither wild jungle fowl nor feral roosters risk their survival in death matches with other roosters. Roosters sometimes struggle for dominance and territory, but the fights are short and rarely lead to serious injury. Certainly, fights such as are seen in cockfighting spectacles, where the victorious bird continues to attack until the loser is dead, do not occur. When a rooster has been bested, he assumes a submissive posture or runs away. The victor then postures or crows, signaling, "I've won!"

Breeders and trainers of fighting cocks prohibit roosters from learning the social signals of conflict resolution. Isolated in cages or tethered to stakes, fed less than they would choose to eat, and kept apart from hens, these roosters are in a constant state of frustrated excitation. Add the stress of transport, the confusing sights and sounds of a busy event, and the injection of drugs or hormones, and it's easy to see how terrified roosters can be brought to fight to the death when faced with a similarly terrified bird armed with steel talons.

This is the secret that cockfighters can't face, and don't want you to know: Roosters fight from fear, not aggression. That's the secret of our rooster rehabilitation program, too.

We rehabilitate fighting cocks by teaching them that they don't have to be afraid of other birds, using the same principles that a psychotherapist might use to help patients overcome phobias or posttraumatic stress. At first, they simply need to be soothed and given time to see and be near other birds without fear. Then, during supervised free periods, such as the one that began this essay, a former fighter is allowed to roam freely until he starts a fight, at which time he is placed back in his spacious rehabilitation cage, from which he can see and interact with, but not hurt or be hurt by, the other birds. Over time, a rooster is able to be free for longer and longer periods (hence the boredom for us) until he can be trusted to mingle peacefully with the other birds all day long. The rehabilitation process takes anywhere from a few days to several weeks. Some birds "get it" very quickly and seem palpably relieved to be out of harm's way. Others take longer to relax. Although personality clashes sometimes have required us to shift birds from yard to yard, we've never had a fighting cock so incorrigible that we couldn't find a place for him to be free. Fighting unto death is not their natural behavior.

People need safety to find freedom, too. More than we realize, we all lead lives structured and constricted by lies and fear. That's why I've tried so hard to tell the truth in this essay, because none of us can be truly free in the context of violent duplicity.

pattrice jones is the cofounder of the Eastern Shore Sanctuary and Education Center and the author of *Aftershock: Confronting Trauma in a Violent World*. She is currently working on a book of creative nonfiction about starting a chicken sanctuary in a rural region dominated by the poultry industry.

2

from rural roots to angels' wings
twyla françois

rural roots run deep

I was born and grew up in a small, religious farming community in Manitoba, Canada. While I lived on the edge of town, many of my friends lived on farms. Here, among these nonhuman animals, my awakening began.

I remember helping my friend milk the cows (even in the 1970s and '80s the milking was done mechanically). When I walked amid cows in the barn, they stopped and sniffed me. They watched what I was doing, much as I was watching what they were doing. I came to see that each of these cows had her own personality. I was also extremely bonded to my pet cat, Mittens (sorry—she came with the name) and began to see that these cows were very much like her. I thought: "If I choose not to eat my cat, perhaps I can choose not to eat cows, too."

In rural Canada, almost all students are enrolled in a program called 4-H ("Head, Heart, Hands, and Health"). With an almost religious fervor (including the chanting of a prayer), 4-H youth are taught about all things rural. The girls learn the domestic "arts"—our final exam was to cook a meaty meal for our instructor's husband; the boys (and some girls) learn how to suppress their feelings of compassion for nonhuman animals, which they are taught to raise and kill for profit. Of course this isn't how "animal husbandry" is presented, but this is the unspoken mandate of 4-H.

My friend, from a dairy farmer family, was enrolled in the livestock program. She was instructed to select a newborn calf, take him as her own, learn to care for him, name him, groom him, and then present the calf at the town fair in the summer. Little did she know that she was not showing her beloved calf for his beauty—those in the audience, bidding on the calf, were meat buyers. As her calf was loaded onto a trailer to be taken away and killed, the full meaning of what she'd done hit her. There was no going back, no matter how many tears she shed or pleas she pled. This is, in fact, stipulated in the rules—no child can have his or her calf back. As quickly as possible, the organizers handed her a check for $1,000. To my surprise, her tears were quickly replaced with thoughts of how she would spend the money.

I don't know how I came to Peter Singer's book, *Animal Liberation*, but I recall reading a copy when I was thirteen. (I still have this tattered, original copy.) My family rarely went to the city, and I didn't know anyone involved in animal rights, so it's a mystery to me how I got this book. *Animal Liberation* shaped my views on nonhuman animals. Singer's words are powerful, and while the philosophy was over my head, the descriptions of what was happening to farmed animals in agriculture shocked me, and much of my teen years were spent thinking about those farmed animals and crying at night because I felt absolutely helpless.

Shortly after reading this book I became a vegetarian—a change I fought with for nearly a decade. Everyone told me I needed to eat meat. In fact, they made the simple act of not eating meat almost painful. School lunches were a nightmare, and I'm sure I was seen as something of a freak. My teen years were particularly painful—there were few people who understood my beliefs, and I wasn't yet able to communicate my understandings and feelings effectively. Only with the perpetual support of my mother was I able to see those years through. My mother greeted each of my new beliefs with a desire to understand. We spent long hours discussing the worth of nonhuman animals. My family has, in fact, always been incredibly supportive. My now sixty-something father and my older sister supported my relatively recent move to veganism, and they became vegetarians in response.

I'd like to be able to say that once I left my rural roots, and moved to the city, I became an activist. But I didn't. In my late teens and early twenties, I was a shell of who I'd been. Society, and rural culture, had crushed me into a demure, unquestioning woman. By their standards, that was who I should be. But the university reopened closed doors, showing me much of what I wasn't supposed to know.

While studying anthropology I learned about evolution (something I'd never heard of before), and I thereby discovered our connection with the other animals. After I recovered from my initial desire to stand up and yell "blasphemy!" I listened intently. Anthropology provided answers to critical questions: Why are we so much like other animals? Why do we share kinship

twyla françois

and common roots? I studied the anthropology of illness and discovered that many of the diseases, conditions, and injuries we are prone to are because of our ancestral/animal past. University life was exciting.

But when I was still a freshman, my world crumbled: My mother was diagnosed with cancer. Every woman in my family experiences (and ultimately dies from) cancer. My grandmother was diagnosed in her late thirties, and my maternal aunt died at thirty-seven. But Mom seemed untouchable. It made no sense.

My mom and I had always been close. We talked daily about what I was learning at the university. As I learned, she learned, too. In her midforties, she was healthy and energetic, and soon she was pronounced "cancer free." But she knew things weren't right.

Over and over she brought concerns to her doctor. Three years later, my mother was still suffering, and her doctor was still dismissing her concerns. By the time her doctor was convinced of the necessity of exploratory surgery, the cancer had metastasized, and she was terminal. During those last few months, I took leave from school, and Mom came to live with me. It was a warm, bonding time that I will always cherish. My mother was an educated, intelligent, and articulate woman. She was ignored in a medical system that was not designed for women. Because one man failed to listen to her, my mother, an incredible woman, died far too young.

Mom's death turned me toward a master's degree in biological and forensic anthropology, where I could study the physiology of the process of dying, and pathology. I was fitting in well, working full time in the office of the president at the University of Manitoba. As a result, I took on increasingly responsible positions with strong, driven women. I worked for the president for four years, the vice president of research for two years, and the vice president for external affairs for two years. But these office jobs ate away at me.

My experience in the office of the vice president of research was particularly troubling. At first the work was exciting; I was able to read cutting-edge research applications. But requests arrived for nonhuman animals to conduct studies on, and the research didn't seem so cutting-edge anymore. In fact, the majority of these studies were simply knowledge-based research—conducted for the researcher's own interest, never to be applied or published.

Around this time the public learned that the university was using dogs, once beloved pets bought from the city pound, for research. Collared, name-tagged dogs were coming to the university and were put through for research—not just acute research, but chronic studies ending with death as a final thanks. (There is no adoption program at the University of Manitoba.) The university had considered using a tissue-sharing network, a system that would drastically reduce the number of dogs killed, but this option was never pursued. It was intensely painful for me to learn that this world of knowledge and academia, a world that I valued above all else, was responsible for countless acts of animal cruelty.

To work through this conflict, I volunteered every spare moment to animal advocacy. But the guilt quietly and insidiously continued to build, and by 2004 I had Stage IV abdominal tumors—which killed my grandmother, aunt, and mother. I took medical leave for two surgeries and six months of chemotherapy. I was thirty-two years old, and terrified.

During this brush with death, I examined my life and pondered where I'd taken a wrong turn. I realized that after fighting through my teen years, I had ultimately succumbed to society's demands. I turned to books like *Reviving Ophelia*, which examines how prepubescent women, before they have been manipulated, are their true selves. Society crushes and coerces young women into being what they are expected to be—submissive and unquestioning, maintainers of the status quo.

Ethically, I couldn't go back to my job at the university. I decided to rediscover who I had been in my preteen years. I met like-minded people and founded a nonprofit, animal advocacy organization called AnimalWatch Manitoba.

becoming an angel

An informant sent AnimalWatch Manitoba a photo of a pig tied up outside Manitoba Pork Marketing Cooperative—a collecting station for pigs in Winnipeg. The pig had been left in the direct sun on a concrete parking lot and appeared to be alive, but dying. I had no income. Yet I decided to conduct an investigation on the pig facility, which lasted for a full year and confirmed our worst fears: Pigs were electrically prodded on their faces, up their rectums and vaginas; and they were tied to posts outside in all elements, left to die. Pigs with broken legs and pelvises were left to die overnight in concrete pens with no medication, food, water, or straw. Pregnant sows were transported close to term, forced to give birth en route, only to have their babies mauled, trampled, and eaten by overcrowded, frightened, stressed pigs.

I sent my final report on the facility to Animals' Angels, an internationally operating organization based in Germany. They answered my questions, and to my astonishment, asked me to join them on their next investigation in the United States. For two weeks I traveled with Animals' Angels, and was exposed to the massive problems of industrial animal agriculture.

Ultimately, they offered me a position; I could see no alternative but to help. In my role as head of investigation for Animals' Angels Canada, and now for Canadians for the Ethical Treatment of Food Animals (www.cetfa.com), I spend roughly half of my time in the field engaged in investigations. I inspect farmed animals in transport, at collecting stations, in livestock auctions, in large production units (which have replaced 'barns'), and in slaughterhouses. I see farmed animals at their most vulnerable—in transport and at slaughter.

As an investigator, I work on two levels. First, at the individual level, advocating for those who are abused or suffering. Often the best I can do for these individuals is to require that they be humanely euthanized because they are far too sick to survive and often in too much pain to tolerate transport for recovery. When possible, I remove these individuals and bring them to a sanctuary where they might recover and live out the rest of their lives as naturally as possible.

Second, I do follow-up work in the office. I write reports, encourage legislative reform, conduct media interviews, attend producer meetings, and work with slaughterhouse directors and transport company owners to advocate for improvements in welfare practices.

One benefit of my position is that I am with the farmed animals—literally—and therefore act as a more legitimate spokesperson for them. I witness what is done to them daily, and I can therefore speak with some level of confidence about necessary changes.

One day, at Winnipeg Livestock Auction, I met a "used up" or "spent" cow from the dairy industry; I named her Emily. She had an excruciatingly painful twisted stomach (equal in pain to a ruptured appendix in a human), torn udder ligaments, and mastitis (painful, inflamed teats). Her mastitis was so acute that her udder was nearly on the ground, yet she was forced into the auction ring, and sold to a buyer who planned to load and transport her to Ontario the following week. Because I was there to insist, she was euthanized, and her painful exploitation at the hands of humanity was over; but it required three days of fighting on her behalf.

Another day I found a dying sow who had been pulled headfirst from the top level of a transport trailer (ten feet high) with the use of a wire cable and tractor. The fall, designed to break her neck, is used to try to kill a farmed animal who is economically worthless, even though this method is illegal and unfathomably cruel. The legal means require workers to enter the trailer with a captive bolt pistol or gun and shoot her, to spare her from being painfully moved.

Yet another day, I saw workers break a boar's tusks with rusty bolt-cutters that shattered the tooth up into the boar's gum-line and cut directly across his innervated pulp canal—a procedure done so that the driver need not bother to separate boars in transport, as the federal transport regulations dictate, to prevent them from fighting in his trailer. Immediately before loading, these boars are also "boar bashed": Men break the boar's snouts with crowbars. With teeth and snouts broken, the boars are in severe agony, and no longer need to be separated to prevent fighting, saving space, which can instead be used to haul yet more boars.

In each of these cases, even with full video footage and the details of each incident meticulously recorded, the authorities did nothing to prosecute the offenders—they would not even write and send a letter of reprimand.

These are just a few of the horrendous cruelties that happen on a daily basis, cruelties that I witness whenever I visit animal industries. One truth stands out from my investigations: Brutality is a natural product of contemporary animal agriculture. Farmed animals are handled in such massive numbers that it is impossible for a worker to recognize them as individuals. When I'm in the field, and see such indifference to suffering, the issues become very clear, as do solutions.

I always assumed that the majority of nonhuman animal suffering was a result of neglect, or mindlessness, but as we improve covert methods of collecting evidence, we find more and more brutality—workers "playing with" pigs with electrical currents in order to hear them scream, birds blown apart by forcing air up their cloacas (where eggs come out), and of course, sows having electric prods pushed into their vaginas.

For me, the most disturbing realization has been that, if you happen to be a female farmed animal, your quality of life drops to near zero. A sow will not know one ounce of human kindness during her entire life. In my experience, these are the most abused of all farmed animals. At breeding operations they are treated as "bacon-makers." They live in crates, row upon row, as far as their eyes can see, throughout their adult lives. They cannot even turn around between these bars. They live in filth, with rats (who sometimes eat the bodies of their dead piglets). Their world is one of such complete, unending hell; deprived of all comforts and stimulation, that they are driven mad. These intelligent, sensitive farmed animals return what they sense from us; even the boars—intact males—have been gentle with me. Their babies, the ones who are slightly too small or slightly too weak, are "PACed"—an industry term meaning "Pounded Against Concrete." These piglets are swung by their rear legs, smashing their heads into a wall or concrete floor in order to kill them—all in front of their helpless mothers. Further, Canada lacks fire codes in hog barns, so fires are common and sweep through entire barns, killing thousands of helpless sows confined in metal crates. When these sows are viewed as "used up," they are loaded onto trailers with electric prods and transported many hours to slaughter. Thirty-hour trips are common, but some Canadian pigs go all the way to Hawaii—a trip that takes nine days. They are generally transported without water, food, or even a rest break.

At the slaughterhouse, these farmed animals, who have had every one of their babies taken from them, who have lived lives of complete deprivation, are often beaten with pipes to force them to the kill floor, where they are slaughtered with methods proven to have high failure rates. Pigs are presumably stunned before they are killed (except for halal and kosher killings, where the individuals are fully conscious while their throats are cut), but "failure" is marked by returning to consciousness during the slaughter process. "Failure" means the farmed animal is not stunned, but stabbed in the jugular, put through the scald tank, and sometimes even butchered while fully conscious, as we recently uncovered at horse slaughterhouses in Saskatchewan, Alberta, and Quebec (www.defendhorsescanada.org).

As women, we must be aware of the suffering of sows (and "dairy" cows, and "laying" hens) and refuse to support such cruel exploitation of female reproductive potential. Just because females have the ability to conceive and give birth—even in the most horrific of circumstances—does not mean that we may imprison and impregnate them throughout their shortened lives. As women, we must reject pork products, especially pork sausages or patties, which are primarily sow meat. The same is true for products that come from the nursing milk of cows or the reproductive eggs of chickens.

My hope is that young women will resist, more and more, society's grip. We are in society, and society is also in us. We internalize so much that is not our own, whether we know it or not. This can lead us down the wrong path and waste years of life. Young women—follow your intuition, what you know is right, whether or not you can verbalize your reasons and understandings. Hold onto your preteen person, and never lose your sense of wonder and compassion.

Women are the heart and soul of the Animal Rights Movement, and the nonhuman animals' best hope for better lives. It is my wish that you become one of these women.

twyla françois, head of investigation for Canadians for the Ethical Treatment of Food Animals (www.cetfa.com), was previously head of investigation for Animals' Angels Canada (no longer in operation). As a farmed animal cruelty investigator, Twyla works primarily in the field, providing food, water, warmth, kindness, medical treatment, and pain relief during transport and slaughter of farmed animals. Twyla is also Central Region Director for the Canadian Horse Defense Coalition (http://www.defendhorsescanada.org/), defending Canada's equines from slaughter and from export for slaughter, through investigation, education, and legislation.

twyla françois

3

are you waving at me?
ingrid e. newkirk

> Coat of fur, hat with feathers
> Lobsters boiled alive
> Who are they, and who am I
> That I may live, and they must die?

I guess it's not very politically correct to start off an essay that has to do with women and their influence by declaring that I detest being defined by the word "woman." Perhaps that sounds a bit strange to anyone who knows that I've been a feminist since forever or, more accurately, since I saw a drawing of a suffragist chained to a railing; that I marched in the bra-burning '60s when women first demanded equal pay for equal work; and that I became one of the first deputy sheriffs in Maryland—I dare say in the country. (During a drug bust or other tricky bit of business, if there turned out to be a guard dog or two on the premises, the men (who lifted weights in their off hours and belonged to gun clubs) would say, "We aren't going in until Newkirk is here to deal with the dogs!"

Of course, I know that women's rights are vital, so don't get me wrong: It's just that I have a "thing" against compartmentalization. I see it as the root of all evil; the labeling and compartmentalization of life have contributed enormously to discrimination. If no one knew we were women, no one could ever have discriminated against us on the basis of that fact.

In one of my favorite books, *Woman and Nature*, the author, Susan Griffin, juxtaposes passages from others' writings from years gone by in which the woman and the "dairy" cow or the mule were regarded in exactly the same supremacist, patronizing ways. Take this gem:

> Girls ought to be active and diligent; nor is that all, they should also be early subjected to restraint. . . . [I]t is, therefore, necessary to accustom them early to such confinement, that it may not afterwards cost them too dear, and to the suppression of their caprices, that they may the more readily submit to the will of others.
>
> —jean-jacques rousseau, *émile*

> The teacher should insist that the horse stand still and on all four legs during the process of mounting and until asked to move on by the rider. Fidgeting on the spot or moving without command must not be tolerated.
>
> —alois podhajsky, *the riding teacher*

In the same way, I can't bring myself (and why should I?) to root for the English drivers when I sit mesmerized, watching international auto races, or for the American (my adopted country) or English entrants valiantly skating for the gold. It's not because they aren't the best—some are—but because nationalism also makes my skin crawl. Funny enough, it was the founder of New York's Vegetarian Feminists' Collective, Connie Salamone, many moons ago, who cautioned me that there are inherent dangers in narrowing our definition of ourselves and about the importance of being ever more inclusive. "Woman" is so narrow a term, a bit like "white," which upon closer examination is meaningless in that it actually means "black"—a long time removed from Africa and now peculiarly depigmented. And isn't the definition of "woman" based on sex? So much emphasis on sex! Yes, the *Vagina Monologues* tell "our" side of the story, mock what needs to be mocked—and mockery of the pathetic is healthy—and let "us" vent, but they point out that at the root of the problem of women's subjugation is the fact that we are the baby incubators, the carriers of men's seed—not equals, but vessels, defined by our sexual organs. One only has to think of why "mammals" are so named!

My appeal is that we not fight only for consideration, respect, and freedom for those we relate to the most, whether they be our family; others of our religion, race, or gender; or even all human beings—for then we will be mimicking the hierarchical, supremacist ideas that have caused the very problems we object to—but that we reject all classifications as much as we possibly can and demand to be part of something bigger, members of the community of all living beings.

This is where the animal rights message comes in: the challenge not to restrict the provision of truly important things in life, like fairness, justice, respect, compassion, and decency, to others by limiting our application of them solely to those we can relate to most closely. It is one thing to live by the old saw that "when you teach a child to be kind to a caterpillar, you do as much for the child as you do for the caterpillar," but quite another to act on principle. The principle being that all violence, all meanness, all prejudice is wrong. As Connie Salamone also said, women who understand oppression on the basis of gender must be the last ones to cause oppression on any other supremacist basis; we cannot seek respect and consideration for ourselves while chewing on the bones of small, tortured birds. Or, to play with Wavy Gravy's words from the Love Generation: War hurts everyone. The victims of war include the birds and camels doused or aflame in the Iraqi oil fields, the mules used to carry explosives to Israeli border checkpoints, the packhorses who were left to perish screaming in pain on the Russian front, and the dogs abandoned by the U.S. soldiers leaving Vietnam.

Almost everyone I work *with* happens to be female—perhaps because of cultural training that makes women less defensive about caring? And almost everyone I work *for* is female. I'm not happy about that. It is, rather, a sad fact of the nature of my work. Sometimes I am reading about, say, the "sacks" riding along in the back of a pickup truck in Afghanistan—yes, women in burkhas, bouncing about on the metal exactly as the poor hobbled camels do when they are driven to market by the men in the often air-conditioned cab—and I think that, relatively speaking, those repressed women are kings (queens?) compared to my employers, my petitioners. Even the word "petitioners" is a misnomer. Those I work for cannot petition; they have no voice at all. (They speak, of course: Elephants rumble warnings over many miles, picking them up through the earth with their sensitive feet, frogs drum on tree trunks, rhinos use a language of breathing sounds, and fish cheep like birds in their underwater languages.) But those in control, the pickup truck drivers, for example, do not usually hear the sounds or, if they do, they find the sounds irritating ("Be quiet!"), or ignore them. Even the farmed animals' death cries in the slaughterhouse are drowned out by laughter at a casual unrelated joke or, often, a joke at their expense: Piglets cut from the sow's body are tossed about like balls, for fun, and the dying turkey's rectum is squeezed in the direction of a coworker so as to get a giggle as her excreta shoots out. We do not hear nonhuman animals. The lobsters, say, waggle their antennae at you the way a paralyzed patient might blink her eyes to convey a desperate message; in the lobsters' case, it's "Don't kill me!" but even I blithely ordered the lobster to the boiling water, once upon a time.

In any case, the majority of factory-farmed animals, more than 20 billion individuals a year, are female. Hens, for example, are kept concentration-camp–style, in cages so small that they cannot raise a wing during their entire lifetime, and sows are chained headfirst to a rail, unable even to turn around to nuzzle their piglets. So are most of the elephants in the circus (because the males would not tolerate the metal spike of the bullhook and would kill the trainer) and the mothers of all species kept as breeding machines on mink and fox farms, in the din of pet bird breeding sheds, and in the cold barren cages in laboratories.

Why is it that the man who committed suicide when he found the calf he loved and played with gutted for meat was noted, at the inquest, as "having taken his life when the balance of his mind was disturbed?" Why is it that the experimenter can continue to insert electrodes into the open skull of his monkey victim after reading, at breakfast perhaps, of the latest study showing how even tiny mice think like humans, enjoy playing, giggle when tickled, run from pain, and crave companionship—and not be called mentally unbalanced? How is it that a woman can lean over the pit wall and cheer on the dog or cock she wants to win the bloody fight, and no one suggests that she is mentally unbalanced?

I wasn't always a "radical," believing that our society is upside-down, selfish, and uncaring and that something urgently needs to be done about it. I was a normal little girl who grew up around nonhuman animals and so came to understand them and read their facial expressions. To me, they did not "all look alike." Yet, just like most children, I petted my dog, nursed the fallen baby bird or injured lizard back to health, and ate most of the rest of the nonhuman animals. In fact, my father and I busily ate our way through almost the entire nonhuman animal kingdom with gusto, while I would have hit anyone back who hit "my" pony and, later, I would have gone to jail, if need be, to defend my beloved dog.

The transformation came at a lobster restaurant in Philadelphia on my birthday, when that lobster really did wave his antennae at me in the same way that puppies, caged inside a restaurant in China, might appeal for mercy as best they could to the diner who is about to choose one of them. I didn't notice it at the time, as I decided whether to have him boiled or broiled (only later did I learn that "broiled" requires slitting the lobster's back open while he is fully conscious and smearing salt and butter into the wound before sticking him on the burning rack under the broiler). But within minutes, he (or she?) was back, and my fork entered his or her little body. I've no idea, to this day, why what I was doing suddenly hit me, but it did: I had ordered an animal killed and was eating his or her flesh to celebrate the fact that I was, some 19 years after my birth, still alive. How bizarre is that!?

Bart Grasulsky, a university professor, told me later that he had had a similar experience with another "odd" nonhuman animal, a fish. He had been on his way to that bastion of civilization, the Library of Congress in Washington, D.C., when he stopped at the Tidal Basin to watch a man fishing. The two exchanged pleasantries. Then the man, rather generously, gave Bart a big freshly caught fish, which he placed on the back seat of his Volkswagen and drove on. Sitting in the library, looking at the statuary and reading quotations about lofty ideals, Bart suddenly thought, "What am I doing sitting here? There's a fish dying on the back seat of my car!" and charged outside to try to get the fish back into the water. Both of us wished that we had grown up as Canadian feminist Harriet Schleifer had, full of the understanding that fish have feelings. Out on a boat with her father or grandfather, at about the age of seven, Harriet watched her family hero as he reeled in a mightily struggling fish. She was horrified. Here was a man she loved, killing a nonhuman animal. Harriet burst into tears and begged him to stop.

What does it take? That is my daily challenge. How can I and all of us here at PETA open people's eyes and hearts? It has happened to each of us, often for very different reasons. The man who runs our marketing department became a vegan when he was broke and couldn't afford to buy a birthday present for his animal rights sister. She was always asking people to go vegan, and he was always mocking her. So he decided that his gift to her would be to go vegan for a week—after all, how bad could it be for one week? For some reason, he found his defensiveness breaking down in those seven days, and he felt better physically. He started to look at what farmed animals endure: chickens having their beaks seared off with a hot wire, pigs having their tails amputated without painkillers, cows having their horns pulled from their skulls with a pair of pliers, and on and on. Now he is a vegan for life.

What is it that will make one woman turn away from fur and another almost spit in my eye when I approach her, as I must (for the victims cannot do it themselves, of course), to ever-so-nicely say: "I used to wear fur too" (it's true—my first fur coat was made of about 100 squirrels), "but I found out about the mothers, who chew off their legs to get back to their young when they are caught in steel traps and how the fox cubs are bludgeoned to death on fur farms."

What is the worst cruelty I have seen? Was it the dogs swinging by their necks in a Chinese slaughterhouse or the horses kicked in the face in Texas or the dog whose face was cut off by a sadist or the cat buried alive or the chicken whose leg was torn from her body as the man pulled her from her crate? Perhaps it was the eel whose throat was torn out of his mouth on the banks of the Schuylkill River as I held him in a towel, trying to help the angler who was impatiently reclaiming his four-pronged gaff back from inside the mouth of this "trash fish." I no longer know, but the cruelty cases keep pouring in, thirty-some years on, with no end in sight. They are on videotape now, captured forever, not in the mind's eye, but on tape so that you can never escape the images.

Women still control most of the kitchens of the world, and I see no reason to object to the situation because food is vital to life. Those places are fonts of power, the rooms in which plans can be laid for dietary domination. Women can control not only what they eat but also what their families eat. Women can get on food committees at work, they can talk to supermarket managers and request what they want to buy and don't want to see (like foie gras and live lobsters—those lobsters again!). They can pack their kids' school lunches, they can choose vegetarian restaurants for gatherings or business meetings, they can cook for workmates and soulmates and so spare farmed animals at every meal. One taste of the Gardein faux chicken, and longtime vegans go pale with disgust that they have eaten an actual chicken; nonvegetarians are amazed. Yes, you can have that fleshy taste without the cruelty. Easy as pie—tofu cream pie!

There are cats in our office because I haven't found a way to accommodate chickens or rescued parrots. Cats keep to themselves a lot and stop doing amusing things when they stop being kittens. Birds are much more sociable. We had two big macaws once who had come out of a grubby pet shop upon which humane officers had served a search warrant. The two of them amused themselves mightily, learning everyone's laugh and then using them at odd moments. At the end of the day, they would position themselves so that they could see out the window at the far end of my office. They would stare down at the street below, waiting for some unsuspecting shift worker to come up the hill. "Hello?" they would call. "Hi, there!" I would see the poor man look around, baffled at first, turning this way and that, finally catching sight of the hollering birds running through their vast repertoire of "hi" and "hello" calls. "Hello!" he would call up to them, smiling. There would follow absolute silence or a gale of bird laughter, and then the birds would retreat to give him time to move on and allow them to return later to play the trick on another human.

Chickens are just as interesting, full of life and character and as individual as the Spice Girls. I've had rescued hens who loved to preen for the rooster, stuck-up ones, "sporty" ones who would play with melon balls and leaves, quiet ones, and gossipy ones. There is a film that we show to junior high school children on the intelligence of hens—how a mother hen will go to great lengths, risk much, and traverse obstacle courses to safeguard her nest and how these dear, gentle birds easily learned to peck at a switch at Bristol University to turn up the heat in a cold barn or turn it down again when they got too warm. Having cats in the office or at home is practical, but more's the pity. If people who love cats came to know turkeys or squabs—the tiny birds who are the apple of their mother and father pigeons' eye and are becoming common even in this country on French restaurant menus—they would be horrified to find them on a menu.

My work is not all about going vegan, although it is hard to justify eating those you work for, or stealing from them. Weren't we all taught the Golden Rule: "Do unto others as you would have them do unto you"? My work is about making kind choices (a shameless plug for my book of the same name) in every pursuit, including:

- How we spend our money at the grocery store. (Will it be meat and dairy products or fruits, nuts, vegetables, grains, and legumes? Will I use ingredients for beef pot pie or for a veggie casserole?)
- How we spend our money in the drugstore. (Were those cosmetics tested in rabbits' eyes?)
- How we spend our money in the clothing store. (Will it be fur or faux? leather or pleather? wool or cotton?)
- How we spend our money in entertainment. (Will we avoid the rodeo, the circus, hunting, and fishing?)
- Which charities will we support? (Will I support the March of Dimes, which has stitched kittens' eyes shut, or Easter Seals, which does not use nonhuman animals?)
- How will we learn? (Will I use dissection or computer models?)
- How will we deal with "pests"? (Will I choose the sticky glue traps to cause suffocation or a humane box trap? Poisons for insects or leafy deterrents?)

There is no end to the choices that we can make, the influence that we can wield just by giving a child or teacher a pamphlet, cooking a meal for a neighbor or coworker, speaking a few enlightening words to a stranger, lending a helping hand in order to draw people closer to the compassionate side of their nature—the side that women are not ashamed to show.

Washingtonian of the Year, ingrid e. newkirk is president and cofounder of People for the Ethical Treatment of Animals (PETA, www.PETA.org). As an activist and author of over a dozen books, including *PETA's Practical Guide to Helping Animals*, *Making Kind Choices*, and *One Can Make a Difference*, Newkirk has been featured in *The New Yorker*, *Time Magazine*, *People*, *Forbes*, *Financial Times* (and numerous other publications) for her work with nonhuman animals. She has appeared on television shows all over the world and is the subject of a film by the BBC and in *I Am an Animal*, an HBO documentary.

4

connections

SPECIESISM, RACISM, AND WHITENESS AS THE NORM

a. breeze harper

In junior high school, he was the boy who used racial slurs against my twin brother, Talmadge, making him cry. He was the same boy who, in my math class, spoke of his distaste for a new sitcom that featured an interracial family. And he was the same boy who made fun of me when I tried to "save" a hornet who was crawling on the classroom floor.

His name was Levi. He and I were in the same algebra class. I was thirteen years old and in the eighth grade.

Mostly during my K-12 years, I remember always feeling angry and uncomfortable about being the only black children (my twin and I) in an all-white working-class school system, in which many of our peers were constantly and openly racist. Many didn't even realize that they were racist.

But Levi was very conscious of the intent of words that unraveled from his tongue, out into the air, for all of us to hear. Only fourteen or fifteen years old, he was already performing his whiteness and masculinity through public acts of sexism, racism, homophobia . . . and often invisible and widely acceptable forms of speciesism.

I don't remember what month or season it was. I do remember, while awaiting the arrival of our teacher, Mr. Rivers, my eye spied a small insect making its way across the dingy carpet, which had not seen a good cleaning in quite a while. As usual, I couldn't resist helping out a smaller creature in need. I tried to persuade this rather lethargic insect onto a piece of line-ruled paper torn from my notebook.

In the Harper household I had a reputation for "saving" insects who were "trapped" inside our home or car. I also had a special affinity for dragonflies, and living in rural Connecticut (the "boonies"), I had the pleasure of being in the presence of a multitude of dragonflies, as well as other crawling and flying wonders.

Once, when I was fourteen or fifteen years old, a thin blue-bodied dragonfly became confused and frustrated in my Dad's old brown van. I didn't know the insect was in the van when Dad and I headed for the bank. Upon arriving, the dragonfly crashed into the windshield, making its presence known. I spent the next thirty seconds trying to help the hapless bug understand that the window was solid by directing her or him towards my open door. The insect however, assuming that I was trying to eat him or her, refused to travel toward the doorway. In my youth, I quickly became frustrated and annoyed, and my father lovingly noted: "There's nothing more you can do. You tried your best to help. It doesn't understand glass."

My father had offered a loving response that made me feel "normal" for putting so much effort into helping a "mere bug" (by most people's standards). In hindsight, I was most upset because, even though I wanted to help the small winged beauty back into the world (and perhaps, to its family), I could not communicate this intent to the insect. Compassion was the best I could do, and when this didn't work, my father did not ridicule me. Instead, his remark honored my best attempt. I was raised by this man, who always told me, "Don't kill bugs just because you're scared of them. What'd they ever do to you?"

Levi's father probably never said this to his son. Compassion for insects would have clashed with the racist rhetoric that he most likely grew up with. Are racist teenagers born "racist," or is this something they learn from others?

It makes sense that Levi would have viciously made fun of me that day in math class, when I got down on my hands and knees, with a piece of paper, to rescue a hornet. No one helped, but a few of my classmates laughed at me, Levi leading the pack. He kept repeating how stupid it was for me to save a bug. I explained, "It's sick and moving really slowly; that's why I'm trying to help it." He ridiculed me yet more, calling me "weird" for thinking that an insect could be "sick" or in need of help.

Twenty years later, I see more clearly how much of a bully this young man was, how he created a false sense of power through bullying, through public assertions of whiteness and masculinity that were predicated on fear of losing his white, male, heterosexual privilege. Right up to the present day, such privileges are maintained and reinforced by taunting and power plays that deny any possibility that whiteness and masculinity can alternatively be expressed through public displays of compassion, loving kindness, and understanding.

I finally moved the hornet outside, but afterward I quietly wondered whether there was actually something wrong with me for putting so much love and attention into safely transporting a little hornet to the outside world. Maybe there *was* something wrong with me. When Levi made fun of me, others laughed along with him, but no one showed any understanding of my point of view. Perhaps, because he was such a bully, students were afraid to defend me. Or perhaps none of them could truly fathom that a "mere bug" could suffer, be sick, enjoy life, or need help. Maybe their mother or father had never said to them, "Don't kill bugs just because you're scared of them. What'd they ever do to you?"

When we drove by the chicken complex that was located down the street from our home, it was also my father who would nod toward the building and say, "That is a concentration camp for chickens." I really didn't understand this until I learned, as an adult, how chickens are (mis)treated in factory farms. Of course my family was omnivorous (and except for me, still is), but I was lucky to have a father who understood and called attention to cruelty.

When Talmadge was a teenager, he experienced a lot of racist violence from boys like Levi. One evening he came home from his best friend's house, annoyed and disgusted. His best friend's little brother had invited another friend over who let them know how much he enjoyed using a gun to shoot "cans." "Yea, I like shooting 'cans': Mexi-cans, Afri-cans, Puertori-cans." He also used his shooting "skills" to kill nonhuman animals for his personal entertainment. Why did this white male child feel the need to unabashedly spit those words out in the face of a black teenage boy in a town that was over 97 percent white? What fears was he acting out through white masculinity, using deadly weapons and racist banter for bullets? Who handed him these fears, and what were they afraid of? Why hadn't someone asked him, "What'd they ever do to you?"

In 2010, I think this question is still seldom presented to most boys in the United States. For example, a 2007 CNN news report explained how a nine-year-old white male child had killed a "wild" boar, and a five-year-old white male child had shot and killed his first bear while hunting with his grandfather. I don't know whether these young boys were raised to be fearful and hateful of human beings who were not "of their race," but I do know that gunning down a nonhuman animal will not help to develop compassion and love for all human beings.

Here in the United States, why do black performances of masculinity, compared to white middle-class performances of masculinity, elicit different responses from the mainstream media? How is covert "whiteness" in the United States maintained by sensationalizing and reprimanding DMX and Michael Vick for animal torture and cruelty, while ignoring the "animal gaming" pastimes of white privileged males, casting them as nondeviant "normative" behaviors? These questions are rarely asked in the mainstream animal rights movement in the United States.

I am a scholar of critical race theory, examining how nonhuman animals are used as part of the United States' ongoing processes of nation-building, whiteness, racialization, and racism. I am emotionally overwhelmed by the clear messages of mainstream media: white male youths who kill "game" animals are "heroes"; black male youths who kill a puppy or engage in dog-fighting are "evil." As a scholar, I wonder, are speciesism and racism in the United States contingent on each other?

My work requires me to engage in uncomfortable—but necessary—"border crossing" in order to explore how critical race, critical whiteness studies, and postcolonial feminist theory can help us to understand the Western world's unique, ongoing, systemic, racist beliefs and acts, in which whiteness, speciesism, and sexism are the norm. Due to my personal experiences as a child in a town where acts of racism, whiteness, and speciesism were clearly "the norm," I know my purpose as an animal rights activist: to push the envelope, to implore social justice activists to see the interconnections of violence and abuse—human-nonhuman animal relationships help shape our relationships with one another, and they help to shape our consciousness of race and ethnicity (as well as class, national identity, gender, and sexual orientation).

A few years ago, French actress and animal rights activist, Brigitte Bardot, openly expressed distaste for the French Muslim community because of religious practices in which they kill nonhuman animals. I wonder, "Why are white French omnivorous nationals exempt from her disgust? Why is she not concerned about nonhuman animals slaughtered for traditional white French cuisine or Christian religious feasts?" Instead, she used speciesism as a means to racialize an immigrant group as "barbaric," as a threat to the white identity of Christian France.

It is crucial that all of us involved with animal rights and critical animal studies notice these inconsistencies and ask these questions, that we all critique how racism, racialization, ethnocentrism, and whiteness-as-norm affect our consciousness and relationships with nonhuman animals (as well as with human animals). This doesn't mean that DMX and Michael Vick are innocent. What this does mean is that each and every one of us must ask how our concept of interactions between nonhuman animals and human beings are connected with racialization, "whiteness as the norm," and racism.

This type of reflection is often difficult even for the most liberal and "post-racial," white, animal rights activist. I would argue that such scrutiny is even tougher for many animal rights people of color—AR people who must battle both speciesism and continuous acts of covert whiteness and racist attitudes in a U.S. movement with only a handful of people of color.

Growing up in the little American town of Lebanon, it was difficult for me to argue with peers and teachers about the importance of addressing racism and whiteness. Simultaneously, I felt isolated and frustrated by speciesism that was also accepted as the norm, and which surrounded me daily. Neither peers nor teachers understood why I refused to participate in dissection, and why I did not "appreciate" deer hunting (a huge "sport" in my town). After I told my fifth-grade teacher that I didn't want to drop a live worm into alcohol to kill it, and then dissect it, he told me repeatedly that worms do not have central nervous systems; hence, they "do not feel pain." Only through repeated stories, in my household, which exposed how our people were treated, did I become fully aware that pro-slavery whites deeply believed that Africans could not feel pain; that we were believed to be "just like animals" who had no feelings, spirits, souls; we were just machines available to serve the purposes of white America. Perhaps my fifth-grade teacher did not know this.

There are many facets to critical animal studies and animal rights activism. It is important to note that, as an activist, I simply cannot ignore the very clear connections among racism, racialization, and whiteness on the one hand, and people's treatment and attitudes toward nonhuman animals (regardless of whether they are vegan, supporters of "humane" meat and dairy, omnivorous, or "big game" hunters) on the other. For me, navigating a country in which speciesism, sexism, racism, and whiteness are an accepted reality, and to stay silent about these acts of indifference and overt cruelty, would precipitate miserable lives for all beings and would continue to create communication gaps and animosity among racial and ethnic communities with differing perspectives on the treatment of certain humans and nonhuman animals.

So, here I am, asking these questions. If you're sincerely interested in ending racism, you must recognize racism's roots in our relationships with, and constructions of, "the place of the animal." And if you're sincerely interested in ending nonhuman animal exploitation, you must educate yourself on the connections between the social constructions of whiteness, racialization, and racisms (as well as sexisms, nationalisms, etc.), and animal abuse.

It's simple: it's all connected.

Animal rights activists are often frustrated when animal exploiters become defensive or downright hostile if asked simply to reconsider what they've been taught about a "normal" diet, or "normal" reactions to animal suffering. I'm asking you to do the same. And if you are white and/or "postracial," and become defensive or downright hostile when I ask you to reflect on the effects of "whiteness as the norm," racialization, and racism on your perceptions, how can you ask others to reconsider—let alone change? How can any of us be exempt from the same critical reflexivity and emotionally difficult self-analysis that we demand from speciesists?

These questions, and their reflective process, are not easy. They are transformative and often take us to places in our minds, and in our pasts, that we have swept under the rug; for some of us, institutionalized racism, whiteness, and/or speciesism have become so invisible in "everyday life" that it is difficult to comprehend or grasp the implications of this ongoing, pervasive oppression.

For many people of color, being forced to accept whiteness as the local and national norm—enduring racism in our daily lives—has become so commonplace that it is difficult even to comprehend why we should take a deep look at how we have built our racial, ethnic, and/or cultural identities around our perceptions of, and relationships with, nonhuman animals.

The last thing that most folks want to admit is that they cause suffering to humans, nonhuman animals, or both, and have for their entire life. This realization can be traumatizing. But the potential for trauma is even greater if those of us in the animal rights movement don't explore these issues carefully, critically—if we are afraid to challenge other, linked zones of power, privilege, and comfort.

Gandhi said, "Be the change you want to see." Educate yourself about whiteness and "postracial" racism. I highly suggest these books: *Unraveling Whiteness: Tools for the Journey* by Judy Helfand and Laurie Lippin, PhD, and *Beyond Fear: Twelve Spiritual Keys to Racial Healing* by Aeeshah Ababio-Clottey and Kokomon Clottey (I also recommend consulting with their center: Attitudinal Healing Connection of Oakland at www.ahc-oakland.org). The powerful Clottey book explains how everyone has been affected by racism and that we all need to heal in order to build true unity. I also suggest, for those interested in understanding white privilege, Tobin Miller Shearer's book, *Enter the River: Healing Steps from White Privilege toward Racial Reconciliation*. Lastly, I would suggest the book *Sistah Vegan: Black Female Vegans Speak on Food, Identity, Health and Society* (Lantern Books 2010). This volume shows how the praxis of black female vegans has been directly influenced by racialized-gendered experience in the United States. These books demonstrate why *all* people—particularly white-identified people convinced that they are exempt from this type of reflexivity—must be mindful of whiteness, colonialism, racialization, and racism, and understand how these function at the conscious, subconscious, and structural level.

a. breeze harper, raised in a working-class household in Lebanon, Connecticut, holds a BA in feminist geography from Dartmouth, an MA in educational technologies from Harvard (2007), and is currently a PhD candidate at the University of California, Davis, studying the application of critical race theory, critical animal studies, and black feminist theory to geographies of food and health. Harper is the author of a novel, *Scars* (Arch Street Press 2008), and the editor of *Sistah Vegan: Black Female Vegans Speak on Food, Identity, Health and Society* (Lantern Books 2010) (www.breezeharper.com).

5

fighting "other"

miyun park

I nervously shifted my weight, first to one foot, then the other, pretending I didn't hear, but he was persistent.

"I said, 'What are you?' Japanese?"

"No," I whispered, staring down at the crack in the sidewalk.

"Chinese?"

"No."

"Then *what are you?*"

"Korean," I said faintly, my cheeks warming.

"I never heard of 'Kreeyan.' You're nothing!"

I was not yet five years old on that first day of kindergarten, yet I remember those words vividly. It was the first time I was forced to be aware that I was different—that because of the slant of my eyes and the color of my skin, I was "other" and could be dismissed as "nothing."

The desire to differentiate—and alienate and subjugate—"other-ness" is one of the greatest sins of our species, and for me personally, one of the most effective motivations for relentless activism to push for change.

Why does it matter if we're male or female, gay or "straight," religious or agnostic, blue collar or white collar, "yellow" (as my birth certificate lists) or "white" (as yours may read), or any other us-versus-them classification? Aside from the convenience of having neat, decisive demographic categories, these differences don't and shouldn't matter. Nor should it matter if we're winged, finned, feathered, hoofed—or not—when it comes to the infliction of unnecessary pain and suffering.

But we like to assess similarities and differences.

Even so, every once in a while the noise dies down to a single note, and we're reminded that our minds need not be so cluttered. Tuesday night, November 4, 2008, as the election results were tallied across the United States, I heard that one, clear note—at least for a moment. For the first time in U.S. history, Americans elected as president someone the majority sees as "other."

Then the noise began to get louder. U.S. Representative John Lewis struggled to hold back his tears as he reflected on the path toward equality, the path that he and so many of his colleagues started down half a century ago, and I couldn't help but think about the oppression and prejudice my parents had been forced to endure after they emigrated to the United States. Reporters, pundits, and interviewees were quick to note that the U.S. presidential election wasn't about race. But with all the tick boxes for skin color and other "demographics," I couldn't help but see how very confused we still are.

That same Tuesday night, across the country from the White House, there was another first in U.S. history. Californians passed—also by a landslide—Proposition 2. This initiative requires that hens used for egg-laying, sows used for breeding, and calves used for veal be given enough space to stand up, turn around, and extend their limbs. Just as it may bring shock and dismay to know that some Americans did not support Obama solely because of his "other-ness," as revealed in exit polls and interviews, it may also shock and dismay to know that a law was needed to ensure that farmed animals can stand up, turn around, and extend their limbs. I cried tears of joy when Prop 2 passed and I was reminded of the first time I set foot inside an egg factory farm as an investigator, where I saw tens of thousands of individuals caged so intensively that they could not even spread their wings.

But we like to assess similarities and differences.

I didn't know that some people see the world divided by "us" and "them" until that first day of kindergarten. As time passed, I began to understand that the fabric of societies is cluttered with prejudices—racism, sexism, homophobia, xenophobia. These prejudices are designed to prevent "others" from enjoying equal consideration. The older I became, the more I felt stifled—at times even smothered—by the security blanket of rough "sameness" that many cling to for comfort, using their blanket to block out those with whom they do not feel comfortable, those they view as "other."

As a child, I felt I couldn't win. Either I was too Korean or too American—an "egg," yellow on the inside, but white on the outside. Either way, I was "other." I grew increasingly uneasy—not only with what I perceived to be injustice, but also with my identity. Was I a Korean kid who happened to be living in America? An American kid who happened to look like a Korean?

Could I be a hyphenated "Korean-American"? While I struggled to keep my balance, embracing Americanisms yet holding onto Korean customs, I became even more confused. Why did I have to be one thing or another? Why couldn't I just *be*? I didn't understand why some people held me to one set of expectations, while others expected something completely different.

Nor did I understand the stories my parents told me when they tucked me in at night. Why had they suffered as children, growing up in a civil war? Why had my father's mother been imprisoned in South Korea? Why was his father a political prisoner in North Korea? Why were there times of hunger? Why were they ridiculed and demoralized by their new fellow Americans? And, as I began reading and writing my own stories, growing into my own life in the United States, I couldn't figure out why some people didn't have safe, warm places to live. Why did we bombard the land, air, and water with pollutants? Why did people fight and die? I could not understand why horrible things happened, for horrible reasons, every moment, all around the world. I was weary, confused, disappointed, frustrated, and I was only a child.

After satisfying an array of standard, first-generation childhood obligations, such as practicing piano, doing laps with the swim team, and struggling to finish homework for both "regular" and Korean schools, I bickered with my sister, volunteered (both to help "society" and for those upcoming college applications), and listened to more stories—or "life lessons" as my parents liked to call them—about terribly sad yet painfully real examples of why I should be thankful. Not thankful *for* anything in particular, just thankful.

Therein lay the problem. I knew I was fortunate—fortunate to have two sacrificing, loving parents, the opportunity for an excellent education, good friends who didn't see me as "other"—and so much more that so many people didn't have. But, instead of feeling thankful for my good fortune, I was angry that *everyone* didn't have what I had. It didn't seem right. I couldn't accept the mindless injustice of it all.

I spent considerable time on my own, pondering how best to make a difference, how to change this flagrant injustice. I protested at the Pentagon against military invasions and against tactics I felt were unfair and harmful, and I demonstrated in front of the White House against apartheid in South Africa. I wrote letters begging governments to release individuals imprisoned unjustly and volunteered at soup kitchens and health care charities. I donated some of my minimum wage earnings to national environmental and wildlife organizations to save the planet and its many inhabitants, and to local advocacy groups to help the D.C. homeless. I adopted a scattershot approach, trying to make *it* a little less painful, a little more fair, and trying to bring about lasting change, to defeat at least some of the *isms* that I abhorred. Yet all the while, a minimum of three times each day, I unknowingly contributed to the *ism* that causes the greatest amount of suffering to the greatest number of individuals.

One week after my father and I docked the chartered fishing boat on which we had caught three hundred pounds of bluefish—I have no idea how many *individuals* we pulled out of the bay that day, since they were merely calculated by the pound—I received an unsolicited piece of mail, a double-sided, trifold brochure that exposed me as speciesist. For the first time in all of my nineteen years, I was aware of the farmed animals who were raised and killed for me to eat. As I read about industrial farming, I stared through tearing eyes at photos of intensive confinement and slaughter and realized the unquantifiable amounts of suffering and pain inflicted on individuals just for me, just for my appetite.

While busy trying to make *it* better, I unwittingly sustained myself on meat, eggs, and dairy products from farmed animals forced to languish in crates, pens, stalls, and sheds—simply because they were "other." They weren't people, or companion animals, or endangered animals, or exotic animals. If they had been, they might have been worthy of consideration, of protection. Instead, they were "food." Because we viewed them as breakfast, lunch, and dinner, we felt justified in "growing" them as quickly and cheaply as possible to fill grocery stores and pantries.

That little piece of unwanted mail stole my ignorance. I could no longer segregate "food" animals as "other." If I did, I would be guilty of the same prejudices held by those who yelled, "Go back to China, you gook!"

I consumed all that I could find on animal exploitation, and I was consistently horrified by what I learned. Dozens of furry animals skinned to make a single coat. Animals burned, blinded, amputated, and fed carcinogens and toxins in the name of research. Mother elephants killed so that their babies can be stolen, broken, and trained to perform in circuses. Manatees, gentle sea cows, mutilated by boat propellers. And billions of farmed animals raised in intensive confinement and killed for human consumption every year.

That flier changed everything. Previously, I had no idea. Now, I could not continue to be complicit in animal suffering. These nonhuman animals truly were—and are—voiceless in our human communities. I could no longer silently accept this injustice. I wouldn't cooperate anymore.

Farmed animals aren't more or less worthy of concern than any others. Nonetheless, their welfare became my priority because of the sheer numbers of exploited animals who were involved. In order to reduce the greatest amount of suffering for the greatest number of individuals—to most effectively make *it* better—I knew I needed to dedicate my efforts to working toward improving the plight of animals raised for meat, eggs, and milk. Their individuality, their sensitive, sentient natures had been largely forgotten in industrial animal agricultural systems that too often deny them the ability to enjoy natural behaviors.

Ethicist Gaverick Matheny first helped me with this utilitarian calculation, and later, with their 2004 essay, "Foxes in the Hen House—Animals, Agribusiness, and the Law: A Modern American Fable," attorneys David Wolfson and Mariann Sullivan penned precisely what that quantification meant on factory farms:

> It is almost impossible to imagine the number of farmed animals. Approximately 9.5 billion animals die annually in food production in the United States. This compares with some 218 million killed by hunters and trappers and in animal shelters, biomedical research, product testing, dissection, and fur farms, *combined*. Approximately 23 million chickens and some 268,000 pigs are slaughtered every 24 hours in the United States. That's 266 chickens per second, 24 hours a day, 365 days a year. From a statistician's point of view, since farmed animals represent 98 percent of all animals (even including companion animals and animals in zoos and circuses) with whom humans interact in the United States, all animals are farmed animals; the number [who] are not is statistically insignificant.

Since graduating with a philosophy degree in 1993, I've worked for non-profit animal welfare organizations. Once again, fortunate—fortunate to have had the opportunities to "professionally" help nonhuman animals. As most "career" animal advocates discover, however, animal advocacy is not merely a job. Animal advocacy is what we do, what we think about, and what influences most if not all of our decisions. For many of us working on behalf of nonhuman animals, change is a collective dream—unemployment our greatest hope. We imagine the day when there is no more work to be done.

Over the years, I've worn several different hats: administrative assistant, publications coordinator, poster-maker, website and print designer, essayist, investigator, narrator, speaker, envelope-stuffer, campaigner, editor, volunteer, president, letter-writer, rescuer, researcher, vice president, fundraiser, negotiator, and then some. I've been afforded incredible opportunities for helping nonhuman animals—some exhilarating, some intimidating, some frustrating, some fruitless, and some wildly successful.

Although people are overwhelmingly opposed to cruelty to animals, including those raised for food, tens of billions of individuals languish in our industries each year. The situation with nonhuman animals is alarmingly the same around the world. Where is the disconnect?

Most often, people just don't know; I didn't know until I received a flier in the mail.

I try not to get mired in the past, in how we allowed this to happen, how we allowed sentient individuals with lives that are important to them, with behavioral needs and desires, to be treated as widgets in a factory. I try not to spin my wheels wondering how we allowed intensive confinement, industrial factory farming to permeate the landscape and then to be exported to Asia, for example, even as these systems are beginning to be phased out at home. Rather, I try to focus on how we can best reduce the suffering of farmed animals.

There isn't one answer, which is why a multi-stakeholder, multi-pronged approach is critical. No one sector, whether it be animal advocates, scientists, consumers, legislators, corporate decision-makers, farmers, veterinarians, or vegans, can change the system alone. Working together, however, we can—and are—making enormous strides for farmed animals.

There is no us-versus-them when it comes to collaborating to reduce suffering. I've sat across the table from farmers, corporate executives, grassroots activists, scientists, and government policy-makers, and delivered presentations in Croatia, Belgium, India, Egypt, Italy, China, France, and across the United States. With every meeting and every lecture, I have just one goal: to find common ground on which we can stand, together, to improve the lives of farmed animals.

When I think back to the very first time I stepped into an egg factory farm, I can still smell the ammonia in the air, my eyes watering from toxic fumes, and I'm once again in disbelief. It's difficult to comprehend the enormity of suffering within a single cage, in a single row, in a single shed, on a single factory farm. When I multiply that suffering by all of the billions of other intensively confined factory-farmed animals, the sum total is simply incomprehensible. I often remind myself of the larger, broader goal: to reduce the greatest amount of suffering for the greatest number of individuals.

To accomplish this, I sometimes must remember a single individual. I could so easily have overlooked her, the hen later named Jane. She was one of about eight hundred thousand hens in a battery-cage egg factory farm in rural Maryland. As I walked carefully down the aisles of one of the eight sheds in the facility, clad in biosecure gear with video camera in hand, I saw so many individuals in such intensive confinement and distress that I'm ashamed to admit that they became a blur. Warehousing individuals in cages so restrictive they cannot even flap their wings may be economically profitable, but such industrialization makes it impossible to provide care for these nonhuman animals. This may explain why I almost didn't see Jane. Almost.

Jane's left wing was pinned under a broken metal clip in the front of a battery cage, where she was immobilized, unable to reach food or water. Who knows how long she had been pinned there. She was emaciated. Unable to move, crowded in that tiny cage with other hens, she was trampled by her cagemates vying for space. Her nearly featherless body had deep, long scratch marks, and she was so weak she could barely hold up her head. As I removed her from the battery cage, my hands encircled her tiny body, and all I could feel were bones. I took her with me.

Jane had struggled so violently to free herself that her wing was dislocated and dragged listlessly along the floor. She had been trapped, immobilized, for so long that gangrene had set in. I found a veterinarian willing to treat Jane, who amputated her diseased wing. Her prognosis was bleak, and I knew that a genetically manipulated, overproducing, battery-caged and factory farmed hen had many human-caused physical challenges to overcome. And now these were compounded by physical trauma. How could she survive, let alone thrive?

But Jane did both. Within six months, she molted and her body was covered with snow white feathers, so full that you only noticed her missing wing when she dustbathed, or basked in the sun. She hopped onto straw bales to roost at night, foraged in fields, and was able to do all that she could not do inside a battery-cage—in essence, be a hen.

The first time I saw Jane step on grass, it was the most remarkable sight. She had only ever felt wire mesh beneath her feet. In awkward, exaggerated steps, she lifted first one foot, then the other. She stumbled a few times, then realized she could not only walk without pain, but she could take more than one or two steps. I cried those deep, body-wracking sobs that feel like they won't ever end. I was crying tears of joy for Jane, and also tears of despair for the hundreds of millions of hens languishing in battery-cages at that exact same moment across the United States and, indeed, in countries around the world. They would never spread their wings and run through the grass, forage, or nest. Inside a battery-cage, they would never be able to be *hens* and to experience their true, natural selves, to engage in their instinctive behavioral needs.

Jane was able to *be*.

Each individual matters and each individual is worthy of moral consideration. I can't change what my parents experienced in Korea or as immigrants in the United States. I can't change how I have been treated. I can't eliminate the concept of "other." But I can help reduce suffering, in whatever ways I am able, and I can do so standing shoulder to shoulder with caring individuals from so many different sectors, speaking in a unified voice, and for this I am truly thankful.

miyun park is executive director of Global Animal Partnership (www.globalanimalpartnership.org), an international nonprofit organization working to improve the lives of farmed animals. Miyun has spoken on behalf of farmed animals around the world and has published extensively on animal agriculture and welfare, including a chapter in *State of the Animals IV: 2007* and *Gristle: From Factory Farms to Food Safety (Thinking Twice about the Meat We Eat)*. Park serves on the editorial board of the United Nations Food and Agriculture Organization's Gateway to Farm Animal Welfare portal. She previously held the post of vice president, Farm Animal Welfare, for the Humane Society of the United States and its global affiliate, Humane Society International.

6

small small redemption

sangamithra iyer

"Small smalls" is what I called them. Small small pikins to be exact. It's the Pidgin English phrase in Cameroon for "little children." Those days I had three of them: Emma and Niete in each arm and Gwendolyn on my back, all shy of one year.

They had just arrived, as I had, at the Sanaga-Yong Chimpanzee Rescue Center in the Mbargue forest of Cameroon, about two hundred miles east of the capital Yaoundé. It was the spring of 2002, and Emma and I made the journey there together. She, like the other girls, was a product of the illegal bushmeat trade flourishing in West Africa, where chimpanzees and gorillas (among other wild animals) are hunted and sold as a delicacy meat to an urban affluent elite both locally and abroad. Their body parts can be found in markets and on menus—eight dollars for a chimpanzee head, ten dollars for gorilla arms. Too little to be made into lucrative meat, baby chimpanzees like my small smalls are orphaned and sold as pets, or otherwise kept captive.

Emma, found tied up and screaming in Yaoundé, was rescued with the assistance of the Cameroon Ministry of the Environment and Forestry by In Defense of Animals-Africa (IDA-Africa), the nonprofit for which I was volunteering. IDA-Africa ran the rehabilitation sanctuary and was waging a conservation campaign for the country's remaining wild apes. As a civil engineer, my role was to provide input on site drainage and the creation of a rainwater collection system for the sanctuary, but at twenty-four I ended up also being a mother of three.

Through our eleven-hour nighttime car journey to the rescue center, frightened Emma clung to me as we bounced along red iron-rich laterite roads and through uneasy military roadblocks. We were traveling with Dr. Sheri Speede, the American veterinarian who started this sanctuary, and her nine-month-old daughter. Sheri had made this journey many times to transport chimps, and she talked our way through the military checkpoints along the route. But on this trip, the last checkpoint was trouble.

There appeared to be a makeshift station set up by three young men who in retrospect probably had no authority whatsoever. I can't remember if they were armed, but they confiscated our vehicle papers and weren't about to let us pass without something in exchange. First they asked for a ride.

"I'm sorry, we have no room. We are traveling with a baby and have this letter from the Ministry of the Environment to transport a chimpanzee," Dr. Speede conveyed.

"Well, give us your baby, then." Uncomfortable laughter erupted from the men.

"I'm afraid I can't do that." Sheri stood her ground.

"Then we'll take the monkey."

Uncertain if they were serious or joking, Sheri responded. "I can't give you either of the babies, and the only money we have on us is for fuel. All I can offer is a few bucks to buy you some beer."

And with that we continued on our way as I tended to the baby in my arms. Emma was indeed a small small with big big ears—almost the size of her whole head. She had a thin coat of fine black hair and a tuft of coarse white hair surrounding her baby bottom. Rope burns were etched into her legs. I tried to imagine what she had been through in the past few months of her life. She may have witnessed her mother's death, which is often the case. With a strong instinct to protect, her mother likely held Emma tight, shielding her from the gunshots to which she herself fell victim.

The only vehicles we encountered that night were large logging trucks. In the past few decades, European and Asian logging companies have built roads into what were previously untouched and inaccessible forests of Cameroon, opening up the wilderness to poachers. Logging crews hire commercial hunters to provide food for them, often supplying the hunters with guns. Logging trucks can serve as conduits for transporting illegal bushmeat to other markets. Even after they leave, the clear-cut lanes remain, providing poachers easy access to now vulnerable wild ape habitats.

I had read about the links between logging and bushmeat, but it all became real for me that night; I entered the forest with an orphaned chimpanzee on my lap while giant tree trunks exited on truck beds. What if the predictions of primatologists were true? Could Emma's species, sharing six million years of coexistence with mine, be gone within our lifetimes? Staring at these trucks full of timber, I wondered just how much they were taking out of the forests. And how much was left.

Shortly after we arrived at the sanctuary, Emma was introduced to her new roommates, Niete and Gwen. They would be quarantined together for a couple of months before joining the other infants in the nursery. Niete was healing from a machete wound on her head that stood out like a part in her thick black fuzzy hair. Too weak to support herself, she hung from my neck like a Velcro plush doll. Gwen was the feisty one, curious and bold, with dark inquisitive eyes. Her baby teeth had rotted, presumably from subsisting on trash at the beach where she was found. At the sanctuary the small smalls were bottle-fed a formula supplemented with local fruits and rice and beans. Emma picked out the rice, Gwen preferred beans, but Niete didn't care for either. They all welcomed papayas and bananas, but on days when guavas and mangos were available, they opted for those treasured treats instead. Emma and Gwen drank from baby bottles. They'd grab on with both hands, lift the bottle up, and lean their heads back. Niete hadn't mastered this skill yet, so she drank from a bowl, but would watch Emma and Gwen with curiosity. I gave Niete a bottle one day, elevating it slightly and she discovered the magic of the tilt. When the bottle was empty, she refused to let go, lifting it higher and higher, applying her newfound knowledge.

My days at the sanctuary were both varied and routine. Claude, the resident rooster, would wake me up every morning at sunrise, and I'd throw on my chimp clothes (the same clothes I wore on engineering field assignments in California, once stained with grey coastal muds and brown sands, now covered with red earth and papaya).

The Sanaga River would wash these histories away. I had left my large-scale water infrastructure projects in San Francisco to help with small-scale water supply and drainage issues in Cameroon. So I surveyed and mapped out the sanctuary. When it rained, I'd stand out and watch where the water ponded, and where it flowed. I sketched plans for a bigger rainwater catchment system. It was an escape from crunching numbers behind cubicle walls, and inhaling diesel fumes behind drill rigs.

In Cameroon, I learned how wonderful a precious drop of sun-warmed rainwater felt on my skin as I bathed right before equatorial sundown. It was at this time I'd think about my afternoon with the small smalls in the forest. I could still feel where their hands latched onto my body.

In the forest I would watch them play and groom. Gwen liked to be tickled, panting "hee-hee-hee" as she giggled. During this time, they gained strength and learned to climb trees. I didn't have to worry about them running away or climbing out of reach. They never ventured too far from their human caregiver.

Chimps, like humans, have a long maternal investment period, so it's natural for them to be attached. Gwen was perhaps the clingiest: Never wanting to separate at the end of the day, she held on tight, using her hands and her even more "handy" opposable toes. It's the kind of embrace that you feel long after it's done, long after you're gone. But it was her high-pitched scream and rotten-tooth grin that haunted me. I had heard the sound before on television commercials and movies, coming out of a smiling chimp. I quickly learned this sound, and that smirks weren't gestures of joy; it was fear that pierced my ears.

Gwen had lost her mother and was terrified of being abandoned again. In the forest I'd sing to her "You Got Me" (written by the Roots), trying to reassure her: "If you were worried 'bout where I'd been or who I saw or what club I went to with my homeys, Baby, don't worry; you know that you got me . . ."

During my junior year of college, when I was supposed to be paying attention in my environmental engineering class, I read *Next of Kin*. It was the memoir of Roger Fouts, a primatologist who was the lifelong caregiver of a chimpanzee named Washoe. Cross-fostered and raised as a human child by Allen and Trixie Gardner in the 1960s, Washoe became the first chimpanzee to learn American Sign Language; she acquired a vocabulary of over three hundred words. What I found most interesting about her use of sign was that Washoe invented her own words. All languages have mechanisms for generating new words. In ASL, compounding—combining two words to create a new word—is the primary generating mechanism, and this is exactly what Washoe did. DIRTY-GOOD was her phrase for using the potty, because it was both dirty and good. Christmas was SWEET-TREE because the occasion was celebrated by eating the treats that decorated her tree.

After finishing the book, I signed up for an American Sign Language class, in the hopes that one day I would meet this remarkable chimpanzee. Several months later, I started a summer program at the Chimpanzee and Human Communication Institute in Ellensburg, Washington, where Washoe greeted me like she did many new visitors, smacking the thumbs of her two fists together and telling me that she wanted to see my shoes. The young, inquisitive, at times mischievous, girl whose childhood I had read about was now in her thirties and transformed into the matriarch of her adopted chimpanzee group of five. I examined her signing hands and marveled at their similarity to mine.

Part of my assignment was to help with environmental enrichment in the chimpanzee enclosures. We simulated forages, placing treats in challenging locations, which required natural behaviors like climbing and using tools. Having been raised as human children, these chimps also enjoyed flipping through magazines, checking themselves out in mirrors, and brushing their teeth.

Roger Fouts presented the ethical implications of using chimpanzees in research. Washoe and her chimpanzee family sacrificed much for human knowledge. Unable to survive on their own in the wild, they could never go back to Africa, and it was up to us to ensure their psychological well-being.

Next of Kin was Roger Fouts's way of sharing "what chimpanzees have taught me [Fouts] about who we are." For me, it confirmed what I had always suspected about animals—we are all, at our core, sentient beings. Not only do we feel our own pain, but we can feel that of others. Washoe illustrated this for me.

Scientists wanted to see whether Washoe would pass sign language on to her offspring, but she suffered the loss of two stillborns, and a third child died shortly after birth. Later, she befriended a graduate student researcher who was pregnant and would often sign with her about the baby in her belly. The woman, however, had a miscarriage. One day shortly after this, Washoe inquired about the baby and the researcher signed that her baby died. Washoe replied with a finger to the eye—CRY—followed later by PLEASE PERSON HUG.

Tatu, another signing chimpanzee in Washoe's family, would greet me by either asking for cereal or wanting to play Peek-A-Boo. Her fingers were slender and her signing was very polished. Black was her favorite color and she'd flip through books and point out all the things that were black—THAT BLACK. She enjoyed puzzles and foraging, but also suffered from an autistic rocking motion that had emerged decades earlier when she was separated from her mother at an early age to be sent off for research.

She loved dairy but was lactose intolerant. She would sign CHEESE or ICE CREAM and on rare occasions she would receive them, only later to complain pointing to her belly and signing HURT.

It was around this time in my life that I too was resolving a love/hate relationship with dairy. I began devouring books and attending lectures about farmed animals, agriculture, and the environment. I was diagnosed with ulcerative colitis and my body started physically rejecting milk. I could no longer eat ice cream, my comfort food staple, and soon I no longer wanted to.

While I was raised a vegetarian, I never really thought much about milk because I didn't think that drinking milk harmed the cow. I learned, however, that most cows exploited for dairy products in the United States eventually become hamburgers. But what seemed worse to me was that to produce milk, cows undergo a cyclical process of forced impregnation (often with an apparatus called a "rape rack"), and repeated separation from their young. Not only are we taking her child's milk, we are taking her child. The male calves will often be crated and killed for veal. The females, like their mothers, will be turned into dairy machines.

A former dairy farmer told me how cows and their calves, once separated, would bellow, calling to each other throughout the night.

A year after the summer with the signing chimps, I moved west, to Berkeley, and started a graduate program in dirt—geotechnical engineering to be exact. I was interested in soil behavior and how the earth responds to human pressures. It was August 1999, and a major earthquake had just devastated Turkey. My professor described the affected area as "smelling like 40,000 dead people," further noting that "engineers who know that smell do their work a lot differently from those who don't." It was this sense of responsibility that led me to pursue engineering. When I entered the workforce, however, I was looking for something more. I was too comfortable and wanted to experience long days of hard work and the sound sleep that follows. I wanted to wake up excited about the day. I wanted to experience living minimally. I read volunteer diaries from this sanctuary in Cameroon, and I wanted to be in that forest with chimpanzees. I decided to take a leave of absence, and applied to volunteer at the Cameroon sanctuary.

It was my engineering background that caught the sanctuary's interest. They had to travel twenty miles to the nearest tap to fill up on water. They had unsuccessfully drilled two wells. They asked me "Where is the water table?" Thousands of miles away, I couldn't possibly know, but I asked a series of questions. Where is the nearest river? What is the topography? How deep were the wells that were dug? What soils did they find? Did they hit bedrock? What are the seasonal rainfall patterns?

I started interviewing staff and former volunteers about site descriptions. I looked up geology maps of the country in the library. I learned about seasonal climate patterns. I compiled these correspondences, maps, and tidbits in a big white binder.

Despite my graduate degree and general familiarity with modern water supply systems supplying millions of people, I was unsure whether I could survive without the Internet and advanced computational software. I was not schooled in small-scale survival solutions, so I tried to school myself. I brushed up on groundwater hydrology, rainwater collection, and tropical residual soils. I started taking classes in French, another language (like signing) that I learned specifically to be in the company of chimpanzees. I had grand plans of preparing more, but arrived in Cameroon with only my "What to (not) order in a Paris café" French and a big white binder. What if this wasn't enough?

I spent my nights in the veterinary clinic at the sanctuary under the protection of a mosquito-net tent, where I'd shine my flashlight to discover the location of the resident spider, look for the visiting gecko, and then climb into my sleeping bag. It was the beginning of the mild rainy season, and we were starting to experience storms in the middle of the night. The chimps sensed them first, and I'd hear their pant hoots when the rains came.

But it was the fruit bats in the tree, who dropped fruit on the clinic, that disturbed my sleep. When the fruit landed on the ground it had the rustling effect of footsteps approaching. But more often, when it landed on the roof, I was awakened by erratic banging from above, and I'd imagine wild chimps dancing on the corrugated tin roof, and smile.

One night I noticed a cobweb-covered book on the shelf of the clinic, a do-it-yourself medical guide, *Where There Is No Doctor*. Thankfully, there was at least a veterinarian, who also served as the village doctor. One of the first patients our vet, Dr. Sheri Speede (the sanctuary founder), tended in my presence was a boy, about nine years old. He had a huge lesion on his thigh, which she treated for infection. His grandmother had brought him in; both of his parents had died of HIV/AIDS.

The origins of HIV/AIDS have been linked to the slaughter and consumption of wild apes, which allowed the benign simian version of the virus to jump species, mutate, and spread, producing the global pandemic we now have. Like my small smalls, the young boy in the clinic was orphaned by the bushmeat trade.

There were many others living in nearby villages with HIV. We'd see them every week on our fruit runs. We took the pickup truck and drove to all the neighboring villages, buying fruit from subsistence farmers: papayas, bananas, avocados, mangos, guavas. We also served as an unofficial postal service, delivering letters from one village to the next. I looked forward to this task because I got to visit with everyone in town, and spend time with my favorite human small small.

Junior is what they called him. He appeared to be orphaned as well. He had a big big smile and liked to hold hands. He mostly spoke Patua, the local dialect. I'd try my French on him.

"*Comment t'appelles-toi?*" (What is your name?)

"*Oui.*" (Yes.)

"*Quel âge-as tu?*" (How old are you?)

"*Oui.*" (Yes.)

But when I was offering treats, his working French came out.

"Donnez moi." (Give me.)

Junior and his buddy, Foris, often rode in the truck with us. They'd sit on my lap, check themselves out in the mirror, and explore the air vents. One day we were listening to a mix-tape, compiled by one of the other volunteers, and these non–English-speaking small smalls started singing "Free Falling." I wondered if Tom Petty would have ever imagined an Indian American girl with two Cameroonian boys sitting on her lap belting out his lyrics while buying fruit for chimpanzees.

Whenever I had the chance, I'd take a walk and visit some of the adult chimps. Kiki Jackson was rescued from a concrete cell at a hotel in a coastal town in Cameroon. He was found emaciated, sharing a room with the body of his female companion, who had starved to death.

When I visited, we'd play chase, running back and forth from one side of the enclosure to the other. I'd bob my head and pant, revealing only my bottom teeth, a chimpanzee expression for play. When we got tired, I'd sit in front of his enclosure. We were always separated by bars. The adult chimpanzees had a forty-acre fenced, forested area to roam freely and would come back to sleep and eat in a covered shelter. I couldn't play with Kiki and the other adults like I could with the small smalls. I knew the adults were strong and could easily injure me unintentionally. I kept a safe distance and respected their space. But one day Kiki offered me his hand through the bars and I held it in mine. He ran his finger over my arm, starting a groom session. He then presented his arm, and I reciprocated, plucking imaginary bugs from his hairy hands.

During this time, I also chatted with Akono and Kanga, the adult chimpanzee care staff. In my limited French, we discussed the old slave trade and the upcoming World Cup. They asked me about veganism. I tried to explain factory farming in America. We talked about race, and they tried to convince me that I was white.

"*Moi? Blanc?* No!" I told them my family was from India.

"Are there black people in India?"

They were certain I was "*le blanc, un peu.*"

I presented my dark brown hands as evidence to the contrary.

To them, perhaps white was not a skin color, but a position of privilege. And maybe I had that *un peu.*

I never felt privileged growing up as a first-generation American in the suburbs of New York City. My father immigrated to the United States in 1969 with seventy-five cents in his pocket. I was a shy, scrawny girl with a funny name that none of the teachers could pronounce on the first day of school. They'd start to stumble when they approached the eleven-letter name on the roll call. Those who dared to give it a try often ended up adding extra letters or syllables. My cheeks slightly flushed, my stomach slightly knotted, I'd raise my hand. "It's Sang-a-mith-ra," sounding out the syllables like they taught us to do, "But Sangu for short."

Both my parents were social workers. They worked hard so that my brother and I would never experience the hardships they had faced. It wasn't until that spring in Cameroon that I fully realized my privilege. For example,

I had brought presents for the Cameroonian chimps, gifts that I knew the American chimps loved—mirrors and toothbrushes. I was embarrassed once I got there, realizing these items could be better used as basics for people than as toys for chimps.

I had studied hard to earn scholarships that would pay my way through school, and I worked hard to save up for my trip to Cameroon, but I didn't realize what a privilege it is to be able to pursue one's dreams.

I remember my parents worrying that I would fall sick in Africa. I was equipped with vitamins, emergency drugs, and insurance that would evacuate me if anything serious happened. But some of the Cameroon people around me were dying, and all they had was a veterinarian. A motorcycle pulled up to the chimp sanctuary one morning and Samuel (I had seen him earlier bottle-feeding chimps in the nursery) let out a loud wail: "*Mon enfant!*" His son, less than a year old, had just died.

CRY. PLEASE PERSON HUG.

"*Mes condoléances*" in my embarrassingly basic French was all I could offer.

Why was I the lucky one? Why should I be rescued?

Disparity was most apparent when visiting the other temporary forest dwellers—Big Big Oil. Several kilometers away, the Chad-Cameroon pipeline was gentrifying the forest. This pipeline, supported by the World Bank and executed by Exxon-Mobil and its subsidiaries, channeled oil from wells in Chad through Cameroon to the Atlantic Ocean to be shipped to refineries and sold elsewhere. They promised it would be a "barrel of hope" for the people of Chad and Cameroon.

On my flight to Cameroon from Paris, I met an engineer working on the pipeline who previously worked on similar oil projects in Burma. I came to know others from the pipeline who visited the sanctuary, and we talked about water and drainage issues. On one occasion, I saw their camp: A small swath of forest was cleared to set up their temporary homes, and in front of each of their trailers was a square patch of grass. Well-secured, stocked with imported food and Western amenities, Big Big Oil was isolated from the surrounding poverty.

Pell, a consultant for the pipeline, stopped by the sanctuary to pick me up one afternoon. "I want to show you my right-of-way," he said, thinking I might enjoy seeing the pipeline. It was a strange invitation, but I grabbed my camera, jumped into his jeep, and we hit the road. Pell was also a geotechnical engineer from UC Berkeley, though maybe twenty years older than I. A classmate of his had written a paper on San Francisco Bay Mud that I was familiar with, and so we talked about dirt.

He showed me his right-of-way, the clear-cut of trees under which the oil conduit was buried. Vegetation was being planted to restore some of the disturbances, and erosion blankets covered the slopes to protect newly seeded areas from washing away. I took in the massive scale of this endeavor.

In our ride back to the sanctuary, Pell was beaming with pride and asked, "Isn't this great, Sangu, to be driving into the sunset in the jungles of West Africa, helping to bring environmental standards to a country that doesn't have any?"

I forced a weak smile but could not muster an adequate response. Did he really believe this?

Despite these environmental measures, the project was disrupting wild forest habitats and impacting the small smalls within. The break in canopy would divide monkey families, who wouldn't cross the pipeline because they would have to cross on the ground. They needed to swing across. Despite its big big promises, Big Big Oil would not be the answer to poverty and health-care in Chad and Cameroon. The wealth, like the oil, would be flowing out of Africa. Did he not see this?

Both Pell and I pursued the same field and ended up in Cameroon, but we were on different sides. These were the things my big white binder had not prepared me for. I didn't have answers. Instead, my binder served as a reminder of what I knew, when I discovered how much I didn't. I did know this: In this world of increasing disparity, I wanted to stand with the small smalls, not the Big Bigs. I stared out the window of his jeep, eager to return to my girls: *"If you were worried 'bout where I'd been . . . Baby, don't worry; you know that you got me."*

sangamithra iyer is a plant-eating primate who is humbled to have been in the presence of great apes. She is a licensed professional civil engineer who served as the assistant editor of *Satya Magazine,* a publication dedicated to animal advocacy, environmentalism, and social justice (www.satyamag.com). She has volunteered at primate rescue and rehabilitation sanctuaries in the United States and in Africa. Iyer is an associate of the public policy action tank Brighter Green where she has been researching the globalization of factory farming. She is working on her first book, blending memoir, family history, and reportage, exploring engineering, activism, and the search for ahimsa in the modern world.

7

compassion without borders
hope ferdowsian

During the summer of 2009, I met a solemn, beautiful, middle-aged mother with deep brown eyes in Washington State. When she was only an infant, she was taken from her own mother in Africa and forced into a life of confinement and repeated harm. As she became older, she was repeatedly impregnated, and after she gave birth to each of her babies, they were taken from her. They were similarly forced into lives of confinement. This understandably somber individual was also kept in solitary confinement in a cement basement for years.

This mother's name is Negra. She is a chimpanzee. Negra was born one year before me, to a species with far less freedom. When she was a child, she was forced into a life of exhibition and experimentation. In addition to breeding, Negra was used repeatedly in hepatitis vaccine experiments. She was held in isolation for at least a couple of years merely due to a clerical error. It is hard for me to believe that she was any less traumatized by these experiences than I would have been.

Thankfully, today Negra lives at a sanctuary in Washington State. In 2009, I had the privilege of meeting Negra and the other chimpanzees with whom she lives, as well as the steadfast humans who try to bring joy and love to the chimpanzees living at the sanctuary. When I heard that Negra loves to watch people dance, I danced for her. I figure that turnabout is fair play, and it was only right that I be on exhibition for her. After seeing the look on Negra's face, I would have danced for her forever. It was another chimpanzee who asked for an encore—admittedly, one of my prouder moments.

Negra is currently one of the many chimpanzees who are part of a purely observational study that I am conducting with my primatologist colleague, Dr. Debra Durham (as well as with the participation and support of many people who work in sanctuaries and conservation around the world). I am a physician specializing in internal medicine, preventive medicine, and public health. But, I've taken a bit of a different path within the field of medicine: I provide patient care for humans, and I also work for human rights and the protection of nonhuman animals.

In the field of human rights, I evaluate and treat human torture survivors. My introduction to the world of torture and human rights came when I was nine years old, when I read *A Cry from the Heart: The Bahá'ís of Iran*, by William Sears. The most vivid story I can recall was about a young boy who was burned to death with his father after he failed to renounce his religion. At the time, I could not understand the complex factors that led to his death, although I understood that these acts were intrinsically wrong. After a few years passed, I learned more about the sociopolitical milieu when my dad's family migrated to the United States to escape the religious intolerance described in Mr. Sears's book.

By the time I reached college, I was very interested in international affairs. I studied the historical events that led to the 1994 genocide in Rwanda, the large-scale genocide in Serbia, and other comparable crises. After college, I continued my studies through books such as Samantha Power's *A Problem from Hell: America and the Age of Genocide.* During my preventive medicine residency in New York, I began volunteering for Doctors of the World (now HealthRight International), evaluating survivors of torture who were seeking asylum. I have since volunteered with Physicians for Human Rights, and my colleagues and I have established a clinic for torture survivors in affiliation with the George Washington University in Washington, D.C. We've also trained others who are interested in providing similar services for traumatized patients.

Although each story is unique, I discovered a thread of commonality among individuals who have suffered significant trauma. I noticed that psychological trauma inevitably trumps physical pain. Fear, vulnerability, and humiliation are, unfortunately, universal themes for trauma victims. Frequently, survivors struggle with chronic psychiatric disorders, especially mood disorders such as depression and anxiety disorders such as posttraumatic stress disorder (PTSD).

In 2007, during a training for health care providers, I began to wonder about some of the psychological effects described by patients who were survivors and whether these symptoms might be found in individuals of other species. I later learned that scientists such as Martin Brune and Gay Bradshaw had already demonstrated that chimpanzees can suffer from psychiatric disorders such as PTSD. My colleagues and I have set out to determine the prevalence of psychiatric disorders in chimpanzees who have been exposed to different forms of trauma. We trust that our findings will aid efforts to protect chimpanzees. Negra is one of the chimpanzees that we are studying.

Early surveys completed by Negra's caregivers revealed a range of psychological symptoms consistent with depression. Surveys demonstrated that she showed limited interest in fellow chimpanzees. Caregivers reported that she often assumed a depressed, hunched posture, sometimes even covering her head with a blanket. Compared with other chimpanzees, she was socially withdrawn, often retreating to places where she could be alone. Like humans who become depressed, Negra slept more than was considered normal. As we might expect, throughout her time at the sanctuary, and with more distance from the laboratory, Negra exhibited fewer of these symptoms. Change is possible. She has become more social, both with caregivers and with other chimpanzees.

From an evolutionary and physiological perspective, it makes sense that other animals experience many of the emotions that we erroneously assumed to be unique to humans. Emotions such as fear, aggression, empathy, and love enhance survival. Why wouldn't other animals share these essential responses to the world around us?

The hippocampus (a very tiny structure in the brain that is found in all vertebrates) aids memory storage and retrieval, and may explain some of the similarities in psychopathology across species. In humans, PTSD is associated with degeneration of the hippocampus (perhaps because of recurrent and chronically elevated levels of the stress hormone, cortisol, followed by down-regulation of the hypothalamic-pituitary axis, which normally controls our response to stress). These findings are not unique to humans, or even to primates—abnormalities of the hypothalamic-pituitary axis have been implicated in animals who have been branded, confined, force-fed, restrained, sheared, isolated, and forced to undergo surgical procedures. It appears that other individuals are vulnerable to many of the same traumas that affect human beings, whether deprivation of water, food, or sunlight; invasive procedures; social isolation or neglect; witnessing harm to others; humiliation; or even something as simple as being deprived of the ability to fulfill natural behaviors.

It is for this reason that I think we cannot only be concerned about humans, or even primates. We, as humans, are not alone in our capacity for emotions such as horror, helplessness, shame, and empathy. Elephants and chimpanzees both experience PTSD, and other forms of psychopathology, as a result of trauma. Learned helplessness has been described both in victims of domestic violence and in rats and dogs exposed to inescapable shocks. Mice in a laboratory become distressed just from being handled. Pigs kept in isolation express depressive symptoms such as withdrawing and refusing to move or eat. Isolated chicks become anxious and depressed, symptoms which have been partially treated with anxiolytics and antidepressants. Nonhuman primates, dogs, mice, chickens, and sheep demonstrate empathy: In one experiment, macaques were fed if they were willing to pull a chain and electrically shock an unrelated macaque whom they could only see through a one-way mirror—almost all of the macaques opted to go hungry rather than shock their fellow macaques.

Most of us have intuitions about suffering in other creatures—simply put, this is empathy. Unfortunately, we often become desensitized and set our empathy and critical minds aside. However, when we start thinking again, and reawaken our sensitivities, it is clear that we aren't alone in our capacity to experience physical and psychological pain and suffering. It is worth noting that experimental research exploring sentience in other creatures, and emotional states such as PTSD and depression, have been seriously flawed from the outset.

Through my mom and dad, I learned of the dire situations in which many humans languish. But even before my parents taught me about infringements of human rights, and human poverty—the suffering of humanity—I was sensitive to the suffering of nonhuman animals.

I grew up in rural Oklahoma with a brother and a sister. We lived with sheep and other animals on our small acreage. I had a friend, Christal, who was a lamb, and my brother befriended a lamb we named Mark. Christal and Mark were as loyal and companionable as our dogs and cats. I never ate lamb. But I did not make the connection with other animals and meat until I was fourteen, at which time I began to choose a vegetarian diet. When I was nineteen, I learned about the suffering that is inherent in the production of eggs and milk products, and I chose a vegan diet.

These empathic tendencies have not changed. They are part of who I am—as they are part of all of us, including my father and my brother. A couple of years ago, my brother found a dog wandering the streets of Oklahoma; my husband and I took him in and named him Charlie. I don't know what Charlie's life entailed before he became part of our family, but it couldn't have been good. One evening when my dad was visiting, he noted how timid and careful Charlie was with people. He presumed that Charlie must have had a hard life before he met us. He asked me if I knew who Charlie reminded him of. I said, "No." My dad began to quietly weep, remembering the hardships his mother faced before her early death. No one felt the need to explain the common vulnerability between my grandmother and Charlie, not in common terms, and not in academic or scientific terms. We all easily recognized the similarities.

When we reflect on Negra, Charlie, the lambs, and billions of other exploited nonhuman animals from a perspective of compassion and empathy, it is difficult to justify their use for science, food, clothing, or other means. They are vulnerable beings who at least deserve our respect and compassion. But I believe we can—and therefore should—do more.

We can start by exercising kindness every day toward all creatures—human and nonhuman—who are in more vulnerable situations than ourselves. This can be as simple as speaking out against injustices, stopping by the side of the road to rescue a nonhuman animal who is in trouble, or donating money to reputable animal sanctuaries such as Farm Sanctuary (Watkins Glen, New York) or Chimpanzee Sanctuary Northwest (Cle Elum, Washington). We can also leave the meat, milk, and eggs of other animals off our grocery lists, and off of our plates, while also keeping their leathered skin and fur off of seats in our cars and on our couches, and off of our own skin. It is now easy to recognize which cosmetics products have not been tested on nonhuman animals (hint: look for the "leaping bunny"). There are hundreds of charities that fund medical services and research and do not test on nonhuman animals. To make a donation, choose any charities at www.HumaneSeal.org, and you will thereby support responsible medical research and avoid contributing to the suffering of individuals like Negra. Change is possible. It starts with understanding, and it starts with each of us.

hope ferdowsian, MD, MPH, is director of research policy for the Physicians Committee for Responsible Medicine (PCRM, www.pcrm.org). She is board certified in general internal medicine and general preventive medicine and public health, and has served medically in sub-Saharan Africa and the Federated States of Micronesia. She is a volunteer physician for Physicians for Human Rights and HealthRight International. Domestically, she is a staff physician at Unity Health Care in Washington, D.C., and an assistant clinical professor in the Department of Medicine at the George Washington University. She lives with her dogs Champ, Charlie, and Lucy, and her husband Nik.

8

theology and animals
elizabeth jane farians

I magine what would happen if the world's religions began to condemn the morality of our beyond-words-horrendous cruelty to nonhuman animals. Imagine what it might be like if theologians wrote about or discussed our unspeakable cruelty to other animals. Both the human and nonhuman animal would benefit greatly. The cruelty would begin to diminish; we would begin to live in a world of peace and harmony. Oh, how sweet it would be!

Most animal rights groups think that religion is irrelevant to their work because truly, it has been. With chicken dinners and Friday night fish fries at church functions, with rat roulette and turtle racing at church summer festivals, most churches have provided nothing but a scandalous example of how to treat nonhuman animals. And nothing comes from the pulpit about morality and our treatment of other creatures, and nothing but contradiction is found in church statements about our treatment of these other beings.

The updated Catholic Catechism, an authoritative statement of doctrine issued by John Paul II in 1994, declares that nonhuman animals must be treated with kindness and respect and then goes on to say that other animals may be eaten by humans. The trouble is, and deep down we all know it: "There ain't no nice way to kill."

Although all major religions claim compassion as a core virtue, nothing on morality and nonhuman animals comes from the pulpit. There has been a growing body of religious literature on animal issues, beginning with Andrew Linzey's work in 1976, but this has had little effect on the actions of religious leaders. For example, it seems incongruous to me to picture the Christ, the

Agnus Dei, the Lamb of God of Christian worship, chewing on a leg of lamb. If there is a god, and god creates sentient beings, then this creator must be a god of love, of kindness, and of compassion for sentient creation. But the fact that this must apply to all of creation, including nonhumans, seems to have eluded most religious people.

Theology itself, as well as the religions it explains, suffers from being anthropocentric instead of God-centered. If our religions were God-centered, humanism would be critiqued: We would begin to realize that human beings are not the center of the universe, nor are human beings the measure of creation.

The topic of ethics and nonhuman animals has eluded most theologians. There is very little religious writing on this subject, and this critical moral issue is not being taught in theology classes. Since over 75 percent of Americans profess Christianity, ethics classes, or even humane education classes in education departments—while very, very helpful—will not solve the problem of violence and cruelty to nonhuman animals. If you ask most Americans why they think it is morally acceptable to eat meat, they will reply, "God gave humans dominion over animals and creation, and God made animals for humans to eat and use." Most people do not know that the creation story in Genesis says that God gave all animals—including humans—the very same breath of life, *nephesh chayah*. They do not think about the fact that nonhuman animals are sentient, like themselves, and that other animals therefore ought to be treated with compassion. Dominion does not mean domination. Rather, in the context of the bible, many scholars say that dominion refers to a loving care, similar to how God exercises dominion over humans.

In truth, religion has not been irrelevant regarding our treatment of non-human animals—religion has been a leading factor in perpetuating cruelty. By ignoring cruelty to other animals, and in some cases condoning such cruelty, religion has exacerbated the problem.

Our cruelty to nonhuman animals is mind-boggling, and it must stop. Our power over other beings is absolute. They live at the mercy of humankind—but we have no mercy. Every year, in the United States alone, more than twenty million animals such as rabbits, cats, dogs, rats, mice, monkeys, great apes, and guinea pigs are killed in biomedical and product testing laboratories; one hundred thirty-five million wild animals such as ducks, squirrels, rabbits, doves, and deer are killed for the amusement of hunters; ten million dogs and cats are killed because they have no homes; and ten billion farmed animals are killed after short, miserable lives spent in prisonlike conditions simply because we like the taste of their flesh. These figures are quoted by Norm Phelps in his book, *The Dominion of Love*.

The issue of nonhuman animals and morality must be dealt with in a religious context. The issue of ethics and nonhuman animals must be discussed at the college level, in classrooms, where this information can influence future clergy and other career leaders. I regret that I have not gotten to this matter sooner; but now the time may be ripe. I came to the idea that I might somehow be able to help other creatures, to bring the subject of animal ethics to the academic world of theologians. This has become my vision and my mission.

It all started when I made an appointment to meet with the chair of the theology department of Xavier University in Cincinnati. When I approached the chair's office I did not know what to expect. My idea was to tell him that the theology offerings at the university were inadequate because there was no consideration of nonhuman animals in the curriculum, and to propose a course on animal theology. Usually new courses or curriculum changes in academe are made only by faculty members. It is unheard of for an outsider to have any influence. But there I was, an unknown woman, uninvited, taking up valuable time, criticizing the theology curriculum because there was no course on nonhuman animals! I could imagine the chair's response: "Animals! Oh, please!"

The theology chair was on the phone when I arrived, so I had to stand awkwardly in the hallway. I felt like a naughty schoolchild outside the principal's office. I waited for quite some time. Obviously, I was not a high priority, just a nuisance. But I was an eighty-year-old woman, a pioneer woman theologian of almost fifty years. I had to remind myself that I was on a new and unique mission—who I was or how I was treated did not matter—I was here to bring change for nonhuman animals.

While waiting, I remembered how lucky I am to be a theologian, and how important my scholarly knowledge is for my cause of helping other living beings. When I earned my degree in theology, women were not allowed to "touch the sacred," so to speak. Female theologians? Unheard of! There was no place for women in the hierarchal dualism of the patriarchal world; women were classified with nonhuman animals and were considered inferior to men in almost every way. As a result, it was permissible to discriminate against them and to oppress them, even cruelly and violently. It was only through the special intervention of an unusual woman, the president of a prestigious woman's college, Saint Mary's–Notre Dame (Indiana), and a world-known educator, Sister Madeleva Wolff, CSC, that a graduate school of sacred theology for women was set up and accredited. That was a tremendous breakthrough for women. This new school meant that women no longer had to listen to men telling them that they were inferior mentally and spiritually, or that women's supposed inferiority was by divine design. Women could speak with authority in religious circles, and even talk back, for the first time!

I realized that, as a theologian, I could argue the theological case for re-thinking our treatment of other creatures. This could help nonhumans (just like it had helped women). When a theology of justice and compassion is lacking, theologians cannot influence practices, or provide necessary guidance to integrate religious life into daily life. Thus the treatment of nonhuman animals did not improve. Actually, it was getting worse with the institutionalization of factory farming and other modern technologies, and with an ever-increasing human population bringing greater demand for animal products.

My reflections were interrupted as the office door opened and the theology chair welcomed me. He was gracious but hurried. The phone call had taken longer than expected, and now *he* was behind schedule. *I* had to talk fast. Luckily I had done my homework; I had researched the introductory theology textbook often used at Xavier, *Faith, Religion and Theology*—of which he was one of the authors. The word "animal" was not in the index, but I was delightfully surprised to find how progressive the theology in this text was. On careful reading, I found nonhuman animals mentioned several times. The last few pages were gems, providing an ecological theological approach that included concern for nonhumans for their own sakes, and not just for human use. Although his text did not go far enough, it was more progressive than most other texts, and the basic principles were there. He had not seen the need to develop these ideas into a new branch of theology, but his theology envisioned nonhuman animals as subjects, not just objects for human use.

I proposed a course designed to show that cruelty to other individuals is morally wrong because it treats nonhuman animals as objects, and that treating these other beings as objects for human use is not acceptable. Perhaps because I rooted my arguments in this textbook, quoting his own words back to him, I was granted the opportunity to request the inclusion of a course on animal theology, which I would design and teach. His schedule was on his mind, and soon he was almost pushing me out the door—but with a promise that we could talk again.

Our talks continued for over a year. Each time it was the same old story: standing in the hallway, waiting like a school child outside his door while he was on the phone. It was very stressful. I was always afraid that I might say something that would give him an excuse to cancel the whole project. I was getting more impatient by the minute (many minutes), always reminding myself to keep cool, that I was making progress, and that I was doing this for the nonhuman animals. Standing in that hallway I became more and more sure of the importance of developing animal theology at the college level, so that future theologians would be educated, so that every student would gain an understanding of God, compassion, and nonhuman animals.

Although the theology chair saw my point, he was hesitant to act. No doubt he thought the rest of the theology department would not take the idea seriously. But finally he authorized a course on an experimental, one-time-only basis with me as the adjunct professor. I developed a syllabus and again waited, this time for him to schedule the course. Finally after several semesters went by, he slipped "Theology and Animals" into a summer, nighttime schedule, where it would be least noticed. However, this also meant that students who needed a final theology course to graduate had to choose this course, whether or not they were interested.

I decided to focus on violence, how violence to nonhuman animals redounds to us in spiritual, psychological, and physical ways. I wanted to emphasize how violence in our relationships with nonhuman animals prevents us from finding peace. I wrote a short poem to express this idea:

Just as there can be no peace without justice
So there can be no peace
Without compassion for every living thing,
Because the human heart can abide
neither injustice nor cruelty.

Though the class went fairly well, the chair did not reschedule my course. I waited and waited as fall and spring semesters went rolling by. In desperation, I scheduled the course as a summer workshop. The evaluations were excellent. This gave new impetus to my proposal and convinced the chair that I was not going to go away. So he scheduled the course again—at the time of my choosing. Again, "Theology and Animals" received outstanding student evaluations, and the chair agreed to send my course to the theology faculty for approval. After the conventional delays, with the help of a sympathetic faculty member, the course was approved, and moved on to the next academic hurdle: the Arts and Science faculty. Again, with help from sympathetic theology faculty, the course was approved and now has a permanent status in the curriculum. Victory at last! Yet this victory is only the beginning.

Animal theology is on the cutting edge of Christian scholarship, and this course owes a debt of gratitude to the chair of theology at Xavier University. Although it took time and work to get the course under way, he did not dismiss the topic, as many in his position might have done. He allowed the course to happen.

"Theology and Animals" is gaining a reputation at Xavier by word of mouth. It is a difficult course to teach because the subject matter does not merely ask that students learn facts, but rather that they rethink attitudes and possibly accept a lifestyle change. No matter how many animal issues the course covers, we always wind up spending a lot of time on diet. Some students resign from the course when they realize that the ideas in the course challenge their dietary habits. Others say the course has changed their lives. As a result of "Theology and Animals," some students have become vegetarians, several have become vegans. Students who have completed this course find ways to help nonhuman animals in their chosen professions. This was my goal. In 2006, a student added the following to the back of the class evaluation form:

HOW I HAVE BEEN IMPACTED BY "THEOLOGY AND ANIMALS"

I strongly feel that this class had the most influence on me as a person over all the classes I have taken in four years at Xavier. I have significantly altered my eating habits and I am more socially aware of the mistreatment of animals. I believe that the influence of this class will stay with me for a very long time. I will be graduating this May and plan on attending graduate school for Health Services Administration in the fall. My ultimate career goal is to run a hospital. If I am determined and fortunate enough to have this happen I would really like to incorporate a much more wholesome food menu into the hospital. . . . Therefore, this class has not only affected me at this time but in the future it will affect and benefit many others. Thank you Dr. Farians for the great change you have been in my life.

Now the challenge is to find theologians to teach this course in the future, and to bring courses like "Theology and Animals" to other colleges. There is broad interest in the subject of theology and nonhuman animals. When announcements for the course are posted in Internet newsletters, I receive inquiries from everywhere—even other countries—from people wanting to take such a course. Perhaps some day this course will be Internet-available.

My work is not over. As in the larger population, theologians are seldom vegetarians. Toward this end, I am now working with the Catholic Theological Society of America, a very prestigious professional society for Catholic theologians. So far I have been able to organize an "Interest Group" on "God, Animals and Humankind." This takes every bit of my eighty-five-year-old, failing energy, as well as all of my time and finances (which I do not have to spend). Much work remains to be done. I hope others will take up the torch, and will help to bring our treatment of nonhuman animals into the classroom, and into theology.

For those who might be interested in taking up such a challenge, below is the beginning of the syllabus for "Theology and Animals."

"theology and animals" (theo 387)

"Theology and Animals" explores the relationship between people and animals with a focus on the violence we inflict on animals and resulting violence in human societies. It reveals how this violence prevents peace, both social peace and personal peace. "Theology and Animals" examines the moral and ethical implications of the way in which animals are treated in our society, including commercial, agricultural, pharmacological, and entertainment industries, and the ways in which this treatment of animals is accepted, promoted, and/ or justified, and how this violence redounds to us in spiritual, psychological, and physical ways. Diet is critical to this analysis, because killing and eating animals is often our most intimate involvement with other creatures. "Theology and Animals" also considers the effects of patriarchy on our treatment of animals, and how women and children may also be adversely affected. This study is made in the context of the Judeo-Christian scriptures and tradition.

"Theology and Animals" discusses alternatives to our current violence, providing solutions such as humane education, highlighting insights for those working in professions such as education, social work, ministry, criminal justice, nursing, science, and law. Students will investigate related scientific findings from disciplines such as psychology and sociology, and materials will overlap with peace studies, women's studies (diversity studies), and criminal justice studies. "Theology and Animals" is also pertinent to parenting and daily life, providing a religious basis for an alternate and compassionate lifestyle, including a dominion of care, rather than domination, of all of creation.

"Theology and Animals" digs deep into the heart of theology. The topics covered in this course are not peripheral, but are central to Christians, and to humankind. This course includes topics such as creation, redemption, the soul, evil, justice, and the nature and divinity of Christ. Although many of these issues are raised in other areas of theology, some of the problems seem to stand out in a unique way when examined in light of animals.

MAJOR TOPICS TO BE CONSIDERED

1. Who are the animals?
2. Are animals relevant to Christian ethics?
3. How do we treat animals in our society?
4. Is our treatment of animals consistent with Judeo-Christian scriptures and tradition?
5. Does the patriarchal nature of Christianity contribute to violence against animals, women, and children?
6. How does the violence we do to animals affect our spiritual, psychological, and physical health?

7. How does a diet including animal products contribute to social and environmental problems?
8. How might humane education (for all ages) help provide a partial solution to the problem of violence?
9. How is violence to animals connected with other disciplines and professions such as Criminal Justice; Social Work; Religious Education; various Health Sciences & Professions, i.e., Nursing, Pre-Med., Nutrition; English; Psychology; History; Sociology; Physical Science; Peace Studies; Business; Philosophy; Economics; Communications; Gender & Diversity Studies; Music; Art; Political Science; Education; Business Administration?
10. What is the peace connection?

Theology and Animals is rooted in class discussion. Material by noted scholars will be provided to introduce topics. Your success will depend on your understanding of the issues presented, not on whether you agree or disagree with class subjects and materials.

elizabeth jane farians, PhD, is a pioneer female theologian, veteran feminist, and animal activist (www.ape-connections.org, Animals, People and the Earth). A long-term vegan, she has written "Dance Lightly With the Living Earth," as well as other articles on nonhuman animal issues. Elizabeth has also designed and is teaching a breakthrough college-level course, Theology and Animals. She is currently working diligently to establish a National Organization for Women Task Force on Animals and an Interest Group on Animals in the Catholic Theological Society of America. Elizabeth notes, "I identify with animals; animals are my passion."

9

freeing feathered spirits
linda fisher

ever since I was a young child, I have had an affinity for painting, drawing, and nonhuman animals. Now, as a professional artist and animal activist, nonhuman animals are still the primary subjects of my paintings. But there is more to my work than love for all animals: Amid my large colorful paintings and hundreds of nonhuman animal photographs, hangs a small black-and-white photograph—carefully placed in a shrinelike niche. This picture of Chief Seattle is the focus of my studio.

an unknown feathered spirit

My ambition to be an artist started early in life. As a child, I would save my allowance and then visit the local department store to buy colored pencils, tablets of paper for drawing, and embroidery thread, just because I loved the colors. The department store sold everything from hammers and nails, to dishtowels and teapots, to live turtles and budgerigars (which we traditionally call parakeets).

I would pause to watch the turtles bob their heads up and down in the water, and sunbathe under their heat lamp, but I especially enjoyed watching and listening to the birds playing and chirping. One day I noticed that a budgie was lying on the bottom of his cage, with labored breathing and eyes half closed. The store was full of mulling customers, but no one seemed to notice the little budgie suffering in their midst.

As a painfully shy child, I was reluctant to say anything. I never liked bringing attention to myself, or asking for help. To me, it was equivalent to raising my hand in the classroom—something I never did. But after long and careful deliberation, I decided to let the store clerk know that the bird was sick. For the sake of this bird, I mustered up my courage. Quivering, I told the sales clerk that one of the birds was sick and needed help. My quiet, small voice, most likely a mere whisper, didn't solicit a response, or even acknowledgment. I tried again, with a stronger voice: "Can someone help the little bird over there. I think he is sick." Still no response. I felt anxious, despairing—I was afraid that the little bird was going to die. I started to cry, but asked again with tearful conviction: "Please help the little bird before he dies!" Again, no response. But this time two security guards approached, took my arms, and escorted me out of the store with a summary command: "Stay out!" I was mortified. I thought I'd broken the law, that I had committed some terrible crime. I ran home sobbing, too fearful to ever return to that store.

ojibway, cherokee

Being part Ojibway and Cherokee, I attend powwows and other Native American functions and proudly wear my inherited Ojibway beaded jewelry. But as I become lost in the hypnotic and joyful sounds of drumming, I cannot ignore the uneasy feeling that consumes me as I glance around: Hundreds of leather goods, feathers, and trinkets made of nonhuman animals' bodies—bear claws, cougar teeth, turtle shells, and whalebones—surround me, all in the name of the proud Indian and commercial trade. I feel torn and saddened by what I see.

In modern Western culture, most of us, including the American Indian, no longer need to hunt to survive. However, we almost always associate the Indian—even today's Indian—with wearing and using nonhuman animals' hides, furs, and feathers. I assure you, even though I avoid hides and furs and choose a vegan diet, my Indianness is critical to who I am. The same is true of my mother, who is both an elder of our Ojibway tribe and a vegetarian. It is not our dark hair, dark eyes, or Indian facial features that speak for who we are, but something much deeper, something not visually apparent: our commitment to the teachings of our ancient Ojibway ancestors.

When I am uneasy, surrounded by furs and hides amid my own people, I reflect on the words of Chief Seattle. His wisdom inspires me, and makes me proud of my Indian heritage. Chief Seattle was alive in the 1700s and was considered one of the greatest Indian orators. A man of great wisdom, he was honored and respected not only by his own people, but also by many non-Indian people. Mostly, he spoke about our ways, traditions, and spirituality; he offered a simple plea to respect Mother Earth and Her living beings.

The Indians of yesterday were true conservationists. They understood the inherent dangers of overtaxing the earth and her creatures. So much so, in fact, that no species would ever be hunted to scarcity or depletion, not even for religious purposes. There was a time when Native Americans were considered heathens because they regarded the land as Mother. They believed that not only nonhuman animals but also rocks and trees had spirit. Indians noted the Earth's messages when they made decisions. They took their direction from nature. They killed only to stay alive.

As early as the 1700s, historical records indicate that the white man's pollution and dirty ways offended Indian people. But as centuries passed and Americans became more aware of their pollution, the Indian concept of conservation and protecting the environment gained legitimacy even among non-Indian people. Native American philosophy, once considered heathen and barbaric, is now an accepted way of thinking; in fact, it is now the politically correct way of thinking.

Yet, when I hear that some of today's Indians are slaughtering whales in the name of tradition, killing eagles for the sake of ceremony, or destroying any nonhuman animal for the sake of vanity and "tradition," I wonder what has happened, what has changed. In a world where most people have traded in guns for cameras, has Indian philosophy become unfashionable and politically incorrect among my own people? Can we maintain such traditions and consider ourselves to be ecologically minded?

lily

The day after I left that little unnamed, feathered spirit dying in his cage, I learned that he had died shortly after I left. With the ease of throwing away a candy wrapper, they had tossed my little feathered friend into the trash, perhaps even before he was dead, and forgotten about him. I have often wondered why some people witness pain and suffering, yet turn and walk away, never giving that suffering another thought, while others empathize, are affected, and are changed by such suffering, forever.

Witnessing an innocent little creature struggling and dying, and seeing that others did not care, made a profound impression on me. I knew that the little bird was a warrior, fighting alone for his life, surrounded by indifference. I asked myself over and over: "Why didn't anyone care?" I also vowed to make a difference for all birds in captivity, and so my animal activism began. I soon learned that he wasn't the only little bird who suffered and died that day—millions of birds, and nonhuman animals of all species, die every day due to our indifference.

As an adult, whenever I visited the feed store I would detour to the bird room to say hello to my innocent, imprisoned friends. Like the rest of the merchandise, the caged birds were stacked on top of each other. Like most feed stores, the building was drafty and dusty, with a large inventory of exotic birds in a small, dingy, and poorly ventilated room with a tiny window. In simple terms, the room was oppressive, and because the birds were trapped in their cages, the room looked like a miniature prison.

Nonetheless, the female Eclectus, whom I called Lily, always appeared to enjoy conversations. She tilted her head and listened as I gently spoke to her, and she responded with soft guttural sounds, while nudging the bars of her cage with her face and beak.

Eclectus parrots are unusual because their feathers look like soft, wispy hair. They are native to Australia, New Guinea, and Indonesia. The females have deep red plumage with dark purple feathers on their lower breast, and their beaks are black. The males have rich green plumage and their beaks are deep golden orange. They are strikingly beautiful.

One day I noticed that Lily was different. Her eyes were not bright, and from my perspective, she seemed depressed. When I told the sales person what I thought, she looked at me as if I were crazy. In general terms, I suppose that Lily looked healthy. But I could see that Lily was not right. I spoke softly to her, asking what was wrong. The sales person, scowling at me, offered an explanation: "Well, maybe she is depressed because her mate of ten years was just sold to a breeder!" I was so focused on Lily that I hadn't noticed he was missing. I immediately sensed Lily's pain, and my eyes welled up with tears. I tried to comfort Lily with familiar words and conversation, but to no avail. Lily's soft, guttural sounds did not come. Lily was depressed and lonely.

I eventually said goodbye to Lily, and left the store, but I could not get her loneliness and heartache out of my mind. I so desperately wanted to reunite Lily with her mate, to see her living freely in the wild, in the trees and forests, raising her babies. Instead, I could do nothing for Lily except pray—and paint.

As a professional artist, I decided to paint Lily's story as a prayer for her.

When I arrived home at two-thirty in the afternoon, I hurried into my art studio, grabbed a large 36" × 48" canvas, and started painting "A Blessing for Lily." I painted all day and all night, and finally finished Lily's painting at five o'clock the next morning. During those hours of painting, charged with emotion, I did not feel the least bit tired until I applied the last touch of paint.

Then I was exhausted. "A Blessing for Lily" was born out of desperation and frustration because I couldn't ease Lily's pain or the pain of millions of other parrots that face the same fate every day.

I decided to check on Lily a few days later, but, when I returned to the feed store, Lily was gone. The store clerk told me that Lily was also sold to a breeder, but not the breeder that had purchased Lily's mate a few days earlier. I have often wondered how long Lily remained in her new environment, what the conditions were like, and how many times this cruel cycle of slavery would continue for Lily. Like millions of other birds who are sold and traded over and over again, like used cars, Lily's fate remains uncertain—a mystery.

It is estimated that the average parrot is bounced from "owner" to "owner" a minimum of five times before reaching his/her final destination. Most "exotic" birds die prematurely after a lifetime of suffering and loneliness. Many more die from starvation, abuse, and neglect. In spite of the suffering and the skyrocketing homelessness of parrots, breeders and pet stores continue to pour millions of baby birds into the marketplace every year, making the lives of these birds cheap and expendable.

A year after I lost Lily to the horrors of the pet trade, her painting was accepted for publication, and graced a publisher's catalog. Now, many years later, Lily's image continues to be popular around the world. Profits from "Lily Products" go toward parrot education and parrot protection. It seems that Lily's prayer, albeit secretly, is being spread worldwide. I pray that Lily's guardian angel is watching over her, and over millions of other birds who endure the pain and tragedy of the pet trade. Parrots are inherently wild creatures who do not belong in homes or cages. They deserve to be left alone and free. Perhaps, if you are reading this, you are one of those guardian angels.

the sacred way

At one time Mayans sacrificed young maidens each season, throwing them into deep pits to appease the gods. Tribes in the jungles of New Guinea and New Zealand have recently practiced cannibalism for spiritual and religious purposes. When Europeans invaded those territories, such religious practices were outlawed. So what about those tribes' right to retain tradition?

Long ago, an American Indian ceremonial drum ended up in a prestigious, non-Indian museum, where it was safely protected in a climate-controlled environment—until recently. One day the original owners began to fight a vigorous legal battle to retrieve their drum. The Native tribe regained custody of their sacred possession, and I felt a sense of vindication for my people. The drum would be used once again for ceremonial and spiritual purposes. On reflection, I realized that this drum—protected and carefully guarded for over a hundred years—was instrumental in educating millions of people about the beauty of an ancient culture. This drum will no doubt offer a sense of spiritual awakening for the tribe, but what about their children's children? How many more decades of pounding can this ancient drum withstand? In time, it will disintegrate, and a piece of history will be lost forever.

Reflecting on the recent renewal of the whale hunt by northern tribes, I can't help but see the analogy. The whale is like the drum. Perhaps it is sometimes better to protect and cherish what we have left so that our children's children can also appreciate and witness the splendor of their history.

The conventional, Hollywood depiction of the Native American diet and lifestyle is false. The Americas were a rich and fertile land, providing plentiful berries, vegetables, nuts, beans, squash, roots, fruits, corn, and rice. Most tribal people survived comfortably eating meat sparingly, while thriving on the cornucopia of the land.

European influence introduced Native people to commercial trade, and fire power, and buffalo began to be killed in great numbers. Only recently has meat become an important staple. Europeans and immigrants believe that meat is a critical part of the human diet, but ancient Native Americans had a much more varied diet. Europeans are carrying their meaty ways overseas to other lands, as well. In China, meat is now served much more heavily in restaurants where European/Americans eat, whereas locals have for centuries eaten a mostly vegan diet. It now appears that this introduced diet of "heavy meat" is harming native cultures and causing health problems such as diabetes, cancer, and heart disease.

Again I reflect on words attributed to Chief Seattle:

> The beasts are our brothers, and we kill only to stay alive. If all the beasts were gone, men would die from great loneliness of spirit, for whatever happens to the beasts happens to man, for we are all of one breath. All things are connected. Whatever befalls the Earth, befalls the sons and daughters of the Earth. Man did not weave the web of life; he is merely a strand in it. Whatever he does to the web, he does to himself.

As the new millennium approaches, it appears that the white man and the Indian are at last on the same course: Both white man and Indian pursue self-interests without listening to Earth and other animals. An ancient Ojibway prayer titled *To Walk in Our Sacred Way* addresses this tendency:

Grandfather,
Look at our brokenness
We know that in all Creation
Only the human family
Has strayed from the Sacred Way.
We know that we are the ones
Who are divided
And we are the ones
Who must come back together
To walk in the Sacred Way

Grandfather,
Sacred One,
Teach us love, compassion, and honor
That we may heal the Earth
And heal each other.

As I sit in front of my easel and a stark white canvas, I gaze into Chief Seattle's eyes and wonder what wisdom he might share with us today. I believe that he, too, would be pained by the death of Lily and the Unknown Feathered Spirit—millions of untold feathered spirits—for the sake of the pet trade, and for the sake of meat that we do not need. And I also believe, if my Indian ancestors could comment on our present "right to hunt" in a world with so many people and so few nonhuman animals, that they, who listened to the land and killed only as was necessary, would not be wasteful. I think my ancestors would tell us that it is time to stop the suffering and the killing.

linda g. fisher, professional artist and animal activist, has dedicated much of her life to educating society about the plight of captive parrots. She was thrust into animal activism at the tender age of eleven, on seeing a tiny parakeet suffering and dying in a department store. Linda soon discovered that she had an uncanny ability to communicate with nonhuman animals and to feel their emotions, and she was consequently inspired to tell their stories through art (www .lindagfisher.com). Linda's sensitivity and remarkable connection to other animals has gained international recognition for her work. Part Ojibway and Cherokee (and a tribal member of the Ojibway Nation), Linda lives with rescues, including parrots.

10

the art of truth-telling

THEATER AS COMPASSIONATE ACTION
AND SOCIAL CHANGE

tara sophia bahna-james

I am humbled by the extensive work of women who labor and serve in the trenches—those who run sanctuaries and shelters, provide foster homes, and risk injury, imprisonment, and even death on a daily basis. By comparison, as a writer, I feel my usefulness in the fight to awaken compassion is elusive. Although I frequently write about nonhuman animals, forgiveness, and healing, my mission is one of truth-telling rather than animal advocacy directly, and in the company of more obvious activists, I sometimes feel like an imposter. Nevertheless, when I consider those who have influenced me, it is clear that the arts have an important role to play in awakening people to the incongruities inherent in our treatment of nonhuman animals.

Initially of course, it was not the artists who were my teachers, but rather nonhuman animals themselves. These animals did not instruct me on what was amiss in society. Nor did they offer me a solution to the problem that I could understand. What they did was bear witness to their soulfulness and intelligence, and to the supreme richness and breadth of their own emotional lives. Since birth, I have watched individuals we call "pets" come into my life and love, smile, play, triumph, ail, grow old, and die. And they taught me the only truth I have ever known—the Oneness of all beings: The certainty of death and the beauty, sanctity, and interconnectedness of life.

It is difficult for me to pose arguments for animal welfare independent of my spiritual beliefs. I use the word "spiritual" rather than "religious" intentionally, because I don't think these feelings were dictated by my religious upbringing directly. Yet, to discuss morality/ethics or why I believe anyone has a right to compassion and autonomy over her body without mentioning divinity, faith, or "that which connects us" seems a little like trying to describe sexual intercourse without referring to reproductive anatomy. I could manage it, but misunderstandings are bound to arise, and my precise meaning is too crucial to forsake.

It is unfortunate that, as a society, we have not yet found a way to bring religion into discourse without highly charged emotions and likely conflict. As scientific method has taken precedence in intellectual circles and public debate, we have, to some extent, chased superstition and dogma from the courtroom. However, in the process, we have lost our ability to discuss spiritual and existential truths in public. Each of us has had experiences that others will never be able to fully understand, since they have not lived in our body. It is fallacious to presume that personal experiences do not inform, or ought not to inform, our political and ethical convictions. For each of us, reality is inherently a combination of fact and personal experience. When we deny our most intimate experiences in public expression, we compromise our ability to express our truth.

This description of truth—the divergence of and coexistence between fact and personal experience—is not unlike the profound dichotomy of Being that governs all living things: We are inherently autonomous—individual beings in autonomous, individual bodies—but we are undeniably and unalterably interconnected and interdependent. On a superficial level it is noticeable that what I do effects you and what you do affects me; on a more profound level, as we breathe the same air and exchange molecules when we regenerate cells, decompose, and are born, it is clear that our physical contents are basically One. Yet, my convictions surrounding this Many-and-One–ness, those which lead me to have faith in its truth—to really grasp, believe, and attempt to recreate it in the world around me—are inherently spiritual convictions and, as such, are in the domain of personal experience.

I have faith in this Oneness of Beings because of my experiences. Life among animals (including humans) and trees has taught me about their spirit and dignity and, consequently, about my own spirit and dignity. In their company, the spiritual and visceral experience of being connected to and in communication with them persuades me that we are truly, as the greatest spiritual teachers have insisted, One. And although this is the single greatest factor that has called me to animal advocacy, I believe that many individuals who would not consider themselves part of the animal liberation movement have experienced this "Oneness."

Compassion is not a character trait to which an individual or movement can lay claim. Rather, it is an ever-available ocean of understanding and identification to which each of us has access. True compassion is not something we can feel merely for a few select individuals, groups, ethnicities, or species. True compassion acknowledges a connection to All; true compassion is inherently inclusive.

To many animal activists, those outside the movement seem almost unreachable. Yet the vast majority of human animals have not built corporate empires rooted in extreme forms of animal exploitation. Nor are most humans so blinded by rage and self-loathing as to derive pleasure from cruelty. Most people are simply well-intentioned mothers, fathers, children, friends, and caregivers who have known love, pain, sacrifice, and kindness. At junctures they may have even been victimized or exploited, and they likely know the sting of abandonment. But most interestingly, like many who do feel called to become animal liberationists, most of them are already aware that they have been deeply moved, taught, and in many cases transformed by the presence or companionship of nonhuman animals.

Yet humans, especially those born to any degree of privilege in industrialized nations, inherit a skewed sense of self-importance from the day of their birth. If I look far enough back in my only-child–hood, I can actually remember the day I learned that I was not the most important person in the world. I was a toddler traveling to Coney Island with my mother. My mom sprained her ankle painfully on the subway stairs, and hating to see her so sad and in pain, I looked into her eyes and, with quite good intentions, declared, "Don't worry mommy. Look on the bright side. At least it didn't happen to me!"

Throughout my brief life, I had noticed that my mother was much more upset when harm came to me than she was when she received harm of equal magnitude. I had watched her sacrifice for me, prioritize for me, lose sleep for me, and be late to work for me. I had come to what seemed a logical conclusion: I was the most important person in the world (or at least in her world). Imagine my surprise when, instead of appeasing her, I earned a stern reprimand: "You're not more important than I am!"

I wasn't upset by her words. I remember processing this information. I thought to myself, "I'm not more important? Oh! I must have completely misunderstood! Clearly this changes everything!" My three-year-old mind reached a new and distinct intellectual and moral understanding.

Not all Westerners are only children doted on by single parents, but we are generally accustomed to seeing ourselves within a spectrum of the more-or-less privileged, respected, and favored. By the time we are privy to what goes on "for our benefit," most of us have fastened our identity to a rung on the ladder of advantage and become defensive and terrified if anyone attempts to dismantle this hierarchy. Most of us were raised to set ourselves above non-human animals.

After watching "An Inconvenient Truth," I heard a viewer ask Al Gore to analyze exactly what it was (other than economic interest) that kept Americans, who claim to care about their environment, from making simple changes in their lifestyles and communities. Gore's reply was simple: "Inertia." Rather than delve into the hearts and minds of those who fail to act and invite us to examine ourselves, he essentially blamed Newtonian physics—and no one batted an eye.

To understand the forces we hope to change, we must look into the lives of those we perceive to be our enemies and opponents, and we must also look at ourselves. In some ways, what makes some people choose not to acknowledge a problem, and others who do acknowledge it choose not to act, is similar to what makes those who *do* take action desperate to convince others that they must follow suit: Most of us are, at one time or another, in denial of the terrifying reality that we are entirely responsible for our choices and actions, *and* we are not responsible for anyone else's.

On some level, we intuitively understand the first part of this equation, which is why we are so afraid. With so much cruelty and suffering in our midst, many are afraid to look behind the veil. How does one continue to serve oneself, to harbor convictions that one is in the right—even to get up in the morning—when one has made, and continues to make, selfish and unattractive choices? Partially, we persist by allowing the second part of the dichotomy to sink in: We are not responsible for anyone else's choices. Yes, we are responsible and culpable for our mistakes, and those mistakes often have disastrous consequences, but no one individual is responsible for the totality of the world's misery. We are, each of us, only responsible for our own action, or failure to act, in any given moment.

This is a liberating realization, but of course it is also quite numbing. Confronting this reality makes us feel helpless—helpless in the face of loss and suffering, helpless because we cannot help those who do not wish to help themselves, and helpless because some individuals are entirely beyond our reach. We are helpless because we cannot single-handedly save the world or those we love. And this is painful because, ultimately, we are those we love. The truth remains that we are connected. And I believe we are all one breath, one spirit.

Most often, fear lies at the root of our "inertia": fear of the unknown, fear that we won't be able to save everyone, fear that we will need to take responsibility for saving ourselves. We fear our own inconsistency, imperfections, and impotence. We fear that we will be deemed judgmental or will be cut off from those we love who disagree. But denying our fear and refusing to come into our compassion and our truth in order to avoid the perceived consequences, only sends us further into an abyss of existential pain and cognitive dissonance.

Our bewildering condition (and, personally, I believe there is nothing exclusively human about this condition, except perhaps that we have developed the tools to systematically deny the realities of this condition) is predicated on paradoxes: We are both separate and one, powerful and insignificant. We must strive for perfection though we are clearly imperfect. Life demands that we exceed ourselves, transcend our mortality, and laugh through tears. As mortals, we must be willing to strive where there is no certainty of success, often where there is every reason to expect failure. If we are not, then how can we be up to the most basic task of living?

Most activities require some degree of faith: faith that we'll make it through the day, faith that kindness matters, faith that one small wholesome action will engender greater ripples of kindness that we cannot see. Teacher and poet Paul Fleishman writes, "Peace is faith in the other." But "other" is just a word for the parts of ourselves that we don't wish to see. Being still, truthful, and open in the company of those from whom we differ, and in the face of our own discomfort, is a crucial step in our development.

This is how artistic work joins the struggle for animal advocacy. More than anger, violence, or aggression, it is fear, defensiveness, polarization, and willful ignorance that perpetuate the cycle of institutionalized cruelty that characterizes our society's relationship to nonhuman animals. The arts are capable of striking directly at the heart of these preconditions.

Theologian Hans Urs Von Balthasar suggested that in order for art to reflect truth (and not simply propaganda or pornography) it must not glorify itself but rather point toward God. I understand this to mean that all true art points to the Oneness of Beings. Similarly, when I see another individual on his or her own terms—or at least make an honest attempt to do so—what I find is no less than God. It is a spiritual revelation, like that which comes when in art or nature I encounter the Beautiful.

Even most nonrepresentational art connects across boundaries. Here the boundary between self and other is between artist and viewer or even between those viewing a work of art together. If the art is successful, an unfamiliar artifact can communicate some otherwise inexpressible experience or sentiment across these imagined lines and elicit an emotional, or even rational, response without the benefit of familiar language. Like a child learning an unfamiliar tongue, we are so occupied with trying to understand what is being communicated that we are caught off guard by a sea of connection.

I am not suggesting that within every artist beats the heart of a committed animal advocate, but I do believe that the arts provide a safe space for accessing the compassionate muscle. With religion having been hijacked in so many instances by those who are power seeking and faithless, perhaps the theater is the next place we can congregate to experience communion—if not with the animals themselves, then with those who have witnessed their tribulations and acknowledged their dignity and love. Let us come to this place with our defenses down and at least begin to listen to stories that might open our hearts.

Although I have always been a theater artist and compassionate toward nonhuman animals, I did not immediately recognize theater as a vehicle to compassionate action and social change. Historically, the power of drama lies in its ability to take a "human" experience with which we can identify (trials and tribulations, desire for relationships, mortality, the necessity of making choices) and relocate that experience in a situation that we do not readily recognize (a family we do not know; a hero of whom we are envious; a setting, time period, or community from which we feel distant or estranged). In witnessing this, our minds are kept entertained like curious voyeurs: We believe we are learning the juicy details of others' lives, but ultimately we learn that these "others" are just like us. Whether or not we would have made their same choices, we recognize the grand strokes, existentially, of where they are and where they have been.

In 2004 I returned from a trip to India, where I was visually exposed to the sanctioned undervaluing of animals within the context of a culture to which I was not already desensitized. Only then was I prepared to contemplate my own society's transgressions. In reading Marjorie Spiegel's *The Dreaded Comparison*, I learned that I do take part in institutionalized cruelty, even as a well-meaning, animal-loving citizen who does not actively condone torture. Institutionalized cruelty is predicated on several conditions, two of which require my sanction: economic complicity as a taxpayer and consumer, and willful ignorance, a virtual "don't ask, don't tell" mentality that assures I will not look behind closed doors to investigate the reality of heinous acts committed in my name.

Breaking down barriers of denial has always been art's forte, and this is no less true of education, travel, and cross-community exchange. But lately, theater has nurtured an extraordinary movement that straddles all these areas and brings with it unprecedented potential for building bridges. It is a shift from story-telling to truth-telling.

Shortly after reading *The Dreaded Comparison*, I came into contact with Eve Ensler's play, *The Vagina Monologues*, and the larger "VDAY movement to end violence against women and girls." Ensler's vision was simply to give voice to that which had long been taboo: women speaking about their vaginas, and by extension, about their sexuality, their power, their abuse, and their bodies. Soon, women from all over the world were coming forward to tell Ensler their stories about menstruation, masturbation, sex, birth, incest, rape, domestic violence, and genital mutilation. When the silence was lifted, many women found that, even if they could not identify with the events described by the narrator, they found familiarity with the character's bewilderment and isolation, and with her prior unspoken agreement to remain silent. Something very important changed when women who had suffered in silence for generations were finally given a pass to communicate with one another and to share their honest accounts of life in a woman's body.

This phenomenon reflects a global revolution in which we as individuals are finally reaching across the boundaries of nations, communities, political factions—and, yes, species!—to reveal to one another the truth about who we are and how we live. As this happens, we are sure to discover that our wars and slaughterhouses, our police states and prisons, our gender roles and age gaps, our uneven income distribution and all polarized affiliations, have been willingly and consciously sustained by only a select few, who have cleverly kept us from tapping into our Oneness by fostering fear of difference. Ultimately, we will see that all are only mothers, fathers, children, friends, and caregivers who have loved and suffered, and would like nothing more than to grow in compassion. It is only our fear of identifying with anyone displaying qualities, actions, or attributes that we loathe in ourselves that clouds our judgment. This is why we recognize the plight of some and have become systematically desensitized to, or shielded from, recognizing the plight of others.

We must develop practical methods of withstanding powerful economic interests that would coerce us into choices that, in our hearts, we do not support—choices that, as they are being made, force us to deny reality and further splinter ourselves. But on a personal level, we must also strengthen our ability to feel compassion in uncomfortable circumstances, amidst inconsistencies, before a solution is evident or available, and in the face of our own imperfections. The ability to hold disparate realities in our heads is crucial if we are to acknowledge what needs to be changed.

When we see human beings step forward in community to share their truth and personal experience, we are liberated to do the same, and there is a collective sigh of recognition and relief. By revealing where we are, we become irrevocably empowered in our vulnerability. We stop hiding. We discover something no one can take from us: An acceptance of ourselves as we are and where we are.

But further alchemy takes place when these revelations occur within an aesthetic context. Here, we can delve into issues or feelings that may feel too dangerous to address otherwise. Due to the conventions of the medium (the audience/performer barrier, anticipation of closure, knowledge that events are "performed" rather than "real," etc.), we are temporarily disarmed.

Culturally, we understand that we have come to the theater, gallery, concert hall, or literary page to experience an aesthetic (rather than literal) reality, and that this will elicit an aesthetic response. Although our response may call up certain emotions, thoughts, or memories, ultimately we understand that we are not here to pass judgment in the way we judge real-life events. Rather, we judge what we see on stage by its "believability," or its aesthetic truth alone—that is its beauty.

Because of this we allow ourselves to sit through things in a theater that we might not tolerate in real life. If we are lucky, if there is merit and truth to the performance, we might experience situations that we would otherwise consider distasteful or intolerable long enough to identify with the players and their experiences. Whereas ideas, philosophies, and politics may divide, understanding human dramas brings us closer.

Essentially, then, theater can present a nonviolent forum in which we might come to understand those with whom we disagree. It is a place where we suspend our judgment in order to witness and understand the experience of others.

When used to examine controversy, theater becomes a very powerful tool. Many movements have employed truth-telling theater with considerable social impact, but it is no mistake that this medium has reached global proportions within the context of the women's movement. Although there are exceptions to this characterization on both sides of the gender gap, women tend to be more comfortable sharing their feelings in community and, as a result, are more likely to have developed a language for doing so. More importantly, women understand what it is like to live in a world where public, political, and economic discourse are dominated by voices that do not understand what it is like to live in their bodies.

Psychologist Carol Gilligan notes that while boys are often conditioned against acknowledging their inner lives from their earliest days, girls' emotional lives are typically encouraged until they approach puberty, at which point they enter into an unspoken social agreement to remain silent with regard to their personal experiences, in order to enter public life in a patriarchal society. Many women remain splintered from themselves and their experiences, but many others have come to understand that "coming into one's truth" requires breaking this social contract and giving voice to repressed experiences. Consequently, it is often easier for women to understand how accessing vulnerability can be a source of power.

On a grand scale, nonhuman animal liberation and human healing are inseparable. Both are furthered each time we open our hearts and our lives to those struggling to acknowledge inconsistencies, struggling to give voice to their experiences, and struggling to reject the unspoken agreement that assures economic complicity and willful ignorance. Because of their experiences, and because of their willingness to speak about those experiences, women are in a unique position to aid this process.

If you are a woman who cares for animals and you wish you could do more to help, especially if you have feared coming face to face with your own limitations along the way, please consider this: In every corner of the globe there lie animals, no less loving, patient, intuitive, and trusting than those you have known. They experience pain and joy, sorrow and fear. Their lives are brief (in most cases briefer than yours), and their bodies, like yours, grow old and die. Most of them are exploited, caricatured, mocked, and malnourished. They are lying alone in abandoned lots, chained to poles in the sleet and rain, boxed into pens with their own feces amid the decaying corpses of their brothers and sisters, strapped down and nonanesthetized in experimental laboratories, worked beyond capacity until their bones give out, forced to mate, trained into aggression, tortured as bait, and hunted for sport. Their bodies are made into luxury clothing items, preservatives for party snacks, and stuffing for pillows. Females are turned into reproductive machines whose young are torn away and discarded. Even those who live in the wilderness, out of reach from subjugation at the hands of humans, experience famine, flood, and disease because we have destroyed their ecosystems.

These animals desperately need to be acknowledged, rescued, comforted, healed, cared for, and appreciated as beings with unique skills, talents, and intelligence in their own right. They need to be given nutritious food, love, companionship, sunshine, and fresh air. They need to be given kindness and patience and time for rehabilitation, and they require our understanding that many, probably most, will never be fully rehabilitated. To do this, we need to step into that uncomfortable place where we acknowledge that the scope of the problem is unfathomable, but the individual act still has meaning. Animals need us to be courageous and curious and to accept the possibility of failure. They need us to have the faith to keep going when we are humbled by our own inadequacy, insignificance, and imperfection. They need us to accept ourselves as we are, and to forgive ourselves and each other so that we have the strength to take the next step, whatever that may be. And they need us to not let things we cannot do stop us from doing what we can. They also need us to tell their stories—not only of how they are dying, but also of how they live. And they need us to be no less brave in telling our own.

But we also need animals dearly. We count on animals to remind us of our ability to give and receive compassion and love—across boundaries, beyond language, in spite of our own undeserved power, and in the face of our dizzying mortality and isolated inner lives. We rely on animals to crack open our hearts to allow for the possibility of relationship, the Oneness of Beings, and the flood of healing that our species so desperately needs.

tara sophia bahna-james is a playwright, performer, educator, essayist, and the founder of Majority of One (www.majorityofone.org), which seeks to inspire humane and ethical practices through marketplace initiatives and outreach programs in the arts, education, and cross-community exchange. Tara contributed "The Journey Toward Compassionate Choice: Integrating Sistah and Vegan Experience" to the anthology *Sistah Vegan* (Harper, Lantern 2009). Tara holds a BA in religion and theater from Yale University and an MFA in musical theater writing from NYU's Tisch School of the Arts.

11

from hunting grounds to chicken rights

MY STORY IN AN EGGSHELL

karen davis

the concentration camps

People often wonder how I started as an academic and ended up as an animal rights activist rescuing and defending the rights of chickens and turkeys.

Before I was an "academic," several things happened that bear on my life as an animal rights activist and founder of an organization fighting for the rights of chickens and turkeys. I grew up in Altoona, Pennsylvania, a railroad town, and I attended two Pennsylvania colleges: Westminster College, which I left in my sophomore year in the throes of a psychological crisis, and Lock Haven State College, where I earned a degree in the social sciences in 1968. As a freshman I graduated instantly from reading books like *Marjorie Morningstar* and *Gone with the Wind* to fervid absorption in Tolstoy's *Anna Karenina* and existentialist philosophy. At Westminster I became interested in Russian and German history, above all in Stalin's slave labor camps and Hitler's concentration and death camps. So immersed did I become in thinking about these camps that I had to leave school. One autumn day, my father visited me and I mentioned going to law school to become a civil rights lawyer. Two weeks later, I called my parents to come and get me. I dropped out of college, unable to carry on as a student while coping with a growing obsession with the human-engineered suffering of people, which had become like a cancer, eating me alive.

I became obsessed with the question of retaining personal identity under conditions intended to destroy personal identity along with the core of oneself. By "identity" I mean one's innermost sense of self, rather than one's appearance to the outside world. I began trying to imagine myself in the concentration camps and inside the skin—the minds—of people forced to live in those camps. Inwardly, I was driven to "go" to places where I imagined how it would be to no longer feel like, or be, oneself, though still remain alive and functioning. I tried to imagine every conceivable kind of human-imposed suffering and at what point one (I) would stop being oneself (myself)—and how that would feel.

"Trying to imagine" is somewhat misleading. My obsessions had a life of their own. I felt as if I had been invaded by an infection of superclarification of abysmalness and horror. Words for these kinds of perceptions lie somewhere in the region of the profane and inane—there are states of consciousness for which no verbal equivalent exists. This is why it irritates me to hear the word "language" used to distinguish humans from other kinds of animals. There are many languages besides human verbal language. There are languages of the intestines and the lungs, as well as of the heart and of the animal being, and I say this as one for whom verbal language is extremely important.

Words—books—helped save me from an ordeal that I thought for a while I might not survive. Back home, my father felt betrayed. He couldn't accept a concentration camp obsession as a reason for leaving school, flouting the education he was paying for. Desperate, my mother arranged for me to see a psychiatrist. When I told the psychiatrist about my need to suffer and how I was plagued with guilt because I wasn't in a concentration camp (and how I felt guilty, too, because I didn't want to be in one), he said, "In a way, you are in one." This was a consoling—almost bracing—thought. Years later I read a book by A. Alvarez, a friend of the poet Sylvia Plath, who described Plath's particular form of mental suffering as a "concentration camp of the mind." This captures something of what I was going through at that time.

I was never in a concentration camp, and I do not pretend to equate my experience with the experience of those who were. Yet the fact remains that learning about these camps affected my perspective, on the threshold of adulthood, more profoundly than any other single previous event. My subsequent preoccupation with the human-imposed suffering of billions of nonhuman animals, far from being an abandonment of the perceptions I gained in the course of my preoccupation with the concentration camps in the 1960s, involved a radical extension of these earlier perceptions to include the largest class of innocent victims on earth.[1]

During those years, I don't recall ever thinking about abused animals in the light of concentration camp victims, although I would have been able to do so because of the cruelties I saw, and in some cases participated in, while I was growing up.

At the time of my obsession with concentration camps, I gorged on hard-boiled eggs because an article in *Vogue* magazine had said that it takes more calories to digest hardboiled eggs than they contain, so the more eggs one eats, the more weight one loses. I had no idea, then, that the eggs I devoured by the dozens were the opposite of a "comfort food," that they came straight from the kind of a hell that I was agonizing over. The battery-cage system of egg production was just then being consolidated as an industry. Perhaps those eggs incubated to hatch my future.

GROWING UP

I grew up in a family and community where sport hunting was normal and expected. When I was in grade school, schools closed on the first day of deer season, and probably still do. My father hunted rabbits and ring-necked pheasants (pen-raised pheasants turned out on the first day of hunting season), then "cleaned" them in the basement. He said he didn't hunt deer because he didn't want to have to lug them through the woods. His defense of rabbit hunting was "everything hunts the rabbit." My father and his friends hunted grouse, squirrels, and small birds, but I don't recall anything about turkeys. Maybe they were "too big" to lug through the woods. We ate some of his killings, and the rest simply disappeared. There was talk such as, "Hell, I don't want them; give them away . . . or throw them away." One of my uncles loved to tell the story about how he threw away twenty pheasant pies his wife had baked.

Not until Tim (the oldest of my three younger brothers) was a teenager and wanted to spend Saturday with his girlfriend, do I recall a family conflict over hunting. My father flew into a rage when Tim announced that he didn't want to "go huntin'" with his dad. He was accused of being "a girl" because he preferred to be with a girl that day.

My middle brother, Amos, had his eye knocked out with a slingshot when he was five, yet he grew up to be an avid small-game hunter with a penchant for killing pheasants and quails. He could admit that some nonhuman animals had feelings. His own family had a golden retriever named Coffee, who was kidnapped from their yard in Baton Rouge, Louisiana. Weeks later, when they somehow got her back, "Coffee's fur had turned white from fright," Amos said.

My father kept a succession of hunting dogs at the far end of the yard. These beagles had a wooden doghouse filled with straw and lived at the end of a long chain tied to an iron stake. Whenever I visited "Nellie," or "Gus," or whoever was there at the time, the dog would cower inside the doghouse or approach me crouching, with his or her tail curled under trembling back legs. My father trained his dogs by hitting them with a work-gloved hand. I'd hear them whimpering from inside the house. I heard stories about hunting dogs who had heart attacks running in the fields because they had been tied up, without exercise, for months between hunting seasons. My father took the beagles out for runs during the year to keep this from happening. In the fall, the men stood in the kitchen in the early morning talking about the great day of killing that lay ahead, and then loaded Dad's dog into the car trunk with the other dogs, all yelping, and off they'd go.

I was an avid meateater. I loved broiled fat, which I would eat off other people's plates: "Give it to me, I'll eat it!" Nonetheless, around the age of thirteen, I started arguing with my father about hunting. We'd be at the dinner table when the fight would commence. I'd be yelling at my father about hunting, and he'd be yelling back—over prime rib or baked ham or broiled lamb chops. Needless to say, my father never changed. He stopped hunting in his eighties only because he could no longer see well enough to shoot, but he hunted for years with poor eyesight before quitting.

I never thought then that I was eating sentient beings. I remember my mother proudly announcing: "I buy fresh chicken from Imler's" (a poultry slaughter market that is still in business). Chickens weren't real to me the way pheasants were. Growing up, I saw ring-necked pheasants dead and alive. Occasionally one flew into our windshield on a country road. As a child, I begged my Uncle George, a cabinetmaker, to carve me a big wooden pheasant. I colored in the pheasant's eyes and neck and carried it protectively under my arm. Now I know that chickens are pheasants.

One of my most vivid childhood experiences was when the white duck who lived up the street with the Mallory family was run over by a car. I cried inconsolably on the couch. I loved that duck, and for some reason it was more painful to me for a duck to be hit by a car than a dog, which I saw often enough, and which was traumatic enough.

As a very young child I spent feverish nights suffering over baby robins that fell out of nests in the trees in our yard. They would be naked and their mouths would be open, crying, and my mother would help me "take care of them." But the next morning they were always gone.

I loved parakeets, too. My parakeet, Wiffenpoof (a budgerigar, actually), loved to push a rubber jacks ball across the rug with his beak. He sat on my father's head whistling loudly while Dad yelled sternly at my brother, on behalf of our neighbor's—Mr. Feathers—flower gardens: "I told you to stay out of Mr. Flower's Feathers!" One day I came home from school and Wiffenpoof was gone. My mother said they gave him away. They bought me a windup canary in a plastic cage to take his place. It still hurts to ponder where they took Wiffenpoof. In those days, no one recognized such parental decisions as both an act of animal abuse and an act of child abuse.

In truth, my mother couldn't stand to see a nonhuman animal hurt and suffering. I still picture her crying in our driveway over a mouse with an injured foot, which she tried to coax (with cheese) into a bucket. At the same time, my brothers and I picked many butterflies off the flower bushes in our yard and put them in jars and cigar boxes, with a handful of grass, until their wings were tattered and transparent, and they died, or we "put them back." We also caught grasshoppers, grass snakes, and worms. Why were we allowed to hurt these creatures? How could *I* do that?

Only years later did I recall seeing my best friend's father pull a brown hen out of a dark shed next to their house one day, lay her on a wooden block, and chop her head off with a hatchet. Her head lay clucking on the grass at my feet while her body ran around the yard. It was definitely a hen. I see her as clearly as if the episode happened yesterday.

When I was eight or nine, my father decided to get rid of the rats under the house by killing them with the whisk of a broom. This project was carried out in the same gleeful spirit as when he and his brother, my uncle Clyde, killed bats in the attic with rolled-up newspapers and tennis rackets. Meanwhile, my mother went through the house shrieking, "God didn't make rats, the devil made rats." That was how she dealt with the cruelty she couldn't bear to watch, much less take part in, but didn't have the courage to speak out against in our household. I can still see a rat deep in a hole in our yard with two bright eyes looking out, and my father bent over the hole with a broom.

racial prejudice and civil rights

A story in the teenage magazine, *Ingenue*, titled "Them!" drew my attention to racial prejudice in the midfifties. "Them" referred to the black students being escorted by police into the all-white high school in Little Rock, Arkansas, in a hate-charged atmosphere vividly evoked by the writer. I remember asking my father about the cause of this hatred, which I couldn't grasp through the writer's depiction of these students. (Perhaps that was the point of the story.) I don't recall his answer, but later, when I was at Westminster College, shortly before my obsession with the concentration camps, I became involved in the racial conflicts that were just then surfacing on campus. I dated a few black students, which was taboo, though it was accepted for a white girl to "fast dance" with a black male student in the student union. At the time—1962— campus fraternities and sororities excluded black students, though a special status, "associate member," was created in one of the fraternities for black football players.

One weekend I was home talking with my father about racial issues at school, and he said that if I ever brought a colored person to the house, male or female, he would not let them in. He said that growing up in Altoona, he and his family used to tip their hat to the single colored family in the neighborhood, but never invited them into the house, and he insisted that the family didn't want to come in anyway. When I questioned my father's point of view, my mother said I should respect other people's opinions. I replied that I was only obliged to respect other people's right to hold an opinion, not the opinion itself.

The opinion at Westminster College (I was sent to this Presbyterian school to satisfy my mother's concern for my "safety," not because my parents were religious—they weren't) was that there were certain lines you must not cross, certain things that were immutable. For example, the school choir's prize soprano, June Singleton, was black, so she had to stay in separate hotels when the choir toured the South. Despite all the talk about Christian love and courage, the administration defended this policy. One day two girlfriends and I went to the college chaplain and urged him to take a stand against racial discrimination on campus; he argued that separate-but-equal was God's will.

Such moments marked the beginning of my intellectual awakening of opposition to much of conventional society's way of thinking. My sensibility began to take shape in the form of ideas and values that were frequently at odds with the norm.

seal hunt

After college, in the early 1970s, I lived in a black neighborhood in Baltimore with my boyfriend and worked at a nursery school at the end of the block called the Little Red Hen. Following that, I became a juvenile probation counselor for the state of Maryland. Out of the blue, I started getting mail from the International Fund for Animal Welfare, (IFAW) in New Brunswick, Canada, about the slaughter of the baby harp seals in the Gulf of St. Lawrence.

Seal slaughter opened my eyes to animal cruelty on a large scale. Brian Davies, then head of the IFAW and the author of *Savage Luxury* (an excruciating book about the Canadian seal hunt),[2] sought to convince the Magdalen Islanders in the Gulf of St. Lawrence that more money could be made by treating the seals as a tourist attraction than by slaughtering them for fur. To this day, the effort to protect the seals, though a major campaign, has been unsuccessful.

In March of 1974, I joined an IFAW-sponsored tour to the Magdalen Islands to see the newborn seals and their mothers on the ice floes off Grindstone Island. For two days we were holed up in the hotel waiting for a break in the weather that would allow the helicopters to land us safely on the ice where the seals were nursing.

I assumed that everyone on the tour opposed the "hunt," which was not really a hunt, just a clubbing of infants. The other visitors were an eye-opener. A retired oilman from Oklahoma had brought a tripod to set up on the ice to film the slaughter for his friends back home as a form of entertainment. A wildlife reporter wanted a piece of fresh-skinned fur to take back to her editor. Several women in our group said that, while they felt bad for these baby seals, they couldn't work up the same emotion for the bachelor seals, who are clubbed to death each year on the Pribilof Islands in the Bering Sea, because they were unattractive (to their eyes). Visitors said things like, "I could never stand to see a dog mistreated, but I don't have the same feeling about cats (or rats)."

These discussions clarified why laws are needed to protect the defenseless against the caprice of human sentiment. The idea that most people have compassion for nonhuman animals, and would be kind to them if society would just encourage compassion, overlooks the extent to which each of us depends on legal protection. Anyway, where does "society" begin if not with people? Who in the United States would surrender the protections afforded them by the Constitution and entrust their fate entirely to human compassion—an easily overridden emotion even when it is present?

On Grindstone Island I met a professional wildlife photographer named Bill Curtzinger, whose color photograph of a baby harp seal's whiskered face on the ice was a beautiful and popular poster at the time. Bill hated the seal hunt. He told me that growing up he'd dreamed of becoming a photographer for National Geographic, a dream that came true. One of his first assignments was to cover a beaver colony. For several days he waited quietly for the beavers to feel safe in his presence before taking pictures. But his editor at the *National Geographic Magazine* didn't like his pictures, and asked him to wreck the beaver colony in order to procure a certain story angle. Bill refused and another photographer was sent to complete the assignment.

On the third day of our stay, we were helicoptered onto the ice floes. Imagine a universe of infants crying piteously in all directions. That's what the ice floes sounded like. Baby seals and their mothers were everywhere, and so was pink-stained ice. Beyond us were the local sealers, the "landsmen," with their long clubs, clubbing the seals—not for "survival," but for sport.

A *Washington Post* journalist to whom I later told this story wrote that I couldn't "process the evil" I'd witnessed that day on the ice.[3] Mistakenly, I thought that the seal hunt would not be taking place during our visit. Indeed,

I was devastated. I couldn't go straight home but instead spent three days blanketed in a Montreal hotel reading Thomas Mann's novel, *Dr. Faustus*.

Throughout my life I have found solace and exhilaration in authors who express my pessimism aesthetically and insightfully, without illusion. Describing Ivan Karamazov's despair in *The Brothers Karamazov*, Dostoyevsky says that Ivan's soul was sunk in a heavy mist, and Thomas Hardy describes Jude Fawley's clairvoyant suffering in his novel, *Jude the Obscure*, in biblical terms—the blackness of darkness. Around the time of the seals, I wrote a pessimistic poem titled "A Confession of Ultimate Night," which ends: "For I am composed of countless unlighted places / that never will know the light of any summer sun / nor feel how warmth can melt even a dark and weighted space of lead and iron / and Age that began to be Old on the very First Day."

becoming a vegetarian

I ate so much steak one summer in the late 1960s, while working as a waitress at the General Putnam Inn in Norwalk, Connecticut, that the landlady of the boarding house where I was staying bought me a steak knife as a joke. After graduating from college in 1968, I spent a semester at the University of Maryland's School of Social Work, in Baltimore. Almost every day after classes, I'd run to the Lexington Market, buy a barbecued chicken, take it back to my room on Cathedral Street, and devour it sitting on the bare floor next to the big iron bed, crunching bones with my teeth, chewing and almost sucking in the skin and then bolting the flesh. Occasionally there'd be a rubbery vein or something which gave pause—not a moral pause, just a kind of distasteful "hmmm, what is this?" Yet the day was approaching when I would discover the meaning of "meat" and become one of those people who, in the words of a former chicken slaughterhouse worker, "just couldn't look at a piece of meat anymore without seeing the sad, tortured face that was attached to it sometime in the past."[4]

Just as I became obsessed with concentration camps in the early 1960s, so in the early 1970s I began to agonize over the suffering and abuse of nonhuman animals. After the seal hunt, I visited a large dark warehouse in Maryland, filled with thousands of parrots, who were stacked in tiny cages waiting to be sent to pet stores. In 1972, I bought a parrot from a pet store simply to get her out of there. My parrot, Tikhon, and I lived happily together until her death, for more than twenty years.

Shortly after I bought Tikhon, I discovered an essay by Tolstoy called "The First Step."[5] In this work, Tolstoy argues that being a vegetarian is the necessary "first step" to becoming the type of nonviolent Christian he aspired to be in his later years. It wasn't Tolstoy's conceptual arguments that convinced me to stop eating nonhuman animals (though they would have, were I a Christian). Rather, it was his grueling description of cows and lambs in the Moscow slaughterhouses. Meat-eating, milk-drinking "egghead" that I was, I needed no further prompting to drop flesh from my diet. I agreed with Tolstoy, and a decade later, with Peter Singer. Because I had never "supported" eating other living beings in the first place, I did not need to be persuaded to abandon one position in order to take up another; I needed only to be made aware.

becoming an animal rights advocate

Three events in the early 1980s brought me into the Animal Rights Movement, which was just then getting underway. A few months after the seal hunt, I moved to San Francisco, where I remained a vegetarian (with a few lapses). I worked for a short time at a no-kill shelter called Pets Unlimited, which was a terrible place for the dogs and cats who died slowly, going crazy in an upstairs room where visitors did not venture. After that, for the most part, I stayed away from animal issues for nearly a decade, fearing their effect on me. But one's temperament follows its own path.

While teaching a writing class to pre-nursing students at the University of Maryland, College Park, I provoked a furor in the classroom over a student paper that sought to absolve the Silver Spring Monkeys experimenter, Dr. Edward Taub, of wrongdoing. Taub was convicted of cruelty to animals in 1981, in Maryland.[6] My request that the student redo her paper sparked a semester-long, emotionally charged discussion about the treatment of nonhuman animals and animal rights. This discussion evolved to include an outpouring of pent-up emotions over the question of how much compassion they should sacrifice in order to meet the demands of impersonal professionalism drilled into them by their instructors. They saw a connection between the experiments they were expected to perform on living beings and the detachment they were expected to cultivate toward their human patients, even those who were dying. As one troubled student wrote, "I would like to be merciful, but I have to be professional."

In 1983, *The Washington Post* published a long, dismissive article about Ingrid Newkirk titled, "She's a Portrait of Zealotry in Plastic Shoes." Ingrid, with Alex Pacheco, had recently founded People for the Ethical Treatment of Animals (PETA).[7] The article sought to discredit Ingrid by describing her compassion: cupping her hands with water for thirsty chickens stacked in crates in the midsummer heat at a slaughterhouse loading dock in Maryland. I saved the article. A few months later, when I saw a newspaper ad for World Laboratory Animals Day in Lafayette Park near the White House, I went.

Lafayette Park was the turning point. As I looked at the posters showing scenes of nonhuman animals suffering in laboratories, two images in particular struck me. One was of a beagle whose body had been burned. The other was of a nonhuman primate whose head had been transplanted onto another animal's body. The look on their faces, the suffering in their eyes, transfixed my attention. It was an indescribable look that said from the depths of their being, "Why have you done this to me?"

The faces of the individuals on posters in Lafayette Park spoke of the terrible things that had been done to them by human beings. Standing there, I remember thinking about what Peter Singer had said in *Animal Liberation*: If you find it unbearable to imagine what these individuals are going through, remember that what you find unbearable merely to imagine, exploited animals are forced to endure in reality. At that moment, I pledged never again to abandon nonhumans to the iniquity of our species simply because I couldn't bear the knowledge of their suffering. From that moment, I became an animal rights activist, a person who seeks and calls for a remedy.

choosing chickens and turkeys

I did not grow up around chickens and turkeys. I did not come to know these birds until I was in my forties.

My first encounter with turkeys took place at Farm Sanctuary in the mid-eighties, where I worked one summer as a volunteer. At Farm Sanctuary, there was a flock of about twenty white females and two bronze turkeys named Milton and Doris. One thing that impressed me then, and has stayed in my mind ever since, was how the turkeys' voices, their "yelps," floated about the place in an infinitely plaintive refrain. Doris wandered about the farmyard all day by herself like an eternal embodiment of a "lost call," the call of a lost young turkey for her mother. Milton followed visitors around on his gouty legs and swollen feet, impressing them favorably—they were surprised at how companionable he was. From behind a bristling armor of iridescent brown feathers, his dark eyes watched us through pendant, heavily wrinkled pouches of colorful, folded skin—like a soul imprisoned deep inside his body.

Soon afterward, my husband and I adopted two young female turkeys named Mila and Priscilla. They both loved to forage in the woods around our house, and sunbathe and dustbathe together, though their temperaments were completely different. Mila was a gentle and pacific turkey with a watchful manner. Priscilla was a moody bird, frustrated by her inability to hatch the many unfertilized eggs that she laid in the wooded nooks, where she nested. When Priscilla got into one of her angry moods, she would glare at us combatively, ready to charge. What stopped her was Mila. Perking up her head at Priscilla's signals, Mila would stand directly in the path between Priscilla and us. She would tread back and forth in front of Priscilla, uttering soft pleading yelps, as if beseeching Priscilla to calm down, and she did.

Over the years, I became more and more interested in turkeys and more and more revolted by the ignominious role that society has assigned to these remarkable birds—and the absolute brutality of the turkey industry.[8] I adopted several more turkeys—Aubrey and Amelia, who still live in our sanctuary even as I write. I was attracted to their friendly (though sometimes prickly) behavior and lively inquisitiveness. Determined to bring the truth about turkeys to light, I researched the matter extensively, and in 2001 I published *More Than a Meal: The Turkey in History, Myth, Ritual, and Reality*.[9]

In 1990, a crippled and abandoned chicken from the meat industry, named Viva, led me to found United Poultry Concerns. From the moment I pulled Viva out of a muddy shack in Maryland, and saw her face, I knew I had a story to tell that would never let go.[10]

When I met Viva in 1985, I was an English teacher completing my doctoral dissertation at the University of Maryland, College Park, and though I was spending more and more time on animal issues, attending protests and learning the facts, I expected to teach English for the rest of my life. At the same time, I was increasingly drawn by the plight of farmed animals; the number of these tortured beings was astonishing. At the very bottom of this gigantic pile of forgotten victims were billions of birds, totally out of sight of consumers. Farmed animals were generally dismissed as beyond the pale of equal—or any—moral concern because they were bred to a substandard state of intelligence and biological fitness, it was argued, and because they were "just food" that was "going to be killed anyway."

My experience with Viva put these matters into perspective. Viva was expressive, responsive, communicative, affectionate, and alert. Viva was cursed with a "man-made" body, forced to bear many times the weight of a normal chicken, resulting in a weak heart, a crippled skeleton, and related genetic infirmities that prevented her—as they prevent all chickens (and turkeys) bred for meat production[11]—from claiming her birthright and earthrights. But there was nothing wanting in her personally. She already had a voice, but her voice needed to be amplified from within the oppressive system in which she was trapped. I knew Viva, but I also knew there were billions of Vivas out there, who were just as special.

Viva's death hit me hard, but she clarified my future. Viva was a valuable being, somebody worth fighting for. She was not "just a chicken." Viva was a chicken, a member of Earth's community, a dignified being with a claim to justice, compassion, and a life equal to anyone else's. I dedicated my book *Prisoned Chickens, Poisoned Eggs* to Viva, and to working for a future in which the voice of every hen is heard.[12]

pessimism of the intellect

I work toward this end, this longed-for future, but I am pessimistic about the fate of chickens. Chickens (and other so-called poultry) are propagated by the billions in industrialized hatcheries around the world. The human species has not shown any significant sign of evolving to a more compassionate way of being.

Though there are places in the world where chickens continue to live the free-roaming life of their jungle ancestors, billions of chickens now live indoors. They do not enjoy even the "pampered" life of farmyard chickens in the Victorian era, when roosters and hens were idealized as models of domestic felicity and decorum. Today the majority of hens and roosters exist only as unrealized potentials, slaughtered as babies without ever knowing the comfort of a mother hen's wing, or the reassuring sound of a rooster's crow.

unnatural suffering

As a college student, I was obsessed with trying to imagine what it would feel like to be in a place that was utterly inimical to one's sense of self, against one's will—to be forced into the abyss of total imprisonment, moral abandonment, and bewildering cruelty—a concentration camp or a death camp where everyday suffering is overwhelmed by human-induced suffering. For me, it is natural to try to imagine what it must be like for a nonhuman animal (like a chicken, or a turkey, or a sheep) to be forced into a human-contrived, inimical universe. For these individuals, the hell they experience is unnatural. There is nothing in the psyche of chickens to prepare them for having their beaks burned off, at birth, and being crammed inside a filthy building filled with toxic gases along with thousands of other suffering, terrified birds. How do these foraging creatures, with the leafy green world of the jungle embedded in their genes, experience entombment? How do turkeys—birds who evolved not only to run and fly, but to swim, roost high in trees at night, and roam with their mothers for five months after they hatch—how do they experience being stuffed into buildings as contaminated as cesspools? How does a grazing animal feel when forcibly herded onto a huge ship, jammed in a filthy pen, and freighted from Australia to Saudi Arabia or Iraq? How is it for a sheep to float sea-sickeningly across the Persian Gulf on the way to slaughter?

keeping faith

In thinking about the bizarre and hideous cruelties that our species inflicts on others, I believe that nonhuman animals suffer in ways that no human has ever dreamed of or experienced, and that there are elements in human nature that exult in creating strange new worlds of misery. With such thoughts, it is tempting to give up on a better world, which is why I find inspiration in the words of the writer Colman McCarthy, a peace advocate whose nonviolent teachings and lifestyle include nonhuman animals and vegetarianism. Asked by an animal rights activist, "Do you think we'll ever succeed?" McCarthy replied: "Don't worry about being successful; just be faithful."[13]

This advice has the advantage of realism over romanticism. Though we hold the moral high ground, and though we work with dedication, we may not prevail over the forces arrayed against nonhuman animals to build the world that we long for. We do not have full control over outcomes, but we do have control over whether we are, and will remain, faithful. And if we are not faithful, we surely will not succeed.

Faithfulness is not about having faith, but about *keeping* faith. This recognition has been a point of light shining into the otherwise dark places to which our species condemns countless billions of our fellow creatures for reasons that, despite various explanations, remain unclear.

karen davis, PhD, is founder and president of United Poultry Concerns (http://www.www.upc-online.org), which promotes compassionate and respectful treatment of domestic fowl. Her articles have appeared in *Animals and Women, Terrorists or Freedom Fighters,* and the *Encyclopedia of Animals and Humans.* Her books include *Prisoned Chickens, Poisoned Eggs: An Inside Look at the Modern Poultry Industry, More Than a Meal: The Turkey in History, Myth, Ritual, and*

Reality, and *The Holocaust and the Henmaid's Tale: A Case for Comparing Atrocities.* She was profiled in *The Washington Post* and is in the U.S. Animal Rights Hall of Fame "for outstanding contributions to animal liberation."

NOTES

1. I developed these perceptions into the argument of my book *The Holocaust and the Henmaid's Tale: A Case for Comparing Atrocities* published in 2005 by Lantern Books (New York).

2. Brian Davies. 1970. *Savage Luxury: The Slaughter of the Baby Seals.* London: Souvenir Press.

3. Tamara Jones. 1999. "For the Birds." *The Washington Post,* 14 November: F1, F4-F5. This article about Karen Davis and United Poultry Concerns won the Ark Trust Genesis Award for Outstanding Newspaper Feature about animals in 1999. www.upc-online.org/991114wpost_karen_davis.html.

4. "Slaughterhouse Worker Turned Activist: UPC Talks with Virgil Butler and Laura Alexander. 2004." *Poultry Press* (quarterly magazine of United Poultry Concerns) 4.3 (Fall): 1–4. www.upc-online.org/fall04/virgil.htm. Virgil Butler died in 2006. See "Virgil Butler, Ex-Tyson Slaughterhouse Voice for Chickens, Has Died. 2006–2007." *Poultry Press* 16.2 (Winter): 5–6. www.upc-online.org/winter0607/virgil.html.

5. This extended essay on "food," animal slaughter, and vegetarianism was written in 1892 as a preface to the Russian edition of Howard Williams's *Ethics of Diet* (1883). Williams's book is a biographical history of philosophic vegetarianism from antiquity through the early nineteenth century.

6. Alex Pacheco with Anna Francione. 1985. "The Silver Spring Monkeys." *In Defense of Animals.* Ed. Peter Singer. New York: Basil Blackwell. 135–47.

7. Chip Brown. 1983. "She's a Portrait of Zealotry in Plastic Shoes." *The Washington Post,* 13 November: B1.

8. A concise summary of turkey industry practices is provided by United Poultry Concerns' "Turkeys" brochure, which is also available on UPC's Web site at http://www.upc-online.org/turkeys/turkeysbro.html.

9. Karen Davis. 2001. *More than a Meal: The Turkey in History, Myth, Ritual, and Reality.* New York: Lantern Books.

10. Karen Davis. 1990. Viva, "The Chicken Hen (November 1985)." *Between the Species: A Journal of Ethics* 6.1: 33–35. www.upc-online.org/viva.html.

11. A concise summary of chicken industry practices is provided by United Poultry Concerns' "Chickens" brochure, which is also available on UPC's Web site at http://www.upc-online.org/chickens/chickensbro.html.

12. Karen Davis. 1996. *Prisoned Chickens, Poisoned Eggs: An Inside Look at the Modern Poultry Industry.* Summertown, Tenn.: Book Publishing Company. This book, revised and updated, was republished in 2009.

13. Bartlett, Kim. 1988. "An Interview with Colman McCarthy." *The Animals' Agenda.* September-October: 7–11. For many years McCarthy was a featured columnist with *The Washington Post* where he wrote outstandingly about animal abuse and animal rights. He continues to write and teach about peace and justice: "An ideal world is where wealth is shared, where love is recognized as the strongest force we have, and where charity is no longer needed because we have justice."

12

isn't justice supposed to be blind?

PRACTICING ANIMAL LAW

christine l. garcia

nonhuman animals are the most
abused individuals on the planet

I am an animal law attorney because there is great need for me to do this work. I often tell people that I am an animal rights attorney not necessarily because I love nonhuman animals, but because I believe that all living beings should be free of pain and torture. Yet nonhuman animals in our country are often not protected from pain or torture.

Humans are not an endangered species. Humans are exponentially growing at a rapid clip and spreading into every natural crevice of this planet—paving new roads in the natural habitat of deer and bunnies and building new homes where coyotes and mountain lions used to dwell. They are pushing other animals into smaller and smaller patches of the earth's terrain, which is reminiscent of the treatment of native Americans, who were "escorted" to barren reservations. Nonetheless, we humans are out to save each and every last human being as if Homo sapiens were on high red alert for going extinct.

The vast majority of our planet's energy and infrastructure serves and represents humans and human interests. This includes our laws. Many humans exploit humans, but I focus on nonhuman individuals because they have the least representation. There are plenty of attorneys who want to help rich companies or human property interests. (All the land on the planet was free in the beginning and belonged only to planet Earth. These plots of land were then claimed under human dominion, ownership, and control.) But there are not enough humans fighting those who routinely exploit nonhuman animals.

Representation is disproportionately in favor of human animals, and therefore it makes sense to represent nonhuman animals, assuming we are interested in justice for all. That's why I do what I do.

Practicing law is by nature unpleasant. I do not practice law for the money or for the joy of working with the lovely personalities attracted to the legal profession. I practice law to attempt to level out the playing field, be a voice for the voiceless: Currently too many attorneys represent only human interests. They shouldn't. The plight of nonhuman animals, imposed by humans, is unjust and unnecessary.

goal: end pain, torture, and oppression—animal liberation!

Another reason I fight for the rights of nonhuman animals is because they are a class of living beings who request only to "be." Nonhuman individuals are not asking for more oil, or a fancier car, or to take over the Middle East. They only desire to be free from harm and injury, to be able to live their lives naturally. Their needs are modest: food, water, shelter, and freedom to build whatever relationships they choose.

I have one rescued animal at this time. Across time, I have fostered at least 100 nonhuman individuals. My apartment has been a halfway house to rats, guinea pigs, pigeons, a chicken, cats, dogs, and fish . . . not to mention activists.

I find it strange that nonhumans can be represented, and have their life spared, only if a human vouches for them and comes forward as their "owner." Just being a dog isn't enough. You need to be dog-as-property, like a slave, with an owner to come forward and say that this dog/slave is yours and you want "it" to live. As slaves were once viewed as property, we continue to view nonhuman animals as property. If nobody comes forward to claim their "property," the dog cannot live. I look forward to the day when a nonhuman is allowed to live because laws protect nonhuman individuals for their own sakes, not because "it" is an object that belongs to a human. Animal liberation!

why are we perceived as anarchists?

I remember giving a speech at the Anarchist Café in Sacramento titled, "Why Every Anarchist Should Be a Vegan." A true anarchist opposes every form of institutionalized oppression, and factory farming is a government-sponsored conventional and institutionalized form of animal abuse.

But this is not my main point here. Government is my point—oppressive government. This essay has been patiently waiting on the sidelines (as well as a seven-layer dip recipe for lauren Orneles' Vegan Mexican Food Web site— http://www.veganmexicanfood.com/), alongside an overwhelming amount of legal work. I am forever bogged down by the government, which brings me back to the point: My legal opposition is almost always a state or city official who is fighting to either

- kill a dog,
- defend police officers who unlawfully arrested animal welfare picketers,
- protect human interests in needless animal testing, or
- resist passing animal protection laws that contain real power for fear of offending humans.

Given this, you can imagine my opposing counsel (the attorneys on the other side). I and my friend give them nicknames to add cheap thrills and laughter to our daily interactions with these repugnant humans, who somehow manage to live with themselves and sleep at night in spite of their indifference to nonhuman suffering and nonhuman lives.

My daily work is encumbered by the government. When I say that the government impacts my career, I am not kidding—it is profoundly true.

government prosecutions of "dangerous" dogs

I spend about 35 percent of my practice defending dogs on death row. City attorneys and county counsel often fight tooth and nail—down to the mat—in order to have a dog "humanely destroyed," rather than give a nonhuman his or her fair shake of justice. I will explain how this comes to pass.

I have clients whose neighbor has poisoned their companion animal, or trapped him or her (usually a cat), and permanently removed the nonhuman because of personal feuding. Complaints on dogs are my most common cases. A human (the Complaining Party) for one reason or another calls the local police station or animal control agency alleging that another person's dog is dangerous. Most of the time, the Complaining Party dislikes the neighbor for some unrelated reason and decides that the most painful and effective way to express these negative feelings is to give the neighbor's dog a death sentence. The Complaining Party reports aggressive behavior to the local animal control agency. Most commonly, officers tell my clients that they will be arrested if they don't hand over their dog. The officers (the government) try to appease my clients by noting that their dog will be returned in ten days (a blatant lie—officers are allowed to lie). The guardian of the dog then hands over the dog.

My clients almost always find out too late about our 4th amendment right,[1] which permits us to hold onto our dogs as "property." As citizens, we can demand a search warrant or court order and retain our dogs in the meantime. Too often, I find myself in court fighting against another self-righteous, callous, and disconnected city attorney or county counsel, hired by the government, who has seized someone's beloved nonhuman companion. This is my most common court scenario: our obnoxious government on steroids out to rid the world of "dangerous" dogs. Might I add, the vast majority of dogs on death row have never bitten anyone. Some dogs have merely "appeared dangerous"—lunged while on a leash or exhibited protective behavior—perfectly natural for a dog. These are tough cases because people in each city and county more or less create their own laws with regard to killing "dangerous" companion animals.[2]

case study: outstanding legal inequities and injustice for nonhuman animals

There is still no American legal code devoted to nonhuman animals. In California, animal laws can be found under the Civil Code, Penal Code, Food and Agricultural Code, and the Health and Safety Code, for example. Also in California, Dangerous Dog Hearings are governed under the California Food and Agriculture Code § 31621, which has relatively decent state definitions. However, as noted, state legal codes allow cities and counties to bypass state law in order to deal with "dangerous" dogs on their own, in a more restrictive manner. These laws are in desperate need of revision.

It astounds me that cities and states can kill a companion animal based on hearsay, such as an irritable neighbor's phone call. Nothing more is needed. "Rules of Evidence" protect humans from being convicted on hearsay alone (i.e., word of mouth—gossip, as opposed to direct personal witness accounts) or by an unauthenticated piece of paper. Rules of evidence do not apply in "dangerous" dog hearings. No simple phone call or scrap of paper will put a human on death row, but a dog can go straight from cozy house to death row—guilty until proven innocent.

Furthermore, for dogs on death row, the required burden of proof is simply a "preponderance of evidence" as opposed to "beyond a reasonable doubt," which is required to put a human on death row. My point is that humans are granted a jury to make sure that testimony is tried under strict rules of evidence, humans have a right to confront all witnesses against them, and the jury must decide beyond a reasonable doubt whether humans are to be convicted. In contrast, a dog is judged by one person, who is often not a judge or has not even attended law school, and that person needs to find only by a preponderance of the "evidence" (51 percent) to convict the dog. When a human does land on death row, the appeal process and options for appeal are nearly unlimited. Nonhuman individuals have no right to a jury, and no right to an appeal.

Let me put this another way. Humans get only eighteen months in jail for vehicular manslaughter, but if a dog merely shows an aggressive stance, she/he can be executed. After a bar brawl nobody gets the electric chair, but a dog will. It is not safe to be a dog in our humancentric society.

One of my most difficult court losses was for a family canine companion named Lucy, in December, 2007. Lucy was a seven-year-old pit bull who lived with loving human parents and three siblings: a mellow cat, an easygoing canine brother, and a two-year-old toddler named Liam. Lucy was truly a loved and warmly appreciated and accepted member of her family "pack." One isolated incident forever removed Lucy from this once happy family.

Lucy had "corrected" a neighboring Chihuahua for repeated aggressions against Liam. Unfortunately, Lucy's corrective action resulted in a deceased Chihuahua. The correction of the Chihuahua was done out of continued provocation and in self-defense of Lucy's brother, Liam. Even though humans can justify aggression—even deadly aggression—for self-defense, this star sibling was not permitted to justify her action.

This was Lucy's only aggressive response in her seven years of life. Prior to this incident, Lucy had been a highly regarded student-teacher dog; she trained other dogs how to behave appropriately around children in particular, and on many occasions conceded to neighborhood children pulling her ears. Expert dog behaviorists sent innumerable letters of recommendation and praise on Lucy's behalf. Nonetheless, the reigning judge refused to see Lucy's actions as justifiable, and the Court of Appeals refused Writ review. Lucy was executed.

government defense of animal testing

Roughly 45–50 percent of my practice consists in defending animal advocates arrested for legal vocal demonstrations and suing cities (along with codefendants such as a university or business) for unlawful arrest of animal advocates. Government universities now seem to have a campaign against free speech (and in favor of animal research) designed to protect unnecessary vivisection on primates, dogs, cats, rats, and so on. For example, universities often convince local police officers to arrest animal advocates for *lawful* picketing. District attorneys ultimately dismiss the university's claims, in the interest of justice, but the end result is the same: In one incident the picket was stopped prematurely, the university got rid of the picketers, and free speech on behalf of nonhuman animals was stifled. Police do not represent picketers' rights, which, from my recollection of law school—and that thingy called the Federal Constitution—is a violation of the Equal Protection Clause, which states that the government will protect everybody's rights equally.

Police protect the university's legal right to test on nonhuman individuals, not the citizen's right to protest against animal experimentation. Officers (the government) never arrest scientists or administrators at the request of picketers, even when picketers are harassed while protesting. At one picketing event, a neighbor beat his dog just to demonstrate that he could. As the dog yelped in pain, a picketer told the southern California officer that the neighbor was violating Penal Code § 597, Animal Abuse, and demanded a citizen's arrest. The police officer refused, laughed at the yelping dog, and threatened to arrest the picketer. The police had decided the right of an institution (the university) was more important than that of the people (the picketers) and the animal.

I have become painfully aware that the police (the government) have become the private security guards for animal testing universities and pharmaceutical companies. In practice, "Constitutional Rights" (such as free speech) have become defenses used to release activists from jail, not rights to be exercised and respected by police officers. In other words, many people believe that you have a "Right to Free Speech" and a "Right to Peaceful Assembly" simply because it is written in the Constitution. However, activists are nonetheless arrested and taken away from pickets for legal, constitutionally protected activities such as chanting in front of a vivisector's house. In court, we turn to the Constitution, which seems to be a document that most judges are not acquainted with. Judges need to be reminded that even animal activists are people protected by the Constitution. Just because they don't like the message of empathy for animals doesn't mean animal activists are excluded from protection. We must exercise the muscles of civil liberties; if we don't use them, we will certainly lose them.

government resistance to appropriate legislation

Another 15–20 percent of my work constitutes drafting legislation and lobbying. I'm not sure when our culture became a culture of conformity—maybe we have always been so. Sitting on the Animal Control and Welfare Commission, I have learned that it is nearly impossible to pass a law unless it has become trendy, mainstream, and noncontroversial. They (the government) won't touch legislation that is controversial. (And this is San Francisco for goodness sake!)

The most recent commissioned request for the city to look into animal welfare at the San Francisco Zoo provides a good example of our legal conservatism. The death of a human and a tiger at San Francisco Zoo called attention to the zoo, and thanks to media coverage, we (the Commission) were able to jump on a wave of public interest waiting to see something happen. In politics, unfortunately, if there is no mainstream public interest, there will be no new law, and no change. Timing is very important if we are to bring legal change.

Here's something else I learned in politics: When drafting a law to protect nonhuman individuals, try not to offend any human being, or all will be lost. My latest trial was an attempt to pass the Humanitarian Art Ordinance, which would have made abuse or killing a nonhuman for the purpose of art, such as creating a movie, illegal. The Humanitarian Art Ordinance did not break new ground; it was based on the existing law against animal cruelty and was both straightforward and constitutionally sound. If you commit animal abuse and cruelty to create art, it would be illegal. Still, the Ordinance did not have enough support to pass; I realize that this sounds like a cut-and-dry case, but this possible legislation kicked up quite a fuss in the community. Artists here in San Francisco, and in New York, were upset by the possibility of their "art" being limited. How can people feel entitled to take the life of a nonhuman animal in the name of "art"?

I drafted another straightforward ordinance for nonhuman animals that invited private attorneys to volunteer under the San Francisco District Attorney's Office to prosecute animal cruelty cases. This "Helping Hands for Animals Program Policy Resolution Proposal" was passed by the Animal Control and Welfare Commission on June 14, 2007, but still needs supervisor sponsorship. Perhaps such simple legislation takes great effort to pass simply because humans know that they benefit by exploiting other animals on a daily basis: for food, for testing shampoos and oven cleaners, for clothing.

Recently I have been dealing with two major government harassment issues. The first is personal. The California State Government is trying desperately to take my law license away to prevent me, a lawyer, from working on behalf of nonhuman animals. The second affects the animal advocacy community more broadly: The federal government, in the form of FBI agents, is questioning parents who are vegans and raise vegan children—with no subpoena and for no good reason. As far as the first issue goes, I will fight for my license in order to fight for nonhuman animals. As for the second issue, I continue to educate parents: We have the right to remain silent under the 5th Amendment of the U.S. Constitution.

human narcissistic entitlement: the source of exploitation and speciesism

I just love that bumper sticker that says "Humans aren't the only ones on this planet . . . We just act like it!"

Human narcissistic entitlement is an underlying belief that allows us to disregard nonhuman beings. Our society supports this human narcissistic entitlement with attorneys, consumer products, laws, businesses, and more. It's all about us! We are the center of the universe! We are entitled to anything that pleases us! That mink is for us to wear; that cow is for us to eat; that tree is for us to cut down and turn into an armoire; that monkey is for us to experiment on; and that elephant is here to entertain us.

Humans support a twisted hierarchy by which we mis-value the world and those around us: "Value" is based on the usefulness of an item or being to us. I call this the Hierarchy of Human Mis-Valuations. Not only do we place humans above other animals and the environment, but we place some humans above other humans and certain nonhuman animals over other nonhuman animals. For example, the life of a homeless person would be ranked lower than that of a wealthy person. Because humans are thought to be "more important," we may exploit all those below us—we may exploit all other creatures. This Mis-Valuation that humans have subscribed to is illustrated by the pyramid in fig. 1.

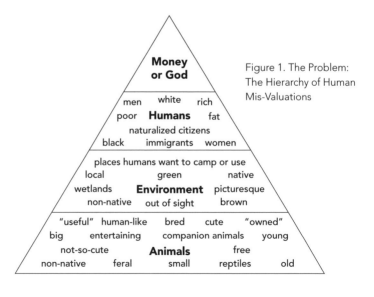

Figure 1. The Problem: The Hierarchy of Human Mis-Valuations

I would like to see a massive philosophical and practical shift in human existence toward respecting *all* life. We need to throw out this old hierarchical model, and when people make discriminatory and speciesist comments and actions, we need to point out what they are doing. It's that simple. For example, Consumer A comments, "Leather handbags are expensive!" and Human B responds: "Actually, leather handbags are underpriced by at least a million dollars when you figure in the misery the cow has endured." Or, Human A says, "Rats are so disgusting!" and Human B responds, "You just say that because their mammary glands aren't large enough for you to steal their milk and make cheddar cheese—I'm sure you'd feel differently if you ate rat flesh." (Hopefully, this response would help people to question the exploitation of cows and goats, and become disgusted with ingesting bodily secretions.) Education. That's how it happens. From person to person. You and me.

I propose a new vision and a new mindset in the form of a spiral (shown in fig. 2).

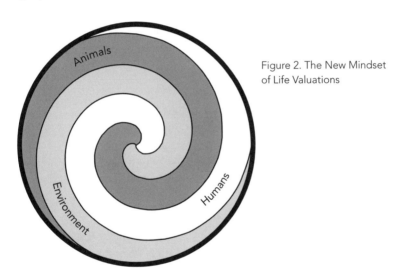

Figure 2. The New Mindset of Life Valuations

In this diagram there is no room for discrimination; humans, other animals, and the environment are all acknowledged and respected as earthly residents. Humans do not own the animals or the environment.

tipping the scales

How do we end government oppression and abandon our old hierarchical mis-valuations?

Change occurs when a few individuals push the masses to a new awareness. Government entities are comprised of individuals who are capable of changing their minds and ideologies. A new philosophy can move like wildfire over entire continents. All we need is a slight tipping of the scales for a new ideology to become mass culture.

It is likely that there will always be many "unconscious consumers" who follow whatever the mainstream establishes. These individuals will watch TV, eat, and buy whatever is on the shelf in front of them. They will continue to act as they do now. Not everybody is an independent thinker.

Those who are thinking must bring change.

Unfortunately, businesses usually don't change because a CEO rolls out of bed and decides to be a more ethical and an ecologically sound person. Businesses change based on consumer demand. Companies change because they want more money, or because they are afraid they are going to lose money. Businesses will pounce on opportunities to make a buck and cut costs. A company can save millions by replacing animal products with plant-based products. Perhaps animal activists can take advantage of our ailing economy by presenting options to companies that will save money and open new markets.

key concept: you are just as capable— and responsible—as others

One key to making changes is to realize that you are the change that you are looking for. Many people wait for opportunity to knock or search for that perfect job description. Why not craft your own job? Why not start your own organization? If you can't find it, create it!

I was a good student who dutifully completed assignments. I think students become accustomed to a pattern of outside stimulus (the teacher) and learn simply to respond accordingly. But this is not a healthy model for life. For me, this unhealthy model began to change at the University of California at Berkeley, where I earned a history major and rhetoric minor as an undergrad. Instructors at Berkeley encouraged students to question the source of the question, to question authority and to create our own theories based on our own understanding.

How does this apply to animal rights? At Berkeley, professors fostered my inner activist. I learned that my brain is just as capable as the brains of my much-admired instructors. I learned not to wait for someone else to say something that sounded right, but rather, to educate myself on the subject and to decide what makes sense for me. Specifically, I learned not to wait for that dream job but to craft my own path to help nonhuman animals. If I had never questioned authority, if I had continued along the prescribed track of attorneys, I would have become just another unconscious consumer in a conventional job and would probably be overweight from eating dead animals.

When the mindless actions of one person infringe on the lives of others, it's not okay, even if those "others" are not our species. We are animals, too. How have we so thoroughly separated ourselves from our roots as children of Earth? Please, begin to make daily choices that honor the Earth and our nonhuman animal brothers and sisters. What are you waiting for?

christine l. garcia, vegan animal rights attorney and founder of the Animal Law Office in San Francisco (http://www.animalattorney .com), earned her BA at the University of California at Berkeley, and her Juris Doctorate after two years at Loyola University in Chicago and one year at the University of California, Hastings College of the Law. Today she represents dogs on death row and activists criminally and civilly, and sues companies that exploit nonhuman animals. She also directs and produces the San Francisco Public Access Television show *Ethics and Animals* and offers presentations on veganism and animal rights. She was recently a Commissioner for San Francisco on the Animal Control and Welfare Commission, legislating locally for nonhuman animals.

NOTES

1. See, *Fuller v. Vines*, 36 F.3d 65 (Cal.) 1994.
2. See, *Cal. Food and Agricultural Code* § 31683, which states "[n]othing in this chapter shall be construed to prevent a city or county from adopting or enforcing its own program for the control of potentially dangerous or vicious dogs that may incorporate all, part, or none of this chapter, or that may punish a violation of this chapter as a misdemeanor or may impose a more restrictive program to control potentially dangerous or vicious dogs."

13

an appetite for justice

lauren ornelas

It was a hot day in North Carolina and the sheds were all locked, except for one, which contained a dead, bloated pig and a smaller pig. As I walked in, I saw what I had been smelling. On each side of me, there were rows upon rows of pigs in pens. Hundreds of them. Looking down the middle aisle, I saw a huge bloated pig and what looked like a plastic bag. I began going pen by pen to videotape the victims—one pig with an injured leg who struggled to lie down, another with an abnormal growth under his belly—all very curious, yet with pleading in their eyes. Finally, I made my way down to the end of the alley, to the bloated pig. As I started to videotape and photograph this poor, diseased individual, I realized that the plastic bag I had seen behind the dead pig was actually a smaller pig who was still alive, but very weak. The pig stretched his hooves under the bars of the pen as if trying to reach the other pigs, who did the same. This pig was very sick. Instead of caring for him, the workers had thrown him in the middle of the aisle where he would have no access to food or water and where he would eventually die. The same must have happened to the bloated pig.

I had investigated numerous factory farms. Why did this incident hit me so hard? Why do those two pigs remain etched in my mind? Looking back, at that moment I came face to face with ongoing, blatant, heartless disregard for millions of sentient nonhuman animals in our food industries.

At each farm I investigated I picked out one individual and did everything I could for him or her. I did not always choose one who was dying; sometimes I would focus on an individual who was somehow able to show a semblance of his or her natural being even while suffering in the worst of circumstances.

If I were caught trespassing, I would remember that individual, and during campaign work on behalf of these individuals, whenever I spoke, he or she was in my mind at all times, keeping me focused on the importance of speaking for those whom we don't hear.

Animal investigations are emotionally draining. I felt helpless watching people in an auction hall in Petaluma poke and prod baby calves whose umbilical cords were still wet. I was horrified watching workers hang ducks upside down on the slaughter line, while some fell off in a desperate attempt to escape. I was deeply saddened by the haunting echoes of confined pregnant pigs banging their heads against bars of crates so narrow that they couldn't turn around.

I grew up in Texas—not exactly a place people think of when they imagine a plethora of vegan options. When I was a kid, I knew nothing about factory farming, or the environmental or social impacts of eating farmed animals, but I did see cows—lots of cows. When we traveled to and from Corpus Christi, I saw fields of cows. Even then I realized that if I ate one, I would destroy their family. Maybe I was sensitive to their families because of my parents' divorce when I was just four. I hated the idea of families being separated; I had an intense desire not to hurt anybody's family. Again, being young, I imagined what it was like for the cow's family when a member went missing, and they didn't know why, or where they had gone.

The first poem I ever wrote was about ants, and how upset I was when people killed them. In my first writing, I was already speaking out for the (very) little critter! I have an old autograph book; friends remember me being a vegetarian in the fifth grade, but I don't think I was exactly consistent. I became a vegetarian (as much as a kid can) after my mom explained to me where "chicken" came from. I decided right then and there that I didn't want to eat anyone. No one else in my family is vegetarian, but I sometimes consider myself to be an extreme version of my mother. I remember her bringing home a little plastic deer and bullet casing from work, and explaining to me how some of the guys teased her because she didn't like hunting. This clearly made an impression on me, and validated my desire to speak up for those who are extremely vulnerable. I became a vegan in the '80s, in high school, at which time I also entered the animal rights movement. During an ecology class slide show on "wildlife management," which explained why hunting was necessary, I repeatedly raised my hand to ask questions. (Without being a troublemaker, I tended to be a bit rebellious.) Finally the teacher responded, "Why don't you talk to someone who cares?"

"I don't know anyone," I replied. The teacher gave me an article from our local paper about a fur protest, and that was my introduction to the animal rights movement. I soon started an animal rights group at the high school, thanks mostly to a couple in San Antonio who ran Voice for Animals, a city-wide group. They taught me much of what I know. Meanwhile, Henry David Thoreau and Cesar Chavez enhanced my growing sense of justice.

I attended two universities and started animal advocacy groups at both. Eventually, a group of us started Action for Animals, in Austin. We were mostly a "seasonal" group—we promoted and honored annual events such as Meatout and Fur Free Friday, and held monthly meetings. We organized only a few of our own campaigns, but I clearly remember our first "victory."

We provided information on school dissection to local school administrators, but their response was sluggish. I called every single week for months until the school district agreed to offer alternatives to dissection in high schools. We got the word out about this new option by placing ads in student papers. While running Action for Animals I learned the importance of persistence, and networking with other groups. This background in grassroots activism brought about a strong sense of loyalty to other individuals and groups involved in the animal rights movement (many of whom I had met or joined when I was in my teens).

Animal advocates speak often of compassion. Compassion is important, but for me, animal advocacy is about fighting injustice and being proactive to help solve the world's problems. Before I got fully immersed in animal rights, I was involved in other social justice issues, such as fighting the death penalty. But I felt I didn't have much impact. I was also involved in the grape boycott and antiapartheid issues, and this is where I realized I could actually make a difference, simply by choosing to buy other products.

In 1995, still living in Texas, I took a job with In Defense of Animals (IDA), and I focused primarily on the plight of nonhumans exploited in circuses, vivisection at local universities, international animal issues, and a long campaign against Procter & Gamble's product testing on nonhuman animals. One of my mentors was a former vivisector who "saw the truth," and began to speak out against experimentation on living beings. Consequently, I focused on fighting vivisection and product testing. (Unfortunately, the campaign against companies that do product testing with these individual beings is not as visible today as it was in the late '80s and early '90s. Household products and cosmetics continue to be tested on nonhuman animals, even though these tests are not required by law. For example, rabbits have toxic chemicals placed directly into their eyes and high concentrations of certain products are put on their skin—even though nonanimal alternatives for such tests already exist. Thankfully there are a handful of groups that continue to work on this issue.)

Less than a year later I moved from Texas to New Mexico, where I had my first opportunity to combine passion for social justice with animal rights. In Albuquerque there is a sacred site called the Petroglyph National Monument, through which the government was planning to build a highway. A small bird would be threatened, and in any event, it was clearly an injustice to build a highway through a sacred site. Though a group of dedicated activists fought a long, hard battle, the road opened in June of 2007.

While still at IDA, I met Juliet Gellatley, founder of Vegetarians International Voice for Animals (Viva!), based in the UK, a group that focused on factory-farmed animals. I was taken by her passion, and felt I had found my calling. She asked me to start Viva!USA, a vegan organization that conducted investigations and created campaigns (mostly against corporations) using consumer pressure to bring change to factory farms. I started the organization as a volunteer, holding temporary jobs to support myself. Soon I was able to work part-time for Viva!USA, while still working part-time for a law firm, until there was finally enough donor support to pay full-time wages.

During this time I conducted my first investigation, focusing on a tiny veal production farm in Northern California. I remember the frustration in the calves' eyes while they were in crates, not able to turn around. Yes, I had seen videos and photos of calves raised for veal, but the reality was much more difficult to bear. When I walked off the property, leaving those calves behind, I felt like a speciesist. I still carry guilt from leaving those calves behind, but exposing these horrific images was important. Still, if they had been human beings, I would not have left until every last one was freed, and/or I would have released them myself. But this time, with these calves, I did not. It would be different in future investigations.

Viva!USA's first major investigation and campaign duplicated Viva!UK's campaign against duck flesh. At first I objected, noting that people in the United States didn't eat ducks. Then I asked myself, "How often do I go by the 'meat' department in the grocery store?" So I did—and sure enough, there it was: duck "meat."

Most ducks killed for food in the United States are Pekin ducks, the white ducks we sometimes see swimming on lakes and ponds. Other ducks killed for food are Muscovys, native to Brazil, who perch in trees. Both types of ducks are kept in sheds, like the chickens we kill for food. But ducks are waterfowl, and need water in order to maintain their body temperature and to keep their eyes clean—to prevent blindness. Even so, these birds are deprived of bathing water, and due to the conditions in which they are forced to live, the tips of their bills are cut off to prevent them from harming each other.

Getting the message out about ducks would be challenging. Our goal was to get footage to U.S. grocery stores and convince them to stop selling duck flesh. Given that duck "meat" was such a small market in comparison with chicken or pigs, it seemed possible. After one letter and video, a few stores dropped duck "meat"—but only "meat" purchased from the farms we had investigated. The small chain Earth Fare, in the southeast, was the first to act. (When Earth Fare wrote to the duck farm we had investigated, to see if our allegations were true, they were surprised when the duck farm would not respond.) Our next targets were Trader Joe's and Wal-Mart. Trader Joe's sold duck flesh from two of the companies we had investigated, and Wal-Mart from one. After about nine months, Trader Joe's stopped carrying all duck "meat." Wild Oats and a few other small chains (such as the Davis Food Co-op), stopped selling duck "meat" from farms we had investigated. Our duck campaign also impacted Pier 1 Imports—they stopped selling products with feathers.

When our duck "meat" campaign was well underway, we received a call from an employee at Whole Foods Market (WFM), telling us that they carried duck "meat" from both of the farms we had investigated. Eventually WFM announced at a shareholder's meeting that they would stop carrying duck from one of the two farms. We wanted both to be dropped, so we renewed our energies against duck "meat" sales at WFM.

In 2003, with the help of animal activists who were WFM shareholders, we attended a shareholder's meeting. We held a protest outside, and a few of us went inside. We spoke, but we were not well received. After the meeting I approached CEO and founder John Mackey. Although he and I have different recollections of this conversation, I remember saying that he seemed compassionate and intelligent and that I couldn't understand how he could accept the horrific conditions on that duck farm. With shareholders all around, he commented on my passion and offered his email address so that we might continue the dialogue. And we did. Repeatedly—until he cut off communication. Then, a number of months later he wrote to tell me that he had done a lot of reading on these issues and had decided to go vegan and revamp WFM policy concerning requirements for raising and killing farmed animals.

John Mackey's decision for WFM gave credibility to the plight of farmed animals; he was willing to listen and open to change. For me, this incident was a valuable lesson in maintaining personal integrity, a lesson that can't be exaggerated. WFM's executives were able to visit the duck farm and see the conditions of the ducks for themselves. If our information had been misleading, we would have been discredited, and WFM would not have changed their policies. Viva!USA didn't gain much media attention until our campaign led WFM to rethink policies regarding the way farmed animals are killed for food.

We didn't have a lot of money, or a large staff; we didn't have celebrities promoting our work. We found success through self-generated grassroots momentum. The power of grassroots advocacy should never be underestimated! Viva!USA was a very small organization at that time, but we made a big difference.

I have been involved in the animal rights movement now for over twenty years. During this time I've also noted issues of abuse against humans. To me, oppression is oppression in whatever form it takes, and although I am far from perfect, I try to do my best not to support *any* injustice.

In 2001, through a BBC news segment, I learned that slavery was endemic to the chocolate industry in the Republic of the Ivory Coast. I knew that labor practices were abhorrent around the world, and I always did my best to avoid products from specific industries, but I knew nothing about the chocolate industry until that day. I distinctly remember a BBC interview with a worker from a chocolate factory who had escaped industry bondage. They asked him what he would like to say to Westerners who eat chocolate: "Tell them that when they bite into chocolate they are eating my suffering."

This is exactly what a nonhuman animal might say to those eating parts of their bodies, and their bodily products. I stopped eating all chocolate.

Later, I found chocolate suppliers that were *not* from the Ivory Coast. I incorporated some of this information into Viva!USA literature. I became more outspoken about other forms of oppression, and in 2006 I had the opportunity to go to the World Social Forum (WSF) in Caracas, Venezuela, to give a talk on Corporate Animal Farms: "Exploiting Animals, Workers and the Environment, and Why You Should Work to Stop It." It was an incredible cultural experience. I met people from all over Latin America: Brazil, Cuba, Mexico, and more. Most of them were activists—like the Bolivian who fought Bechtel's attempt to privatize their water. I heard President Hugo Chavez speak about the importance of protecting land. Being a Chicana, I felt very comfortable there but was surprised at how different Latin American food is from traditional Mexican food. (Still, I found that eating vegan is not difficult—especially if you can speak Spanish.)

Many of the issues being discussed at the WSF involved food—from labor and immigration issues to water, nonhuman animals, and the environment—and I began thinking about what would eventually become my new focus—the Food Empowerment Project. Responsible eating seemed key in fighting against many injustices. In fact, my time at the WSF helped me create the tag line for the Food Empowerment Project: *Because Your Food Choices Can Change the World.*

I was further inspired by the South Central farmers in Los Angeles, who created a 14-acre urban farm and community garden in industrial Los Angeles, which fed around three hundred and fifty low-income (mostly Latino) families. The farm instilled pride in community, as well as self-reliance and power. Unfortunately, the farm was torn down for development.

At last I had found a movement in which almost anyone could participate through consumer power, and it didn't take me long to focus on creating an organization to fight oppression and injustice involving food issues.

Everyone has a chance to address the most significant problems facing animals—human and nonhuman—and the environment through food choices. Every dollar spent is a vote. People need to recognize the power of food choices, not only to represent what they believe, but also to change the world. Every dollar is either a vote for cruelty or a vote against cruelty. When you buy something, you reveal your values. No one is perfect, but everyone ought to remember that food is power, and everyone ought to use this power to work for justice and compassion.

In 2006 I began the Food Empowerment Project (F.E.P.), a vegan organization that focuses on justice issues involving farmed animals, workers, and the environment. In many communities of color and low-income communities, there are few healthy food options. In some areas, there are few, if any, grocery stores, yet fast-food and liquor stores abound. One goal of F.E.P. is to limit fast-food outlets, introduce healthier options in grocery stores and local markets, and help people become more self-sufficient by growing their own food and reconnecting with the land. F.E.P. recognizes that food justice requires access to healthy food—healthy food is a right, not a privilege.

We especially hope to reach out to the Spanish-speaking community, as well as highlight the plight of workers, locally and internationally. As a vegan organization we encourage people to eat more fruits and vegetables, so we need to be sure that field workers who harvest these foods are treated with dignity and paid fair wages. Additionally, we attempt to highlight other food injustices, such as slavery in the cocoa (chocolate) production of the Ivory Coast, and Coca-Cola's responsibility for privatizing water in India.

We also work to raise awareness concerning environmental racism in the United States, where policies and laws allow a disproportionate number of high-pollution industries (i.e., trash incinerator projects, refineries, factory farms, etc.) to locate in low-income communities and communities of color. This includes calling attention to factory-farm waste and pollution, which harms ecosystems, as well as nearby communities and individuals.

As the Food Empowerment Project continues to evolve, and I support myself by working for an organization that focuses on issues of human and environmental justice, I have been pleased by those in the animal rights movement who see F.E.P.'s goals and offer enthusiastic support. Martin Luther

King Jr. became a significant threat to the status quo only when he began to connect various social justice issues, speaking out against the war in Vietnam, and bringing awareness to the plight of the poor. Similarly, animal advocates will draw more people, and become part of a more viable movement, when we explicitly connect injustices affecting the animals—human and nonhuman—and the environment. We are all comrades in our quest for justice, and the more social activists recognize this, the stronger our voices will become. In this way we will create a force to be reckoned with, a strong force bent on change, determined to secure justice.

Strength. Strength reminds me of Taylor, whom a friend and I met at one of Foster Farms's turkey slaughterhouses. We sometimes cruised by these slaughterhouses to see whether anything noteworthy was happening—turkeys being shackled, beaten, or neglected—anything we might witness. One day, when we drove by en route to rescue chickens and roosters in a cruelty case in Southern California, my friend interjected, "There's a turkey!"

My first thought was, "No way. We are on a long road trip; how can we take a turkey with us?" Even as I hoped she was wrong, I drove back to look. There she was, running around in front of the office, peering at her reflection in the windowed door. (Turkeys are most inquisitive and personable individuals.) But we also noticed that she was covered in something.

There we were. There she was. "We don't have a choice," I noted out loud. "We need to take her." I stopped the truck right in front of the "No Trespassing" sign. A security guard stared vacantly out—apparently not noticing us—while my friend jumped the fence. Understandably, the frightened turkey ran away. My friend, wishing she could communicate with the bird, chased her around at a frantic pace. Eventually, she threw her jacket over the frightened escapee, subdued her, and handed her over a very high fence into my arms—right over the "No Trespassing" sign.

Taylor was covered in blood. More than likely, she had fallen from the shackles at the slaughterhouse into the blood of fellow turkeys . . . then ran away. We also noticed that her beak, and all of her toes, were cut. Turkeys and hens raised for eggs suffer the nightmare of having the tips of their beaks cut off; turkeys have their toes cut off as well but hers were cut so close. In fact, it was difficult for her to eat or walk. I pondered all that she had been through: born in a sterile hatchery, her beak and toes cut; sharing a shed with thousands of other turkeys; her body growing too large for her to walk comfortably (cut toes and all); transported to slaughter and hung upside down; falling, and witnessing her mates slowly moving forward to have their throats slit. Driving with this poor turkey seated beside me, I just couldn't fathom her suffering.

Taylor was one of the lucky ones; she lived out her life at a sanctuary.

More importantly, she was a survivor. And I tell her story because it needs to be told for her, and for others—for each individual who experiences injustice and pain. It is important to remember that every day, each one of us has the opportunity to save a life and make a difference. That is why it is important that we all understand that "Food Is Power!" and that our food choices can change the world for the better.

lauren ornelas, an animal rights advocate for more than twenty years, is the founder and executive director of the Food Empowerment Project (www.foodispower.org, www.veganmexicanfood.com), which seeks justice by recognizing the power of one's food choices. After four years as the National Campaign Coordinator for In Defense of Animals, Viva!UK asked lauren to start and run Viva!USA, a national nonprofit vegan advocacy organization. As Viva!USA's executive director, in cooperation with activists across the country, she brought corporate changes to such powerful companies as Whole Foods Market, Trader Joe's, and Pier 1 Imports. She is currently campaign director with the Silicon Valley Toxics Coalition.

14

a magical talisman

allison lance

Twenty years ago, my life changed when I happened onto a Last Chance for Animals TV commercial on vivisection. I looked up the word "vivisection" in the dictionary, phoned the number on the screen, and the next day I was off to my first protest, called "World Week," in front of Cedar Sinai in Los Angeles. Although I didn't know exactly what I wanted to do for nonhuman animals, I knew I had found my purpose, and I had left the "Clydesdale Horse World" behind—you know, the Budweiser Horses with the blinders on, which is my view of how most people walk through life.

I bounced from one animal rights organization to another, until I found PRISM—People for Reason in Science and Medicine. PRISM was a group of extremely bright women focused on the abolition of vivisection. I leaned heavily on the women at PRISM for knowledge. Wanda Ballard, Sandra Bell, Debra Goldsmith, and Sue Marston became my mentors. Wanda also became my best friend.

I still find vivisection to be the most horrible of all wrongs committed against nonhuman animals. Torturing other beings in laboratories is evil and sinister beyond what I am able to imagine or describe. These individuals sit in cages for years, hooked to electrodes and injected with poisons. Experimenters even strap monkeys' penises to car batteries and surge high voltage through their most vulnerable body parts. A human being willingly inflicts this unimaginable pain, often leaning against a wall, writing down "data," perhaps chewing on a piece of gum, and calmly observing the suffering. Scientists in laboratories poke, prod, inject, smash heads—and are unmoved by a sentient being's painful reaction. How do these people go home at night and sit down to dinner with their families and pet dog? Anyway, everyone with a brain knows that you cannot safely extrapolate substance tests, or any test for that matter, from one species to another.

Soon I was hunt sabbing in Arizona. To sabotage ("sab") a hunt, we bring air horns, pots and pans—and no weapons. We stalk hunters as hunters stalk nonhuman animals, and just when they're ready to shoot, we set off air horns and bang pans, and send the would-be victim running full speed to safety.

During this time, as chance would have it, I came upon a "blind" in the mountain ranges of Arizona. A blind is usually a wood shack designed to blend into the natural environment, where a fearless hunter/murderer sits with his penis in one hand and his trusty weapon in the other. As a thirsty individual arrives for a drink of water, the fearless hunter, hiding in his blind just a few feet away, opens fire. Perverted hunters build these blinds next to watering holes to assure victims—a hunter in a blind can kill without even letting go of his penis. (Hunters/murderers tend to be very lazy; blinds make killing very easy.) When I spotted the blind, my duty was clear: "destroy." I removed the wood shack plank by plank, knowing that this watering hole would be safe for bighorn sheep, at least for a while, at least until small-minded cowards built a new enclosure for masturbation. [Marc Gaede, an anthropologist and dear friend, has written a fascinating article on the sexual perversion of hunters and killing (*High Country News*, Vol. 31, No. 4, March 1, 1999).]

Hunters/murderers feel tough and fearless, though they shoot unarmed individuals who are unaware, as they go about their daily tasks (drinking, foraging, or lovemaking), falling under the fire of modern weaponry. I watched a video of two grizzly bears making love, while hunters, yards away, were filming and laughing into the camera. When the bears were finished, the two giants rolled in the tall grass, and the men opened fire. I felt every bullet those bears endured—as though I were a voodoo doll, taking each shot the bears received. The hunters were elated with their kill. I suppose they posed and stuffed the bears, in a pose towering on their hind legs—you know, the pose with canines gleaming, as if the hunters had killed a ferocious and dangerous bear that was about ready to attack them.

Hunt saboteurs know the inherent risks they face, but are driven to protect the innocent. More than once when I was sabotaging a hunt I have come face to face with hunters. In my experience, hunters are not sane: They are cowards with weapons—twitchy individuals, like armed crack addicts—not a good combination. I have had a rifle pointed at my chest and belly, and once between my eyes, and a knife held at my gut, all by men that have daughters, wives, girlfriends, sisters, and mothers. Every year, in a field next to my home in Riverside, California, a group of adult men dress up in full—and I mean full—camouflage, like a military SWAT team, to hunt the most dangerous of creatures—the dove, the Bird of Peace, a symbol of love worldwide. These yahoos drink beer, pack lunches, and have a kid or three in tow. Several of the men bring baby daughters to this bizarre "family day" of killing doves. Desensitize your children, and why not get drunk while you're wielding fire-arms? These breeders are laying the groundwork early on: follow in daddy's footsteps—kill the innocent and defenseless.

I have been arrested for disrupting hunts. In northern California, after a successful day of sabbing, we came back to our car to find a hunter posed to slash our tires. I ran up and pushed him down, and he came up swinging a knife frighteningly near my gut—the madness of hunters. Yet *I* was arrested, and did community service at my local shelter—no harm done. Sabbers are protecting life, and yet we are called violent. Unarmed, we use our bodies as shields to protect nonhuman animals in their homes, and yet we are arrested.

I am proud of being arrested for protecting the defenseless. Once I was arrested for disrupting a "'lab animal' torture death test," which they tried to disguise as safety testing at the University of California in Santa Barbara. To add insult to injury, these tests were done on the most innocent and defenseless of creatures: rabbits. Rabbits were being bled out by their ears under the guise of drug tests, I think the drug was aspirin. For hours we successfully blocked these rabbits from entering the lab. Frustrated, the vivisectors loaded the rab-bits into a truck to take them back to the vivarium. We hopped in the back of the truck, but the Santa Barbara Police had arrived, and off to jail we went.

I also protested the fur and cosmetics industries. From luxury coats to dyed pink underwear, Fendi's fur store in Beverly Hills on Rodeo Drive sells skins from anally electrocuted, clubbed to death, and leghold-trapped animals to human beings who have too much money and too little compassion. My friends and I chained our arms together in heavy steel cylinders, and refused to leave. For our efforts, we were hauled off to jail for six days, during which time we remained on a hunger strike.

Nordstrom's is no better than Fendi's, so I decided to sit on a ledge above the escalator with my feet dangling, where I could gain the attention of women in the cosmetic department *and* the fur salon. With my booming voice I gave shoppers an earful of statistics on fur and cosmetics to help them rethink their consumer needs. I had their undivided attention, with a U-shaped bicycle lock around my neck, locked to a pole that seemed conveniently made for a protest. The LAPD were soon my escorts—another day, another arrest.

Just in case you were wondering, let me say clearly that I support and believe in the ALF and ELF (Animal and Earth Liberation Front, respectively). I support direct action for nonhuman animals and the earth. I had somehow traveled from big-eyed, fuzzy animal-lover to a deep-hearted, comprehensive view of animal liberation. When I became an animal rights activist, it was the beginning of the end of my relationship with the true love of my life. He "liked" nonhuman animals, but my commitment to animal activism eventually took its toll. My ex is a beautiful man: big, strong, gentle, and as tough as they come. He is the president of an outlaw motorcycle club, whose world I thoroughly enjoyed. He and his club brothers remain the funniest, most loyal bunch of men I have ever known. My hunk of man had three children. I am not big on kids, but these three found a place in my heart . . . soooooo, I had to teach them about social activism, right?

When I heard that Eva Park of Orange County People for Animals (OCPA) was directing a rodeo protest, off I went with my husband's three children. Before I even got home, my husband saw his three little ones and his activist wife on the news, holding banners and protesting rodeos. Did I mention that his nickname was "Tex" (from Texas), or that his family is fond of rodeos? Tex and I eventually went our own ways.

Some time after I left my husband, I read an article about a man who owned a submarine and a boat, and sank whaling ships. I told my friends, "One of these days I am going to marry that man."

"Yeah, sure," they said. So in 1997 I attended an animal rights conference in Washington, D.C., where I met Paul Watson of the Sea Shepherd Conservation Society (SSCS). After his speech I approached and said to him, "My name is Allison Lance and I have always wanted to marry you." He just looked at me.

Six months later I received a phone call from a friend: "Paul Watson is looking for you." I phoned him that day. The next night we met for dinner; we were inseparable—our marriage lasted ten years.

During my time on the high seas with Paul, I saw major changes: fewer birds, whales, and dolphins, and an astounding amount of pollution. It infuriates me to watch a sandal float by, or a plastic jug, when we are on a major ocean crossing, in the middle of nowhere. These days human "footprints" go everywhere.

On my first SSCS campaign, I was arrested for protecting gray whales against the "red-haired freckle-faced" Makah Indians of Washington State. Under the aboriginal clause of IWC regulations, in order to hunt whales a tribe needs to have an unbroken tradition of whaling, and they also need to prove that such killing is necessary for subsistence. The Makah could do neither. Consequently, the Makah did not have permission from the IWC (International Whaling Commission) to conduct an aboriginal hunt. So, I and another SSCS crew member climbed into a Zodiac and motored off to protect the whales. When a thug from the Makah tribe stood up to throw a harpoon—breaking international law—I maneuvered the Zodiac between the whale and the harpoon. In doing so, I swamped their boat with water. Luckily, the government was there to be sure all laws were upheld—okay, not the laws, but rather illegal "traditions." The U.S. Coast Guard brought their big ship alongside our tiny zodiac, and told us to come aboard. We thought about running, but our boat was no match in size or speed, so we were pulled from our boat. Why was the Coast Guard protecting the Makah's illegal slaughter of the world's most intelligent being?

Despite Biology 101, brain-to-body ratio is not an indication of intelligence. If this were so, the hummingbird is the world's most intelligent animal—beating out many others, including the human animal, by a good bit. Brain size in itself, however, is important, and the largest brains ever developed on this planet belong to whales. The quality of brain tissue is even more important for assessing intelligence. With greater, more pronounced neocortex convolutions—four lobes—and overall greater size (the brain of the sperm whale is 9,000 cc; the brain of the orca is 6,000 cc.), whale brains are paragons of brain evolution. By contrast, the human brain is a mere 1,300 cc.

Whaling is illegal, and has been since 1986. Only one whale hunt remains legal in America, an Inuit bowhead hunt in Alaska. Although we detest the Inuit slaughter of whales for mere "tradition," SSCS does not intervene because this hunt is considered legal.

The Makah, however, were not engaged in a legal hunt. These thugs killed a defenseless three-year-old (baby) gray whale. A speedboat hauled their lazy asses close enough for a shot; they threw the traditional harpoon—just for a show of tradition—and then blasted the life from the young gray whale with a fifty-caliber tank gun.

A gray whale is a bottom feeder, and not very tasty. The Makah call this whale "the whale that makes you shit." Most of the whale meat ended up in the dump. I also watched the Makah shoot a Stellar sea lion, a protected species. Though I dove over the side of our small boat, I could only hold the sea lion as she took her last breath, bubbles pouring from her lips. Working with SSCS was just as heartbreaking as working to protect nonhuman land animals.

SSCS protects the seas from illegal operations. Catching poachers in the act is ominous. This work requires that we take on both individuals and nations, but at least sometimes we have the law on our side. With SSCS I had a chance, sometimes, to remain free while *killers* were arrested. In Cocos Island we apprehended an Ecuadorian longline operation. SSCS members gathered these illegal skiffs into a nearby cove to prevent fishermen from dumping their catch, or making a run for it. They could not run far, in any case, because we had arrested the mother ship, which carries the skiffs, and the closest land is

Costa Rica, some three hundred miles away. They never see us coming in our big, black ship. Out of the dark, out of the fog, SSCS emerges to close down illegal killing operations. SSCS seizes the mother ship of a long-lining operation, collects skiffs and catch, and hands the perpetrators over to authorities.

Though my actions were legal, they were no less painful. What I witnessed on that Ecuadorian longliner ripped my heart open, and remains one of the saddest moments of my life. I was the only SSCS crew member who went aboard the mother ship. In their hold I witnessed hundreds of beautiful sharks, from hammerheads to white tips, their gorgeous bodies thrown one on top of the other. Most were still alive, but the men had cut their fins off, and they had cut the eyes out of the hammerheads. The eyes are some sort of a good luck charm, and the fins are cooked in soup by compassionless, brain-dead people. The cartilage is sold as some snake-oil remedy to ward off cancer and to those willing to buy glucosamine that is made with shark's fins. People will swallow anything that they think will provide an easy fix.

The gullibility of humans is astonishing, and too often we buy into things at the expense of other species and the planet. Stay away from all animal products—that includes fish; fish are not vegetables! (I am aghast when people say "Yes, I am a vegetarian . . . I only eat fish." Go vegan! Guaranteed, you will live a healthier life, as will the planet and our fellow beings.

But I digress. The illegal fishermen were angry with me, and with SSCS. Luckily, I was with rangers armed with rifles (provided by SSCS). I told those fishermen how despicable they were and that they needed to find a new way to feed their families.

I am sick and tired of hearing about poor fishermen. These men were breaking the law. Why should I feel sorry for them? I could see that they were indifferent to the suffering and death they caused, which made me feel hateful toward the human species. At such times I try to remember the words of John Quincy Adams (1767–1848): "Courage and perseverance have a magical talisman, before which difficulties disappear and obstacles vanish into air." They were arrested; I walked free, back to our ship, confident that they will kill no more sharks.

My most visible campaign with SSCS was with Alex Cornelissen, Nik Hensey, and Thomas Heinemann. In 2003 Alex and I were arrested for freeing fifteen dolphins in Taiji, Japan. We did our reconnaissance—scouting out the situation before planning our action. We rented a dumpy little trailer in Taiji, and patrolled the harbor every day, waiting for the killers to make the first move.

We spent so much time with these killers that I learned a little bit about one of them. Dolphin killers are not impoverished fisherman, as they would like us to believe. One of the dolphin killers told me that he travels to America to hunt buffalos on a ranch in Wyoming. (Where is that asshole Ted Nugent's canned hunt ranch?) This dolphin-killer pays for canned hunts, where wild animals are trapped in an enclosed area so that even the worst hunter can walk up and fire away. Some of these nonhuman animals are so accustomed to people that they don't even run. Others have been injured, or declawed, so they can neither fight nor escape.

Finally, one morning we watched the dolphin killers head out to sea with thirteen boats, and we waited. In the early afternoon they came back with a pod of dolphins. Dolphins are extremely loyal, and will not leave injured members behind. To catch a pod, killers injure a couple of dolphins. This keeps the pod nearby, trying to help the wounded. Dolphin hunters also use "sounders," long metal poles that are dropped into the water, that disrupt the dolphins' sonar—their ability to communicate and travel. First, part of their community is injured, and then the dolphins are disoriented by the sound of men banging on metal pipes. Ultimately the killers drive the dolphins into a bay and rope off the bay.

Alex and I hid in the hills that surround the bay on each side, and waited for the dolphin catchers to leave. Frightened and hurt, the male dolphins desperately tried to find an escape route for their pod. We could see them swimming back and forth against the lines. We sat up in the hills, very still. I had my wet suit on under my clothing, saddened to tears. I watched the pod, knowing how many thousands of dolphins are captured in this way when we are not waiting to help.

Just then a passing woman spotted us from a trail below. "What are you doing?"

"Bird watching," I replied.

"Ah yes, bird watching very good here," she noted in broken English as she turned to go. Phew! Not arrested—yet!

We waited a bit longer, not knowing whether the dolphin killers would be back straight away. Normally such bloody capitalists would kill the dolphins the next morning, after the dolphins' adrenaline had settled. They would be easier to kill, and the meat would not be affected by the adrenaline rush from the stress of capture. But they knew SSCS was likely nearby, watching and waiting.

Alex and I decided it was time to move. We had to act fast. Down from the hill we rushed in our wet suits. The dolphins were roped off by two sets of lines. Alex took the line closest to the open ocean and I took the one closer to the shore. Alex untied his line, but I had no luck, so I cut my line. We dragged the lines to the side to make an opening for the dolphins to escape. The nets were heavy and weighted. We were in view of each other, within earshot, and agreed to release the other side of the line as well, just to be sure the dolphins escaped. We swam to the other side, where the lines were wrapped around a stake in the rocks. We untied the lines and were dragging the heavy netted lines aside when someone on shore spotted us.

Within half an hour the whole town arrived on the site, including the police. The fishermen came zipping into the cove in skiffs, and one of them tried to pull the line from me. An angry killer wrapped the line around my neck and started to drag me underwater. I put both of my feet against the side of his skiff, and pushed to keep myself from going under, while struggling to remove the noose from around my neck. He pulled his finger across his neck—you know, the sign for "you're dead," or "I will kill you."

Alex and I were pulled from the water and hauled off to jail. Alex was charged with "interfering with commerce." Apparently dolphins are nothing more than "commerce" in Japan. I was charged with "interfering with commerce using force." We were fined US$15,000, and spent three weeks in jail, where they allow prisoners to smoke. Oh dear god! I was locked in a very tiny cell, squatting over an Asian-style toilet, where the smoke overwhelmed me. Ugh!

When they took me into custody, they exchanged my street clothes for jail clothes. They took away my bra because it contained wire. I am not a girl who prefers to go braless, yet they refused to give me my bra, so I stripped naked and marched in a circle in my tiny cell, stomping my feet on the wooden floor, refusing to put my clothes on until I was given a bra—any bra. This lasted for more than an hour. Meanwhile, Alex was yelling from his cell that my treatment was out of line with the Geneva Convention—I was being treated unjustly. My reaction was something the Japanese officials simply did not know how to deal with—and they were all men. They were frantic, yet we could not communicate, as I spoke no Japanese, and they spoke no English. But my methods worked. Soon a female desk clerk entered with a sports bra—no underwire. I still have that bra hanging in my office.

Our hunt sab in Japan, the long hours of recon, sleepless nights, cold rainy days under constant surveillance—it was all worth every penny and every moment to save a pod of dolphins. Furthermore, by the time Alex and I left Wakayama Prefecture, the police, detectives, and interrogators respected us. Although we had broken the law, they understood our reasons, and what we did was honorable. Yet no attorney in the Wakayama Prefecture or in the surrounding prefectures would take our case. The local attorneys did not want the heat of the dolphin killers—they are a powerful bunch, and bullies to boot. Through Sean Penn's recommendation, we found an attorney in Tokyo, who noted that "we were acting on what was right, not on what was legal."

I would like to thank my dear friends Nik Hensey and Thomas Heine-mann who stood by Alex and me, at great risk to their own lives. Thomas took punches and was spat on—not just by angry fishermen, but by ignorant town folk as well. He filmed our entire arrest. Nik, one of my best friends, would not leave his post, where he filmed me being dragged under the boat by dolphin killers (available on YouTube).

In ten years with SSCS I freed many nonhuman animals, and I am proud of my work. In fact, when I was summoned to appear before a grand jury to provide information on possible ALF and ELF members and activities, I gladly confessed to my "illegal" acts. When they asked, "Have you been involved in releasing animals?" I said, "Yes! Sharks, swordfish, marlin, turtles, dolphins, and (unfortunately) dead albatross."

This was not the answer they were hoping for, but I am no snitch.

As I write, I am in the Galapagos with my comrade, Alex Cornelissen. Alex is in charge of SSCS's operation in the "Enchanted Islands." From sea cucumbers to lobsters to shark finning, nothing wild is sacred; nothing is safe. We work with the National Police, and we board ships to report what products are coming in and what products are going out of the Galapagos. We are determined to stop the poaching of sea lions for their penises. (Yes, just like harp seals in Canada.) Fishermen in the Galapagos Islands kill beautiful, brown-skinned sea lions to sell their penises on the Asian market. Apparently they have not heard of Viagra. Why do some men have so much penis trouble?

What comes into the Galapagos is just as devastating as what goes out. In spite of a "special law of the Galapagos," which states: "No dogs or cats are allowed on these islands," there are both dogs and cats. Importing "pets" is dangerous to indigenous wild animals, and it is also unfair to Saint Bernards, huskies, shepherds—hairy, hairy dogs in a hot, hot climate. Do people ever think?

Until just a few years ago, the streets of the Galapagos were full of stray dogs and cats fending for themselves: eating iguanas and lizards, and wiping out those famous Galapagos finches. You can't blame the strays for eating, and of course they were breeding. Luckily, a few dedicated women—Shelly Thomas with Wild Aid, and Emma Clifford and Alice Ng with Animal Balance—launched a very successful spay-neuter program. I have worked on four different campaigns with Emma and Alice, and I am amazed at what these young women can accomplish. (You have got to hand it to women!) For my part, I have adopted six dogs and four cats from the islands.

I travel quite a bit in the process of helping nonhuman animals. I have swum with dolphins, whales, seals, sea lions, sharks, rays, turtles, crazy beautiful electrifying jellyfish, and penguins. I have rescued many a bird blown out to sea, providing refuge on our ship. Yet I have rescued dogs and cats that are now waiting for me at home. They count on me, too. When I look into their eyes and tell them that I am off, again, I see their hearts sink. It hurts me to hurt them. Sometimes I think how great it would be not to be tied to critters, or a home. I think it is best to be an activist with no ties. I think activists without ties are more effective. But I also know how wonderful it is to come home to my furry family, put my jammies on after a day of wild activism, and settle into my big comfortable chair surrounded by—covered in—dogs and cats. Then I am in heaven . . . heaven as I know it.

People often ask, "Do you think there is hope?" I find this a very strange question, very anthropocentric—hope for whom?

Hope is a human construct meant to provide us with satisfaction and comfort. If I answer truthfully: "Hell no! I don't think there is any hope!" But I am driven to do what is right—not what is right for humans or what makes me feel good, but what is right for all sentient beings. I am driven almost to the point of insanity by what I see happening around me—hunters, whalers, consumers, poachers, flesh-eaters, and breeders who are overpopulating the earth with human beings. I don't know how having a baby can be the number one reason for a woman's existence. Is it smart or loving to bring a kid into this down-spiraling world? I am sick of hearing: "My baby could grow up to change the world!" Bullshit. There are already a lot of good people trying to bring change, but there are too many people consuming, using resources, living without thinking or feeling. Bringing a child into the world is selfish, dangerous, and totally irresponsible. What are you looking for—someone to take care of you in your "golden" years? Are you afraid of being alone?

I never wanted children, and once I became an activist I knew I had made the right decision.

I am driven to work for change. I am not working for humans or to make myself feel good. As I said at the outset, if I walked through life with blinders on, life would be "grand"—at least for me. I am driven by what is right for nonhuman animals. Period. And when I look back on my life of animal advocacy, I could live no other way.

allison lance has been an animal advocate for more than twenty years, fighting animal exploitation in lab cages and forests, in cosmetics and fashion industries, in foreign lands and on uncharted seas. Allison worked with Sea Shepherd Conservation Society (SSCS) for ten years, and in the words of Paul Watson, she "has devoted her life to the protection of the most defenseless and disenfranchised sentient beings on this planet—the nonhuman citizens of the land, the sea and the sky." Allison recently founded Galapagos Preservation Society (www.gpsociety.org), to humanely remove dogs and cats from the Galapagos Islands and ensure a safe haven for iguanas, lava lizards, seal pups, and Darwin Finches.

appendix
FACTORY FARMING AND FEMALES

lisa kemmerer

Many people are of the opinion that animals are generally well cared for in animal industries, that laws protect animals, and that it is in the industry's best interest to treat other creatures well. Nothing could be further from the truth.

No federal laws regulate the treatment of animals raised for meat, eggs, or milk, and almost all customary agricultural practices, no matter how painful, are exempt from extant animal cruelty statutes. Animal welfare takes a back seat to economic interests. Animals are not individuals on factory farms; they are units of production—"livestock." The cost of veterinary care, the cost of housing, and the cost of feed are all weighed against profits; profits are the purpose and the guiding principle, not the individual animals themselves.

This section explores the exploitation of females on factory farms to expose why the consumption of animal products is a critical issue for feminists in particular, and for people of conscience in general.

cattle

Every year, thirty-five million cattle are destroyed for beef, nine million cows are exploited for milk, and one million calves are destroyed for veal.

"DAIRY" CATTLE AND THE VEAL INDUSTRY

Cows, like humans and other mammals, lactate only after giving birth. In order to produce milk, cows are artificially impregnated. They carry their young for nine months, and their calves are taken shortly after birth. Cows have a strong mothering instinct, as do most mammals, and cattle try desperately to protect and keep their offspring and then bawl for days after their calves have been stolen from them.

The veal industry exists because of the dairy industry and was created to take advantage of an abundant supply of unwanted male calves. If you support the dairy industry—if you eat dairy products—you help to support the veal industry.

Male "dairy" calves are either killed shortly after birth and sold as "bob" veal for low-quality meals (like frozen TV dinners), or they are chained by the neck in two-by-five-foot wooden crates, where they are unable to turn and where they can neither stretch nor lie down comfortably. The veal industry confines one million calves in these small crates annually, feeding them a liquid milk substitute that is deficient in iron and fiber and thus designed to create an anemic, light-colored flesh that is prized by veal consumers. Calves exploited for veal are usually slaughtered when they are just four months old.

Life is no better for mother cows enslaved by the dairy industry. With their calves gone, milking machines are attached to the cow's teats morning and evening. Dairy cows endure mechanized milking for ten out of twelve months per year (including seven months of their nine-month pregnancies). One in five factory-farmed "dairy" cows secretes pus from her udders, which invariably mixes with her milk. Genetic manipulation and dietary controls cause extraordinary and unnatural milk output. Cows naturally produce just over two tons of milk per year, but Bovine Growth Hormone (BGH/BST) has increased milk flow so that cows now provide as much as thirty tons of milk annually, enough for ten calves.

Cows are so exhausted by the dairy process that they are "spent" and sent to slaughter after just four or five years of repeated impregnation, giving birth, and constant milking. (Those few cows who escape the animal industries and find their way to sanctuaries can live upward of twenty years.) Most cows are pregnant when they are slaughtered. "Dairy" cattle are not considered to have high-quality flesh (most "beef" cattle are slaughtered at a much younger age, when their flesh is tender). The flesh of "dairy" cattle is therefore used for soup, burgers, or processed foods.

Those who believe that consuming dairy products is acceptable (because only flesh requires slaughter) are mistaken: "Dairy" calves and their mothers are slaughtered for human consumption at a young age. Cows exploited by the dairy industry suffer for many years at the hands of capitalists who impregnate them, steal their young and then their milk, and ultimately send them off to slaughter—capitalizing on their reproductive abilities, their nursing milk, their calves, and finally their flesh. In the dairy industry, cows suffer for years, while their calves are among the most mistreated and neglected of all factory-farmed animals.

When making changes in your diet, please do not become a vegetarian who consumes *more* dairy products. Please cut back on all animal products to avoid increasing and encouraging the exploitation of cows and their calves.

SLAUGHTER

Four corporations slaughter more than 80 percent of the thirty-five million cattle killed annually in the United States. A standard slaughterhouse kills two hundred and fifty cattle every hour, a rate at which it is impossible for workers to assure a quick or relatively painless death. In any event, killing cattle all day at high speeds does not create an attitude of caring or compassion. Hidden videos testify to the many animals that are hoisted onto the slaughter assembly line kicking, struggling, and fully conscious. The *Washington Post* (April 2001) related the words of a slaughterhouse employee and his friend, Moreno: The cattle were supposed to be dead before they got to Moreno. But too often they weren't. "They blink. They make noises," he said softly. "The head moves, the eyes are wide and looking around." Still Moreno would cut. On bad days, he says, dozens of animals reached his station clearly alive and conscious. Some would survive as far as the tail cutter, the belly ripper, the hide puller. "They die," said Moreno, "piece by piece" (*Washington Post* [April 2001] in "Factory Beef").

Legislation offers only minimal protection for animals sent to slaughter. Mammals are supposed to be "stunned" (rendered unconscious) before they are killed (federal Humane Slaughter Act, 1958), but slaughter (like most contemporary businesses) is shaped and driven by economic factors: In the slaughterhouse, the quicker each animal is killed, the higher the profit margin. Time is money. Workers must be paid for their time, and while one animal's body is on the dismemberment line, no other body can be processed. Consequently, economics encourages speed, which works against effective stunning. Not surprisingly, a USDA survey concluded that stunning was either "unacceptable" or a "serious problem" in 36 percent of sheep and pig slaughterhouses and 64 percent of cattle slaughterhouses. (Even more remarkable, chickens, turkeys, ducks—all poultry—are exempt from the federal Humane Slaughter Act. Yet 90 percent of those killed in U.S. slaughterhouses are birds.)

DOWNERS

Like every aspect of the animal industries, transport methods are dictated by cost analysis, but what is cheapest is rarely best for animals (or consumers). As a result, animals arrive at slaughter exhausted, thirsty, hungry, and terrified; many arrive injured, and some are unable to stand or walk.

Slaughterhouse workers refer to arrivals who cannot or will not rise or move as "downers." Every year, one hundred thousand factory-farmed cattle arrive at slaughter injured or too disspirited to walk (Kirchheimer); undercover investigators have repeatedly documented downed animals being kicked, beaten, pushed with bulldozers, and dragged from transport trucks with ropes or a chain. These animals are often fully conscious, in pain, and bellowing pitifully.

pigs

One hundred million pigs are raised and slaughtered every year. Pigs are intelligent and social, in many ways similar to dogs. They are also very tidy: When pigs have sufficient space, they do not defecate in areas where they sleep or eat. On crowded factory farms, where a few extra feet reduces profit margins, pigs must live in their own feces, urine, and vomit—even amid the corpses of other pigs (as discovered by many undercover agents). Pigs are more than 95 percent factory farmed, spending their entire lives crowded in small, concrete, indoor pens.

SOWS

Like cattle exploited by the dairy industry, sows suffer a continuous cycle of forced impregnation, giving birth, forced nursing, and loss of their young. During their four-month pregnancy, breeding sows are isolated in gestation crates—small metal pens just two feet wide—where they stand on cement floors. A lack of space prevents them from turning, or even lying down comfortably, and the sides of larger sows rub incessantly on the ever-present metal bars.

When it is time to give birth, sows are transferred to similarly cramped farrowing crates, with concrete or metal floors and bars that prevent mothers from reaching their piglets but still allow the young to reach their mother's teats. Short chains or rubber straps are sometimes used to immobilize the mother; this allows perpetual nursing in order to fatten the piglets, which can cause lacerations and painful infections on the sow's udders.

When the piglets are born, identification notches are cut from their ears. Pig farmers also cut off their tails, clip their teeth, and castrate the males—all of these invasive procedures are performed without anesthesia. Not surprisingly, by two to three weeks of age, 15 percent of the piglets have died.

Normally, piglets would nurse for about fifteen weeks, but factory-farmed piglets are taken from their mothers at two or three weeks of age. They are weaned in crowded, concrete "nursery" pens surrounded by metal bars, with little more than one square yard of floor space per pig. Here they have one purpose in the farmer's eyes: to gain weight—every pound gained is also a gain in profits. They are slaughtered at about six months of age, though pigs lucky enough to find a home in a sanctuary can easily live beyond fifteen years.

Thanks to the benefits of hormone injections, five days after her piglets are stolen, a sow is again impregnated. Sows endure at least two pregnancies, birthings, and nursing stints per year, giving birth to more than twenty piglets annually. When the sow is no longer considered to be a productive breeder, after producing somewhere between four and seven litters, she is sent to slaughter at about four years of age.

Factory-farmed sows, who are repeatedly impregnated and perpetually confined, have weak bones and muscles, heart problems, and frequent urinary tract infections. Unnatural flooring and a lack of exercise cause obesity and crippling leg disorders, which also lead to arthritis. All of these problems are enhanced by pig farmers seeking a high profit margin, who breed and feed pigs to grow as quickly as possible. (Transgenic farmed animals—farm animals with the genes of other species inserted—grow even faster.) With barely enough room to stand or lie down, and no bedding to speak of, many sows have chronic sores on their shoulders and knees. Respiratory diseases are also common: 70 percent of factory-farmed pigs suffer from pneumonia. Despite these common problems, throughout the course of a complete year, one in four commercial pig operations never summon a veterinarian.

Deprivation, chronic pain, and frustration also cause sows to adopt neurotic coping behaviors. It is natural for sows to build a nest of leaves or straw before giving birth. In their barren cells, sows repeatedly and desperately try to build a nest and often fall to nervous chewing (chewing without anything in their mouths) and/or moving their heads backward and forward in a rhythmic fashion, gnawing on the metal bars that confine them.

Overcrowding and boredom also lead to aggression, which is why their tails are docked and their teeth cut. It is much cheaper to dock tails and cut teeth to prevent the injuries that will be caused by aggression than it is to provide pigs with adequate space to satisfy their most basic needs. Space would allow them to create nests, root, and wallow—engage in normal pig behaviors—which would prevent injuries from aggression and thus eliminate the need to dock tails and cut teeth.

As with all factory-farmed animals, pigs are not provided with food, water, or protection from extreme weather when they are transported to slaughter. Each year, eighty thousand pigs die in transit. At the slaughterhouse, "downer" pigs are dragged from transport trucks. Survivors face questionable stunning methods before they are shackled and hoisted by their hind leg onto a belt that moves them to the "blood pit." There, a worker cuts the pig's throat, sometimes at the remarkable rate of nine hundred pigs per hour. Needless to say, at such speeds throat-slitting cannot be achieved with any precision. Nor is there much incentive among workers. Undercover videos show conscious pigs moving along the processing line, kicking and struggling, hanging upside down by one leg, while workers try to "stick" the terrified victim. Sometimes the unfortunate pig remains conscious all the way to the scalding tank to be boiled alive.

poultry

Nearly ten billion chickens are hatched annually in the United States. More than 95 percent of U.S. hens are factory farmed. These hens are raised in giant warehouses, where they live out their short lives in confinement and deprivation.

"LAYING" HENS

Factory farmers exploit three hundred million "laying hens" each year. Hens lay eggs (and cows produce milk) as part of their basic biological functioning— not because they are well cared for or contented. Even miserable humans, if provided with food, are likely to menstruate (pass eggs) and lactate after birth. Common sense should tell us that the same is true for chickens (and cattle).

Shortly after hatching, without anesthesia, female chicks are "debeaked"— the tips of their sensitive beaks are sliced off with a hot blade, cutting through bone, cartilage, and soft tissue. This procedure is intended to reduce injuries caused by stressed birds, who squabble in their overcrowded conditions (as do pigs, and as do humans). Debeaking causes some chicks to bleed to death or die of shock.

When they are just eighteen weeks old, young hens are crowded into 1.5-square-foot cages (slightly bigger than your average microwave oven) in giant sheds, where they remain until they are sent to slaughter. Although the average hen's wing span is 2.5 feet, four or more birds are stuffed into each of these small cages. Hens exploited by the egg industry cannot stretch their wings, and their wings constantly rub against wire, which causes featherless sore spots.

Though hens have a strong urge to create a nest and sit on their eggs, factory-farmed chickens can do neither. They must lay their eggs on the cage floor. The eggs roll onto a conveyor belt and are taken away to be boxed. Hens in the wild lay roughly twenty eggs per year, but factory-farmed hens yield two hundred and fifty eggs (or more) annually. Consequently, factory-farmed hens sometimes suffer from "cage layer fatigue," a condition in which they become "egg-bound" and die because they are too weak to expel even one more egg.

When hens' egg production begins to decline, which it naturally does after a few months, they are put through "forced molt," in which they are starved and kept in total darkness for as long as eighteen days. This procedure shocks the hens' exhausted bodies into yet another egg cycle, but also causes some hens to lose more than 25 percent of their body weight. Forced molt kills 5–10 percent of the hens, but it is economically worthwhile for the farmer because the process brings on another cycle of egg laying, and the hens who die during forced molt are otherwise of no value because their egg production has declined.

Factory-farmed hens suffer from prolapses (the uterus is expelled along with the egg), egg peritonitis, cancers, infectious bronchitis, and severe liver and kidney disease. Because eggshells require a tremendous amount of calcium, hens commonly suffer from calcium deficiencies, and so they often suffer from broken bones, as well as paralysis.

Chickens at sanctuaries can live for up to fifteen years. Factory-farmed hens continue laying eggs in their tiny cells until they are "spent" at just over a year old. "Spent" hens are transported for slaughter, or more commonly, simply thrown away. Egg-laying chickens are bred for egg production; they don't grow fast or large enough to bring a profit on the flesh markets. Consequently, it is not cost-effective to send these birds to slaughter, and many spent hens are thrown into a wood chipper. Undercover investigators documented Ward Egg Ranch (California) throwing more than fifteen thousand spent laying hens into a wood-chipping machine, alive. Despite tremendous outcry from a newly informed and horrified public, the district attorney declined to prosecute, noting that disposing of hens in a wood-chipper is legal and is a "common industry practice."

Because we buy eggs, two hundred million newly hatched male chicks are discarded every year. These chicks are of no economic value, since they are of egg-laying stock, and they are therefore discarded the day they hatch. They are gassed, crushed, or simply thrown into garbage bins to die of dehydration or asphyxiation. Others, like their mothers, are tossed into a grinder or chipper. Eyewitness accounts describe struggling, peeping chicks dismembered by metal blades. Their little fluffy bodies can be used as fertilizer, or as feed for other farmed animals (despite the fact that these animals normally eat grains).

Some "laying" hens are sent to slaughter, where they join the "broilers." Though mere adolescents, "laying" hens are still much older than "broilers" when sent to slaughter. Consequently, the flesh of "laying" hens is of less value, and their flesh is used for soups, baby food, stock cubes, school dinners, pot pies, the restaurant trade, animal food, or other low-grade products (for which their "spent" bodies are shredded).

"BROILER" HENS

More and more people are moving from red meat to poultry in hopes of staving off heart attacks, strokes, and cancers that have been linked with the consumption of red meat. This means that yet more females will be exploited: Male and female pigs and cattle are raised for slaughter, but among chickens, only hens are exploited for flesh.

Chickens raised for flesh, called "broilers," are crowded by the thousands into warehouses that hold up to one hundred thousand birds. Their floor is covered with excrement, creating an overpowering, lung-damaging odor. Broilers, who must stand and lie in their own droppings, develop blisters, ulcers, and burns on their feet, legs, and breasts.

Chickens have natural sleep rhythms, determined by daylight and darkness. Light deters hens from sleeping, which encourages them to eat and helps them gain weight rapidly. Most windowless sheds are equipped with artificial lighting that remains on for most of a twenty-four hour period.

Like hens raised for the egg industry, "broiler" hens who have been raised for the flesh industry are debeaked and sexed just after they hatch. Male chicks are cast aside to die, or thrown into a chopper because they are too aggressive to be raised in close confinement.

Hens raised for flesh are genetically altered to grow twice as fast, and twice as large, as their ancestors. They reach four pounds—slaughter weight—in just six weeks by consuming high-protein feed and growth-promoting antibiotics. Their immature bones cannot support such weight, so they live in chronic pain for the last weeks of their short lives. Hens do not move much "because it hurts" when they walk (John Webster, *The Guardian* [October 14, 1991] in "An HSUS").

Because hens in broiler sheds are confined in crowded, unsanitary conditions, thousands succumb to heat prostration, infectious disease, and cancer. Hens raised for flesh frequently die of heart failure because their heart and lungs cannot sustain such fast and excessive growth (*Feedstuffs* in "Viva!USA").

Hens raised for flesh reach market weight just forty-five days after they hatch, though they might otherwise live for fifteen years. When they reach market weight, workers grab the overweight hens by a wing, leg, or head—whatever they can grab—and cram them into crates stacked on trucks. The terror-stricken, plump birds, with weak hearts and fragile bones, struggle desperately to escape. In the process, they dislocate and break hips, legs, and wings; hemorrhage internally; and suffer heart attacks.

As with other factory-farmed animals, it is cheaper to absorb high transportation mortality rates than to pay for enclosed transport trucks. Though they travel as much as eighty miles per hour in all weather conditions, hens are transported in open cages or in crates stacked on open trucks, without food, water, or protection from rain, snow, or sun. Some birds inevitably freeze to death, while others die of heat stress or suffocation during their prolonged transport.

At the slaughterhouse, hens are dumped onto a conveyor belt, but some flapping and frightened birds inevitably miss the belt and fall onto the ground, where they are either crushed by machinery, or die of starvation or exposure. Hens who land on the belt are hung upside down by their legs, in metal shackles. For the sake of efficiency, most slaughterhouses attempt to stun the birds—it is much easier to kill a bird who is not struggling. As the birds move along the assembly line, hanging upside down, turning their heads to see what might befall them, their heads are supposed to touch an electrified basin of water. Some birds, particularly smaller ones, raise their heads to avoid the water. Furthermore, even if they touch the water basin, the shock is of questionable value. As with electric tongs on cattle, the amount of current needed to properly stun birds is uncertain. As noted, U.S. laws do not regulate the slaughter of fowl (though 90 percent of the animals killed for food in the United States are birds). Too much power damages the flesh, reducing profits, so managers tend to err on the side of lower electric current. As a result, birds are usually immobilized by the electric basin, but remain fully sentient.

After they pass the electric water basin, a hen's throat is cut either by hand or with a mechanical blade. Slaughter lines run up to eighty-four hundred chickens per hour, so accuracy is the exception rather than the rule. The Livingston plant (California) kills nearly six hundred thousand chickens daily (Morrissey 12). After their throats are (presumably) slit, birds are submerged in scalding water (with the intent to loosen their feathers), and those whose throats were not slit, or were not slit properly—millions annually—are boiled alive.

Roughly one million factory-farmed hens are killed each hour for human consumption. When adjusting one's diet on behalf of animals, please do not reject red flesh in preference for poultry flesh. Compassion does not permit us to become vegetarians who consume yet more eggs—please do not buy eggs or poultry. Compassion ought to guide us away from poultry products in light of the sheer numbers of hens affected, because of the intense suffering forced on hens and chicks, and because of their premature, unregulated demise. Compassion requires us to cut back on (or eliminate) all animal products.

Two hundred and fifty million female turkeys are slaughtered for flesh each year. Forty-five million turkeys are killed each year for Thanksgiving alone. More than a quarter billion turkeys are hatched in the United States annually, though almost all of the males are quickly discarded. Most of the remaining female turkeys are slaughtered after just four months, when they reach market weight, and are shipped to slaughter. (Turkeys who live in sanctuaries can live up to fifteen years.)

Poultry Press, a publication of United Poultry Concerns, provides a first-hand account of what happens to a newborn turkey on a factory farm:

> The newborn turkeys were dumped out of metal trays, jostled onto conveyer belts after being mechanically separated from cracked eggshells, then sorted, sexed, debeaked and detoed, all without anesthetic. Countless baby turkeys were "mangled from the machinery," suffocated in plastic bags, and dumped into the "same disposal system as the discarded egg shells they were separated from hours earlier." (Davis 6)

Like chickens, turkey chicks are placed in large sheds with as many as twenty-five thousand other birds, allotting less than three square feet per turkey. Also like their smaller cousins, turkeys suffer from burns and ulcers because they live in their own excrement.

Turkeys are debeaked by removing half of the upper beak, but less of the lower beak, making it extremely difficult for factory-farmed turkeys to peck food. The last section of each toe is also clipped off. Toe-clipping removes the toenail, which reduces the danger of fights between overcrowded, bored, stressed turkeys. All surgeries are performed without anesthesia.

Like chickens, factory-farmed turkeys are genetically manipulated: They are selectively bred for extremely large breasts so that neither their bone structure nor their internal organs can withstand the rapid, excessive growth of their breasts. Consequently, millions of baby turkeys die prematurely from heart attacks, and many turkeys have problems standing upright. When they fall, they are trampled in their crowded quarters. It is more profitable for factory farmers to absorb this loss of life than it is to allow turkeys to grow more proportionally or to send smaller turkeys to market. Losses caused by stress or trampling are easier to absorb than the cost of providing poultry with adequate space.

Male turkeys grow so large that they cannot mount hens and therefore cannot reproduce naturally. Consequently, turkeys are artificially inseminated, known in the turkey industry as "breaking the hens" (Davis 7). To "break" a turkey, these large and cumbersome females are tipped upside down and injected with semen that has been stripped from males. Breeding turkeys continue to grow long after their peers have been shipped off to slaughter, reaching such massive weights as twenty-five pounds before they are worn out by the breeding process, at which time they are transported to slaughter in crowded, open trucks, for low-grade products like turkey "ham" and turkey "sausage."

"free-range," "cruelty-free," and "organic" animal products

These three labels are neither regulated nor monitored by our government, which means that we have no dependable standard for any of these claims. Even if these labels were monitored, they do not address the vast majority of problems facing factory-farmed females.

"Free-range," "cruelty-free," and "organic" industries are inherently exploitative—they exploit farmed animals for flesh, nursing milk, and reproductive eggs. Animals exploited by "free-range," "cruelty-free," and "organic" producers are routinely debeaked, dehorned, detoed, detailed, castrated, or branded, according to species. "Free-range," "cruelty-free," and "organic" milk labels do nothing to protect cows from perpetual impregnation, pregnancy, birthing, calf-snatching, transport, or slaughter at a young age. These labels do nothing for male calves, who are snatched at birth and sold into the veal industry. What would "free-range," "cruelty-free," and "organic" farmers do with thousands of male calves—calves who cannot produce milk and have not been bred for "beef"? Calves that cannot be exploited for a profit are not wanted.

Similarly, "free-range," "cruelty-free," and "organic" egg labels do nothing for male chicks, who are discarded at birth. Nor do these labels help "spent" hens, who are sent to slaughter at the same youthful age. Eggs and chickens' flesh marketed as "free range" or "cruelty free" may or may not have more space than hens raised in battery-cages, and they may or may not be allowed to step outside into natural light and fresher air. If they can step outside, their outdoor pen is likely to be very small, crowded, and barren—it is not profitable to keep fewer hens on more land; it is profitable to keep more hens on less land. And of course the animals behind "free-range," "cruelty-free," and "organic" products are sent through the same slaughterhouses, via the same rough transport system, when they are "spent" or reach market weight.

"Organic" producers do not even pretend to care about animal exploitation; "organic" products are designed to optimize human health or to address environmental concerns on behalf of human interests. They are not designed to alleviate the suffering of farmed animals, and they certainly do not do so.

"Free-range," "cruelty-free," and "organic" labels cannot satisfy the compassionate consumer.

summary

North American flesh eaters generally consume more than 35 nonhumans each year, amounting to 2,600 individuals over a seventy-five-year lifetime, including some 2,460 chickens, 96 turkeys, 32 pigs, and 12 cattle/calves. Most of these are females who have suffered egregiously.

Factory-farmed animals—whether cattle, chickens, pigs, turkeys, sheep, or ducks—are habitually deprived of fresh air, sunlight, mobility, their young, and the fulfillment of their most basic tendencies and urges. They are genetically manipulated, warehoused, and transported as if they were objects—stock—rather than sentient individuals. Females who are exploited for their nursing milk, eggs, and flesh are routinely maintained, transported, and slaughtered in ways that maximize misery. Factory farms are designed and managed for profit; they are not conducive to the health, let alone happiness, of the exploited individuals. Furthermore, uninformed health-conscious humans are buying more poultry, and due to the smaller size of these individuals when compared with cattle or pigs, this trend has exponentially increased the number of females who are exploited by food industries.

Whether or not we eat cows and their nursing milk, chickens and their reproductive eggs, sows, or turkeys—and their young—intimately affects the lives of other females.

NOTES

This appendix is an abbreviated excerpt, with permission from Oxford University Press, from *Religion and Animals*, by Lisa Kemmerer.

Information included in this appendix can be accessed on Web sites, including VIVA! USA (http://www.vivausa.org/visualmedia/index.html), PETA (http://www.petatv.com/), HSUS (http://video.hsus.org/), PCRM (http://www.pcrm.org/resources/), Farm Sanctuary (http://www.farmsanctuary.org/mediacenter/videos.html), and Vegan Outreach (http://www.veganoutreach.org/whyvegan/animals.html), to name just a few. Information on dairy cattle and laying hens was taken from the following sites: HSUS Factory Farming Campaign (http://www.hsus.org/farm/resources/research/welfare/welfare_overview.html#76), Farm Sanctuary's FactoryFarming.com (http://www.farmsanctuary.org/issues/factoryfarming/), and VIVA!USA Guides (http://www.vivausa.org/activistresources/guides/murdershewroteı.htm#).

To understand the importance of this topic, it is important to view undercover footage that shows what happens behind the scenes, when those who deal with animals think that no one else is watching. Undercover footage can be found on many Web sites. Here are some suggestions: For U.S. footage see Mercy for Animals at http://

www.mercyforanimals.org/ and Compassion over Killing at http://www.cok.net/. For Canadian footage, see www.cetfa.com and www.defendhorses.org. For Australian footage, see Animals Australia at http://www.animalsaustralia.org/. For European footage, see Vief Pfoten (Four Paws); for Western European footage see http://www .vier-pfoten.org/website/output.php, L214, and for footage from France see http:// www.l214.com/, Eyes on Animals at http://eyesonanimals.com/ and Varkens in Nood at http://www.varkensinnood.nl/. For excellent footage from the Netherlands, and also for an overall view, see the Web site of Compassion in World Farming at http://www .ciwf.org.uk/. I also highly recommend these two short online videos: http://www .youtube.com/watch?v=vCX7f_s1CA4 and http://www.petatv.com/tvpopup/Prefs .asp?video=mym2002.

REFERENCES

"An HSUS Report: The Welfare of Animals in the Meat, Egg, and Dairy Industries." *Factory Farming Campaign*. Aug. 7, 2008. http://www.hsus.org/farm/resources/research/welfare/welfare_overview.html#05.

Davis, Karen. "The Mother Turkey and Her Young." *Poultry Press*. (Winter 2008–2009): 6–7.

"Factory Beef Production." *FarmSanctuary: FactoryFarming.Com*. Aug. 9, 2008. http://www.farmsanctuary.org/issues/factoryfarming/beef/.

Kirchheimer, Gabe. "US Cows: Sacred or Mad?" *High Times*. July 1, 2001. *Organic Consumer's Association*. Online. Internet. June 22, 2009. http://www.purefood.org/madcow/cows7101.cfm.

Morrissey, Christine. "Christine Morrissey, Director of East Bay Animal Advocates." *Poultry Press: Promoting the Compassionate and Respectful Treatment of Domestic Fowl*, 17:4 (Winter-Spring 2007–2008):12.

"Viva!USA Guides: Murder She Wrote." *Viva! USA*. Aug. 14, 2008. http://www.vivausa .org/activistresources/guides/murdershewrote1.htm#.

Index

hunting, mentality behind, 129–30
"hunt sabbing," 162–63

Inconvenient Truth, 120
In Defense of Animals [IDA], 154
In Defense of Animals-Africa, 87
Indianness, as separate from tradition, 111
International Fund for Animal Welfare
(IWAF), 132
International Whaling Commission [IWC],
164

John Paul II, 102

Kheel, Marti, 32
King, Martin Luther King, Jr., 13, 26, 28, 35,
37–38, 159
Kwate, Naa Oyo A., 23

laboratories: animals in, 59, 161–62; and
animal testing, 154
language: in nonhuman animals, 67; sex in
relation to women and hunting, 18
Last Chance for Animals TV commercial,
161
Lewis, John [U.S. Representative], 80
Linzey, Andrew, 102
Lippin, Laurie, 77
Living Among Meat Eaters, x
Lorde, Audre, 13, 24, 25, 27
Loyd-Paige, Michelle, 4

Mackey, John, 156–57
Magdalen Islands, 132
masculinity, media portrayal of black vs.
white, 74–75
McCarthy, Colman, 139
Methany, Gaverick, 83
More Than a Meal, 137
multiculturalism: as assimilation, 9; in
feminism, 9–10

National Geographic, 133
Newkirk, Ingrid, 135–36
Next of Kin, 90–91
Ng, Alice, 169
nonhuman animals: similarity to humans,
21; statistics on deaths, 103

oil industry, in Cameroon, 95–96
Oneness of Beings, 117–26
oppression: definition of, 10–11; difficulty
recognizing links, 5; importance of recognizing links, 13; and objectification, 26;
and violence, 24–25
oppression of nonhuman animals: and environmental degradation, 22; and human
rights violations, 21–22
Orange County People for Animals [OCPA],
164
organic, 183

Pacheco, Alex, 135
patriarchy, 10–13; and pastoralism, 48;
violence in, 24–25
Penn, Sean, 168
People for Reason in Science and Medicine
[PRISM], 161
People for the Ethical Treatment of Animals
(PETA), 33, 71, 135
personality: in chickens, 70, 137–38; in
turkeys, 136
Pharr, Suzanne, 48
Phelps, Norm, 103
Physicians for Human Rights, 98
pollution: and economic status, 15; and race,
14–15; and sex, 15
Pornography of Meat, 2, 12
Powers, Samantha, 98
Premarin, 19
Pribilof Islands, 133
privilege, ignorance based on, 4–5
Problem from Hell, 98
Procter & Gamble, and animal testing, 154
Proposition 2 [California], 80
protesting: cosmetics and furs in stores, 163;
at shareholder's meeting, 156; at universities, 146
psychiatric disorders: in chimpanzees, 99;
examples in nonhuman animals, 99–100;
hippocampus role in, 99

race, influence on worldview, 2–3
racism: black experience with, 72–74;
environmental, 158; Korean experience
with, 79
Regan, Tom, 21
rehabilitation, of roosters, 45–46, 55
religion, role in animal advocacy, 102–3
Republic of the Ivory Coast, industrial slavery in chocolate trade, 157
responsibility, limits, 120
Reviving Ophelia, 60
Rich, Adrienne, 25

Saint Mary's-Notre Dame, 104
Salamone, Connie, 66, 67
Sanaga-Yong Chimpanzee Rescue Center,
87–88, 89–90, 92–93
San Francisco Zoo, 147
Santosa, Melissa, 5
Savage Luxury, 132

lisa
kemmerer

associate professor of philosophy and religion
at Montana State University, Billings, is an artist,
activist, and wilderness adventurer who has
traveled the world extensively. She is the author
of *In Search of Consistency: Ethics and Animals* and
Curly Tails & Cloven Hooves, a poetry chapbook,
and *Animals and Religion*, and is the editor of
several anthologies, including *Primate People, Call
to Compassion*, and *Speaking Up for Animals: An
Anthology of Women's Voices*.

the university of illinois press

IS A FOUNDING MEMBER OF THE
ASSOCIATION OF AMERICAN UNIVERSITY PRESSES.

DESIGNED BY kelly gray
COMPOSED IN 9.75/14 ICS SCALA
WITH AVENIR DISPLAY
BY jim proefrock
AT THE UNIVERSITY OF ILLINOIS PRESS
MANUFACTURED BY CUSHING-MALLOY, INC.

UNIVERSITY OF ILLINOIS PRESS
1325 SOUTH OAK STREET
CHAMPAIGN, IL 61820-6903
WWW.PRESS.UILLINOIS.EDU